1,2 Kings

BOOKS IN THE BIBLE STUDY COMMENTARY SERIES

*Not yet published as of this printing.

BIBLE STUDY COMMENTARY

1, 2 Kings

HOWARD F. VOS

Lamplighter
Books Grand Rapids,
Michigan
Zondervan Publishing House

BIBLE STUDY COMMENTARY: 1, 2 KINGS
Copyright © 1989 by Howard F. Vos

Lamplighter books
are published by
Zondervan Publishing House
1415 Lake Dr., S.E.
Grand Rapids, MI 49506

Library of Congress Cataloging-in-Publication Data

Vos, Howard Frederic, 1925–
   1, 2 Kings / Howard F. Vos.
       p.   cm. – (Bible study commentary)
   Bibliography: p.
   ISBN 0-310-33921-9
   1. Bible. O.T. Kings—Commentaries. I. Title. II. Title: First, second Kings.
III. Series: Bible study commentary series.
BS1335.3.V67   1989
222'.507–dc 19   88-13842
                                                            CIP

If not the author's own translation, then Scripture quotations are taken from the
Holy Bible: New International Version (North American Edition), copyright ©
1973, 1978, 1984 by The International Bible Society. Used by permission of
Zondervan Bible Publishers.

Edited by John D. Sloan, Mary McCormick

Printed in the United States of America

89 90 91 92 93 94 / CH / 10 9 8 7 6 5 4 3 2 1

Contents

Prologue

Though the books of Kings may not be the most popular books in the Old Testament, they contain stories of some of the best-known figures and events in Western civilization. The glories and wisdom of Solomon, his visit from the queen of Sheba, unscrupulous Jezebel and apostate Ahab, the prophet Elijah and his contest with the prophets of Baal, the miracle-workings of Elisha, the rescue of the baby king Joash from the murderous clutches of queen Athaliah, and the destruction of Sennacherib's army are only a few of the more dramatic accounts reported in these two books. Episodes from Kings have caught the fancy of painters, musicians, literary artists, and craftsmen over the centuries and have become the subjects of some of the greatest works of art in Western civilization.

More interest has centered on Solomon than on any other personality depicted in these books. His coronation, judgment of the two prostitutes, construction of the temple, and meeting with the queen of Sheba appear frequently in the unsigned stained-glass windows of the cathedrals of northern Europe. Solomon welcoming the queen of Sheba forms the subject of one of the panels of Ghiberti's fifteenth-century bronze doors on the Baptistry of Florence; Michelangelo called these doors the "Gates of Paradise." In the same century Gozzoli painted a fresco of Solomon and the queen of Sheba in Campo Santo in Pisa. Veronese in the sixteenth century painted the *Reception of the Queen of Sheba*. Rembrandt also produced a *Queen of Sheba* and the artist Claude Lorrain, *Embarkation of the Queen of Sheba* (1648). Rubens and Giorgione each painted a *Judgment of Solomon.*

Musicians, too, have immortalized Solomon. F. T. Richter composed an oratorio. *Coronation of Solomon,* in 1696; and Handel's oratorio, *Solomon,* premiered in 1749. Mendelssohn reworked Handel's composition and added an organ part, "Entry of the Queen of Sheba," which has become a standard concert piece. In the nineteenth century Gounod (1862) and Goldmark (1875) each produced a biblical opera entitled *The Queen of Sheba.* Handel composed his famous musical description of Solomon's enthronement, *Zadok the Priest,* for King George II in 1727. It is still sung by a choir at the coronation of British monarchs in Westminster Abbey. In a different medium, the Inbal Dance Theater of Tel Aviv has produced a ballet, *The Queen of Sheba.*

The ministry of Elijah has also furnished abundant inspiration for artistic creation. In the third century (ca. A.D. 245), unknown artists painted frescoes on the wall of the famous Dura-Europos Synagogue in Mesopotamia depicting Elijah humiliating the prophets of Baal and reviving the widow of Zarephath's son. Tintoretto painted an Elijah at the Scuola di San Rocco in Venice. Antonio Caldara's oratorio *Elijah* (1729) was followed by Mendelssohn's better known *The Elijah* (1846) with its immortal arias and choruses. Other examples of the many works that have drawn themes from the ministry of Elijah include Martin Buber's novel *Elijah* and Norman Nicholson's biblical play "The Old Man of the Mountains" (1946). The latter transposed Elijah to a setting in the north of England, where he becomes a champion of the working masses.

Of course, the name "Jezebel" has come into the English language as a noun with a dictionary definition of "a shameless woman." Legion have been the works devoted to her infamy, but a few examples will suffice. Hans Lufft produced a wood engraving of the infamous queen for Luther's Bible in 1534. Goethe wrote a drama about her in the last century. James Smetham's contemporary painting *Naboth's Vineyard* appeared on one of the biblical stamps of Nicaragua in 1971. And earlier in this century the new rationalism of the period tried to rehabilitate Jezebel. Clemence Dane turned this classic villainess into a kindly, reasonable woman in his play *Naboth's Vineyard* (1925); and John Masefield in his deliberately iconoclastic drama, *A King's Daughter* (1923), entirely rewrote the biblical story to whitewash Ahab and his queen.

Though a lesser-known figure, the good king Joash, too, has attracted artistic interest. For example, Louis Pendleton wrote a biblical novel *Lost Prince Almon* (1898), based on the survival of the infant Joash after the massacre instigated by the infamous queen Athaliah. And Antonio Caldara composed an oratorio, *Joash, King of Judah* (1726).

Hans Holbein the Younger sought to depict the split of the Hebrew kingdom in the days of Rehoboam in his painting *King Rehoboam* (1530). In it he portrays the king threatening the elders with a lash worse than his father's (Solomon's), and some of the Israelite spokesmen turning away in consternation to form a separate kingdom.

Two of Lord Byron's collection of poems known as *Hebrew Melodies* beautifully describe major events in 2 Kings. *The Destruction of Sennacherib* tells of divine decimation of the great Assyrian's armies while they were besieging Jerusalem. *By the Rivers of Babylon We Sat Down and Wept* depicts the Jews weeping while in Babylonian captivity after Nebuchadnezzar's destruction of Jerusalem.

Of course, these are only a few examples of the tremendous inspiration that creative artists have drawn from the books of Kings down through the centuries. Bible students have drawn great inspiration and sober warnings from them, too, and the following commentary attempts to spell out those truths.

Chapter 1

The Biblical Drama on the International Stage

God's Movement Behind the Scenes

The biblical drama unfolded on the stage of history. On that stage during the period of 1 and 2 Kings, Assyrians and Babylonians played the major roles with Egyptians and Phoenicians as supporting cast. From God's point of view, those actors did not merely come and go as kingdoms have a way of doing. Rather, God moved according to His will among the inhabitants of earth (Dan. 4:35) and deposed and set up kings as He pleased (Dan. 2:21). In fact, He sought to use those empires to wreak judgment on the Hebrews as they strayed from divinely appointed paths. Again and again the prophets thundered that Assyria would serve as an agent of God's judgment on the Hebrews because of their idolatry and other sins. And Nebuchadnezzar of Babylon was even dubbed "my servant" (Jer. 25:9), for unknowingly he did God's bidding as he carried the inhabitants of Judah into captivity for their apostasy.

Fluctuations of power in Mesopotamia related to the sinfulness of the Hebrews, and to the sinfulness of their adversaries and oppressors as well. The Middle Assyrian Empire began with Tiglath-pileser I (1115–1077 B.C.), but his successors could not equal his military and administrative accomplishments, and Assyria slipped into a weakened condition, leaving a power vacuum at the eastern end of the Mediterranean. (The Egyptian and Hittite empires had come to an end by 1100 B.C.) Thus, there was opportunity for the Hebrew united kingdom to develop and flourish under Saul (1050–1010), David (1010–970), and Solomon (970–931). Then, as idolatry began to make its inroads in Israel during Solomon's reign, God announced that in His judgment the kingdom would be split. Just as that division occurred (931), Ashur-dan II of Assyria (934–912) was bringing about the reemergence of Assyrian power, and his son Adad-nirari II (911–891) went on to launch military campaigns to reestablish Assyrian control in the northwest. But Ashurnasirpal II (883–859) was the real founder of the Neo-Assyrian Empire, and his son Shalmaneser III (858–824) met Ahab of the Northern Kingdom in battle and reduced Ahab's successor Jehu to tributary status.

After a considerable show of force in the west for a couple of generations, Assyria again lapsed into a period of weakness (782–745). This corresponded to the reigns of the good king Uzziah in Judah (792–740) and Jeroboam II (793–753) in the Northern Kingdom. Between them those two kings controlled most of the territory that David had ruled at the height of his kingdom. This half century of respite from external threat led the people of Israel and Judah into a false security, and evidently they increasingly concluded that the denunciations of the prophets were empty threats. But then arose Tiglath-pileser III (745–727), who launched the century of the greatest expansion of the Assyrian Empire. He destroyed the kingdom of Damascus and chipped off a chunk of the Northern Kingdom; his successor, Shalmaneser V (726–722), besieged and probably took the city of Samaria. Subsequently, the Assyrians almost toppled the kingdom of Judah.

God's movement in history appears not only in His judgment on Israel for her sin, but also on Assyria both for her idolatry and her treatment of Israel. Divine condemnation pronounced against Assyria appears in such passages as Isaiah 10:12–19; Nahum 1:1–3:19; and Zephaniah 2:13–15. The reason for that condemnation may be found in a general way in the Abrahamic covenant (Gen. 12:3) and more specifically in Isaiah 36 and 2 Chronicles 32:13–21. Judgment fell on Assyria as the Babylonians and Medes destroyed Nineveh (612 B.C.) and then went on to divide the Assyrian Empire. Expansionist Babylon next conquered Judah. Nebuchadnezzar, as "my servant" (Jer. 25:9) to bring judgment on the Jews, torched the city of Jerusalem, broke down its walls, and carried off most of its inhabitants into slavery (2 Kings 25:4, 9–11). But again God caused a great empire to fall because of her treatment of Israel and her other sins (Gen. 12:3; Jer. 25:10–14, 50, 51; cf. Isa. 13:17–22; 45:1–3). In magnificent fulfillment, the forces of Cyrus the Great of Persia marched into Babylon on October 12, 539 B.C., almost without shooting an arrow.

Near Eastern Developments During the Hebrew Monarchies

That God was moving behind the scenes to accomplish His purposes in Israel and among the nations is clearly stated in Scripture. It remains now to tell the story of Near Eastern developments for periods of the united and divided monarchies.[1]

Near Eastern power vacuum. As already noted, the Hittite and Egyptian empires had fallen by 1100 B.C. Though the Assyrians under Tiglath-pileser I had made an imperialistic thrust around 1100 B.C., the effort was short-lived. For the next 150 years Assyrian kings were weak. Thus, in the days of David and Solomon there was no power to stand in the way of Hebrew expansionism. Nor was there any curb on Phoenician commercial activity, and the Phoenicians launched joint ventures with the two great Hebrew kings. King Hiram of Tyre was especially involved in helping to build palaces for David and Solomon, the Hebrew temple, and the Hebrew merchant marine and port of Ezion-geber on the Red Sea.

Assyria, threat to the Westland. Then, as the Hebrew kingdom split into the separate kingdoms of Israel and Judah, Assyrian power reemerged. Ashur-dan II (934–912) restored the virtually nonexistent central administration of Assyria, reestablished Assyrian military control within Assyria's natural borders, and improved the economic base of the kingdom. His four able

---

[1] Books especially helpful in reconstructing this narrative are Jack Finegan, *Light from the Ancient Past*, 2nd ed. (Princeton: Princeton University Press, 1959); A. T. Olmstead, *History of Assyria* (Chicago: University of Chicago Press, 1951); H. W. F. Saggs, *The Greatness That Was Babylon* (New York: New American Library, 1962); H. W. F. Saggs, *The Might That Was Assyria* (London: Sidgwick and Jackson, 1984); D. J. Wiseman, *Chronicles of the Chaldaean Kings* (London: British Museum, 1961).

successors built effectively on the solid foundation he laid, and within a century Assyria became *a* (perhaps *the*) major world power.

While Ashur-dan was refurbishing Assyria, a Libyan soldier, Sheshonk I (945–924) established a dynasty in Egypt. Ruling from Bubastis in the eastern delta, he mustered enough strength to launch a devastating invasion of Palestine in the fifth year of Rehoboam of Judah (probably 926–925), according to 1 Kings 14:25 (where he is called "Sishak"). The Twenty-second Dynasty that Shishak founded lasted for some two centuries, but the country was loosely organized in an essentially feudal way during most of that time.

Ashurnasirpal, founder of empire. As we turn the spotlight back on Assyria, we find Ashur-dan's son and grandson greatly expanding Assyrian holdings to the north, south, east, and west, but Ashurnasirpal II (883-859) gets credit for being the real founder of the Neo-Assyrian Empire. He converted Assyria into a ruthless fighting machine, and his voluminous records boast of the merciless cruelty of his campaigns. The fierceness of the king's countenance, as preserved on his statues and bas-reliefs now in the British Museum in London, supports the image conveyed in his inscriptions. Some have argued that the Assyrians may not have been more cruel than other ancient peoples but allege that their cruelty is just better documented. Admittedly, reliefs on Egyptian temple walls show piles of body parts of enemy warriors, and the Hebrews also engaged in mutilation of their enemies (e.g., 1 Sam. 18:25, 27). Presumably, Assyrian brutality resulted not so much from their bloodthirsty nature as from the desire to intimidate their enemies so thoroughly that they would surrender without a fight. A case in point is the treatment of Tur Abdin, northwest of Nineveh. When the vassal ruler of that territory rebelled and attacked an Assyrian garrison town, Ashurnasirpal responded with such terrible atrocities that other petty kingdoms in the area submitted without resistance.

In any case, Ashurnasirpal had considerable military success. First, he secured a hold on territory to the north of Assyria, then subdued the region to the northwest, and next subjugated lands to the northeast. Then, after a show of force in the south

which secured the border with Babylonia, he conquered the
region in the bend of the Euphrates in the west. Finally, he
pushed west to the Mediterranean, winning submission of all
the kings of north Syria and receiving tribute from some of the
Phoenician city-states.

Expansionism of Shalmaneser. Shalmaneser III (858–824)
effectively continued the expansionist program of his father. He
secured the Mediterranean coast, and Phoenician city-states
paid him tribute. But when he tried to move into inner Syria, the
story was different. At Qarqar on the Orontes (853 B.C.) he met a
powerful coalition of Syrian and Palestinian kings, including
Haded-ezer of Damascus and Ahab of Israel. His monolith
inscription says that Ahab contributed 10,000 men and 2,000
chariots to the joint effort. Though it is not at all certain that
Shalmaneser won the great victory at Qarqar that he claimed, he
was eventually successful in the region. A few years later,
Ahab's successor, Jehu, became a vassal to Shalmaneser; Shalmaneser's Black Obelisk portrays Jehu bowing before him and
paying tribute. Shalmaneser also moved across the Amanus
Mountains into Cilicia, thus securing the principal source of
iron in the Near East and important trade connections with
Cyprus and Greece. In other campaigns he crossed the Zagros
Mountains to the east and reduced the Medes to client status.

Assyria in decline. Near the end of Shalmaneser's reign a
power struggle developed between two of his sons. This was
accompanied by widespread revolt from which Shamshi-Adad V
(823–811) emerged victoriously, and completely restored order.
Subsequently he settled some scores with the Babylonians and
wrought havoc in the cities of northern Babylonia. His wife was
Sammurammat, the famous Semiramis of Greek medieval tradition. She was the person behind the throne not only during the
reign of her husband but also her son Adad-nirari III (810–783).
Adad-nirari had trouble with more than his domineering mother; the kingdom of Urartu arose to the north of Assyria and
expanded into north Syria at the expense of the Assyrian
Empire. Urartu continued to gain power during the reign of
Adad-nirari's three successors (Shalmaneser IV, 782–773; Ashur-dan III, 772–755; and Ashur-nirari V, 754–745). The
Assyrian kings mounted only minimal military campaigns, and

provincial governors tended to assert increasing amounts of independence. Under these circumstances, Aramaean states of Syria tried to build alliances against Assyria, and Israel and Judah were free to enlarge their holdings. As noted, Uzziah of Judah and Jeroboam II of Israel benefited from the changed international situation.

Tiglath-pileser and Assyrian resurgence. Then the governor of Calah (capital of Assyria at the time) took the throne and assumed the name Tiglath-pileser III. It is not clear whether he was a usurper, but he was certainly of royal blood. His personal name was Pul or Pulu, and that is the way he is referred to in the Old Testament (2 Kings 15:19; 1 Chron. 5:26). The reign of Tiglath-pileser III (745–727) introduced a century of great imperial expansion. He came on the scene with a burst of energy, carried out an administrative reorganization that gave him effective control of the empire, and set up an efficient communications network and an intelligence system.

Tiglath-pileser campaigned effectively against Urartu in the north, took control of most of Babylonia in the southeast, and gradually overwhelmed the coalitions pitted against him in Syria and Palestine. On one occasion, probably in 743, he put Menahem of Israel to tribute (2 Kings 15:19–20). Later, Pekah of Israel and Rezin of Damascus allied against Assyria and tried to force King Ahaz of Judah to join them (2 Kings 16:5–9). In order to stop their attacks, Ahaz appealed to Tiglath-pileser for relief. The Assyrian was only too happy to oblige. He descended on Damascus, killed Rezin (2 Kings 16:9), and annexed his kingdom in 732; and about the same time he annexed the northern part of Israel and carried off thousands of captives (2 Kings 15:29). With Samaria and Judah in tributary status (2 Kings 16:7), Tiglath-pileser had gained control of the Palestine coast as far south as Gaza, and by the time he died he controlled an empire that extended from the Persian Gulf to the Sinai Peninsula and through Syria to Cilicia.

Assyria and the end of Samaria. Shalmaneser V (726–722) followed his able father, and like his father, faced trouble in Israel. Hoshea rebelled against Assyria in 725 and Shalmaneser launched a three-year siege against the city of Samaria, finally destroying it and the Northern Kingdom by the end of 722. All evidence points to Shalmaneser's capture of Samaria, but another son of Tiglath-pileser, Sargon II (721–705), claimed to have destroyed the city and to have hauled off its survivors in fetters. Presumably, he conducted the mopping-up activities after his brother's victory. About seven years later, Sargon crippled Urartu on the north after a fierce contest with that inveterate enemy. Shortly thereafter, he faced serious difficulties in Babylonia. There he finally forced Merodach-baladan, a Chaldean who had overwhelmed much of the earlier Semitic population, out of his capital city of Babylon into his base in the marshes of southern Babylonia. Sargon established his control in Babylon just in time to meet a new wave of Indo-Europeans from the north, the Cimmerians (Gomer of the Bible), and possibly he died in battle fighting them.

Sennacherib and the greatness of Nineveh. The Cimmerian threat led Sargon's son and successor, Sennacherib (704–681), to a rapprochement with Urartu in order to use them as a buttress against the new and more dangerous enemy. Sennacherib soon busied himself with building a new and permanent capital for the Assyrian Empire at Nineveh. His beautification of the city, fortifications, and aqueduct made it a fit capital for a proud and powerful empire. Though building his new capital was Sennacherib's ongoing project, he was forced to meet several enemies on the battlefield. In 703 Merodach-baladan again organized a Chaldean insurrection in Babylonia, with Elamite support. Sennacherib's response was to force Merodach-baladan out of Babylon, to set up a puppet king in the city, and to devastate southern Babylonia. Two years later, Sennacherib had to deal with Hezekiah's bid for independence in Judah. After initial successes against the Hebrews, Sennacherib's forces suffered a crippling plague at Jerusalem (Isa. 37:36–37), and news of another insurrection in Babylon led by Merodach-baladan required withdrawal from Palestine by the Assyrian army. When Sennacherib's forces attacked (700), Merodach-baladan fled to Elam and disappeared from the pages of history. Sennacherib then installed one of his sons as king in Babylon and launched an attack on Elam, wasting the southern part of the country. The Elamites counterattacked against the north of Babylonia and carried off Sennacherib's son. In the

ensuing warfare (693–689) Sennacherib's patience wore out.
After the loss of his son and some fifteen years of warfare against
Babylon, he finally decided to destroy the city utterly. Eight
years later (681) factionalism within the royal family led to
Sennacherib's murder by two of his sons in Nineveh (2 Kings
19:37).

Assyrian conquest of Egypt. Esarhaddon (690–669) was a
son of Sennacherib, who had had no part in his father's
assassination and whom his father had designated as crown
prince. Under the circumstances, however, Esarhaddon was
forced to fight for the throne against troops raised by the
regicides. After establishing himself in office, he reversed his
father's policies toward Babylon. Evidently he was of the pro-
Babylonian faction in Assyria, and sought to gain the goodwill of
the Babylonian populace; therefore he decided to restore the
ruined city. He helped to rebuild the walls and the temple to
Marduk, and resettled many of the people who had fled Assyrian
attack.

Next, he established an alliance with Medes in Iran and
renewed the alliance with Urartu, evidently in an effort to
marshal forces against Elam and the Cimmerians and Scythians,
who were pushing south out of Russia. In the northwest, Syria
and Palestine remained generally loyal to Assyria; only Sidon
rebelled, and Esarhaddon dealt sternly with her. With the
corridor to Egypt firmly under control, Esarhaddon decided to
conquer that land. Presumably the reason was to head off the
dynamic threat of Pharaoh Taharka or Tirhaka (a Nubian ruler of
the Twenty-fifth Dynasty) against Assyrian holdings in Palestine
and Syria. After incredible difficulties with desert conditions, he
took Memphis in 671 and secured the submission of the delta
region soon thereafter. But no sooner had Esarhaddon left the
country than the Egyptians rebelled. Taharka retook Memphis.

Ashurbanipal (668–627) had to take up the sword against
Egypt to complete his father's conquests there. First he recap-
tured Memphis and then moved south against Taharka's successor Tanutamun, conquering Thebes and thoroughly looting it in
663 B.C. (see Nah. 3:8–19). Thus the Assyrian Empire had come
to its greatest extent in the southwest. But Assyrian control in
Egypt was short-lived. Psamtik I established the Twenty-sixth

Dynasty and cleared the Assyrians from Egypt by 651. Ashurbanipal was unable to maintain an empire there because of trouble with Elam in the east. There King Teuman mustered a powerful force but Ashurbanipal worsted him, and the Elamite king met death in battle. Elam continued to be a threat to Assyria, however (in part as a supporter of the rebellious forces in Babylonia), and Ashurbanipal eventually totally devastated Elam and even deported some of the Elamites to Samaria (Ezra 4:9–10). He was also forced to put down rebellion in Babylonia. In dealing with all uprisings or opposition he was harsh, ruthless, and vindictive—devoid of human kindness or even statesmanlike qualities.

But Ashurbanipal had another side to him. He had a passion for building the great Assyrian library, sending his scribes throughout the length and breadth of the empire to copy texts of various sorts. This library, found in the mid-nineteenth century, constitutes the major single source for modern knowledge of ancient Babylonia and Assyria. Ashurbanipal is known as Osnappar or Asnapper in the Old Testament (Ezra 4:10 KJV).

Decline of Assyria. Soon after Ashurbanipal's death in 627 B.C. the empire began to fall apart. Nabopolassar, a Chaldean and possible descendant of Merodach-baladan, established an independent state in Babylonia at the end of 626. Meanwhile the Medes had moved into Elam and had begun to infiltrate Assyria proper. The Babylonians and Medes made a treaty of alliance, and evidently the Scythians and other tribal hordes joined them later. These confederates then besieged and destroyed Nineveh in 612 B.C. The remnant of Assyrian forces fled westward to Haran, where they proclaimed Ashur-uballit of the Assyrian royal family as king. With Nineveh destroyed, the allies withdrew. This gave Nabopolassar a chance to consolidate his holdings in Assyria, and Ashur-uballit time to regroup. Meanwhile the Medes were taking control of Assyrian territory east and north of the Tigris. The desperate Assyrians now called on Egypt for help, which was eventually to be generously given. When the tribal peoples advanced from the north against Haran in 610, Nabopolassar joined them to protect his interests. The Assyrians moved southward to meet their Egyptian allies and the Assyrian-Egyptian forces now made their base at Carchemish in Syria. At this point a new pharaoh, Necho II (610–595) came to the throne of Egypt. Presumably, his new commitment to support for Assyria involved Egyptian imperialistic designs. As Necho marched north to join Ashur-uballit, King Josiah of Judah sought to prevent the meeting. For his efforts Josiah paid with his life (609 B.C., 2 Kings 23:29), and Necho put Josiah's son Jehoiakim on the throne of Judah (2 Kings 23:34).

Nebuchadnezzar and Babylonian ascendancy. For a few years Egypt dominated Syria and Palestine, but in 605 the aging and perhaps infirm Nabopolassar turned over control of the armed forces to his able son Nebuchadnezzar, and a new dynamic came on the scene. The Babylonian army made mincemeat of the Assyrian-Egyptian army at the battle of Carchemish in the spring of 605. The remnants of Assyrian power disappeared forever from the pages of history, and Necho's Syrian empire came to an end. Jones explains the demise of Assyria in part by the failure of Assyrians to participate meaningfully in the economic structure of their empire and the gradual extinction in constant warfare of the sturdy peasantry, which served as the recruiting base for the army. Assyria could not get the same results with mercenaries and subject levies.[2]

Immediately after the battle of Carchemish, Nebuchadnezzar took control of all Syria and Palestine. Jehoiakim of Judah, who had been a vassal of Necho, now submitted to Nebuchadnezzar, and some Jews, including the prophet Daniel, were carried off as captives or hostages to Babylon (Dan. 1:1–7). Then, in August, Nebuchadnezzar rushed back to Babylon to establish himself on the throne after his father died. In the following year Nebuchadnezzar returned to Palestine and Syria, "marched about unopposed" and collected "heavy tribute." He made a further show of force in the region during each of the following two years, evidently in an effort to establish firm control of territory through which military supply lines would have to pass when he launched an attack on Egypt.

Finally, in his fourth year (601/600), Nebuchadnezzar was ready for the Egyptian offensive. After a fiercely fought battle in

---

[2]Tom B. Jones, *Ancient Civilization*, rev. ed. (Chicago: Rand McNally, 1964), 135.

which casualties were heavy on both sides, Nebuchadnezzar and his army "turned back and returned to Babylon"[3] (his words), apparently admitting defeat. With this evidence of weakness on the part of Babylon, Jehoiakim seems to have thought he could get away with a move for independence. He rebelled against Nebuchadnezzar in that very year (601/600, 2 Kings 24:1). Nebuchadnezzar did not respond in person immediately, largely because he was busy rebuilding his shattered military establishment, but he was probably responsible for urging guerrilla attacks on the borders of Judah (2 Kings 24:2). Finally he mustered his troops, besieged Jerusalem, and took the city in the spring of 597 B.C.

During the siege, Jehoiakim had died and his eighteen-year-old son Jehoiachin became king. After he had ruled for three months, Nebuchadnezzar took the city, deposed him, and put his uncle Mattaniah (renamed Zedekiah) on the throne. He deported Jehoiachin, the officials of the court, and the leading citizens of Jerusalem, and hauled off many of the temple treasures to Babylon (2 Kings 24:12–17).

But though the light of freedom flickered in Judah, it had not gone out. After nine years as vassal of the great Chaldean, Zedekiah rebelled against Babylon. Nebuchadnezzar was determined to extinguish this spark of independence, and Zedekiah did not possess the resources the Jews had enjoyed earlier. Finally in Zedekiah's eleventh year, in August of 586, the Babylonian siege of Jerusalem broke the back of Jewish resistance. The invaders torched the houses of the people and the palace of the king, destroyed the temple and the city walls, and carried off into captivity all except the poorest elements of society along with the objects used in temple worship (2 Kings 25:1–21).

Nebuchadnezzar continued to rule in Babylon until 562, beautifying the city, building the power of empire, and enhancing his reputation. His successors were not of his caliber, however, and they were able to maintain the empire for little more than twenty years after his death. Meanwhile Judah and Jerusalem lay prostrate, waiting for the deliverer Cyrus, who

---

[3] Wiseman, 71.

would found the Persian Empire, destroy the Babylonian Empire, and launch the restoration of the Jews to their homeland.

For Further Study

1. Trace the military campaigns of Shalmaneser III, Tiglath-pileser III, Sargon II, Sennacherib, and Nebuchadnezzar as they affected Israel. For this, consult especially the *Macmillan Bible Atlas*.

2. Write a brief description of how developments in Babylonia during the Assyrian Empire and Neo-Babylonian Empire periods affected Hebrew history.

3. If the Hebrew kingdom had not fallen under divine condemnation and if the kingdom had remained united and powerful, how would the history of the Near East have been different? Write a brief imaginative piece.

Chapter 2

Introduction to First and Second Kings

Purpose and Message

The obvious purpose of the books of Kings is to trace the story of Israel from the latter days of David (where the books of Samuel leave off) to the Babylonian captivity. But the author did not merely write history; he sought to drive home moral and spiritual principles. His chief concern was to show that Israel as the people of God, in covenant relationship to Him, were expected to keep His law. They would be blessed for keeping it and punished for failing to do so. Especially, Israel must worship no other gods but Yahweh (Exod. 20:2–6). Idolatry is highlighted as the worst of sins; when persisted in, it would lead to destruction of the kingdom and deportation from the land. Such an attack on the sin of idolatry is quite logical because it involves dethroning God from first place in the life of the believer; all other evils flow from that. Throughout these books of Kings the prophets thunder at the sins of kings and people, and call them to repentance before it is too late. The prophets proclaim loudly and clearly the principle that righteousness exalts a nation and sin is a reproach to any people (Prov. 14:34).

Since the kings stood at the head of the nation and had the power to influence it in the direction it would go, the author narrated his history by giving an account of the reigns of the kings. He evaluated them in terms of whether they did what was evil or right in the sight of God—in terms of how well they fulfilled their covenant responsibilities. Therefore, the author refrained from glorifying national heroes and even from mentioning many important political or economic facets of the royal administrations. For example, Omri, one of Israel's greatest kings, is dismissed with eight verses and is condemned for the evils of his reign (1 Kings 16:21–28). Jeroboam II, who ruled for forty-one years and enjoyed great prosperity, rates only seven verses and suffers condemnation for his idolatry (2 Kings 14:23–29).

In addition to judgment on idolatry, several other theological themes surface in the books of Kings. It is enough only to mention them here; they receive further treatment in the commentary: (1) God's faithfulness in fulfilling the Abrahamic covenant (Gen. 12:1–3; 13:14–17, etc.). As promised, He did protect and preserve His people and judged those who afflicted them; destruction came on the Assyrians and Babylonians for their treatment of Israel. (2) God's faithfulness in fulfilling the Davidic covenant (2 Sam. 7). Even though God judged the Hebrews for Solomon's idolatry by splitting the kingdom (1 Kings 11:11–13), He preserved a king in David's line on David's throne in Jerusalem during the continuing history of the Southern Kingdom. (3) In preserving David's line, God preserved the line of the Messiah. (4) God will never permit the truth to be snuffed out entirely. During the darkest days of the Northern Kingdom, He called and protected Elijah and Elisha and other prophets in their conflict with their idolatrous society. (5) God operates on the principle of proximate justice—justice on the near term for sins committed. Even though there is eternal justice and God promises ultimate blessing on Israel in the land, people may expect to suffer for their sins in this life and on the near term. Individual kings and the people as a whole would suffer for their faults in specific ways, and Israel would be hauled off captive before a glorious day of restoration to the land and the ultimate fulfillment of the promises of the Abrahamic and Davidic covenants.

Outline

  I. The Reign of Solomon (1 Kings 1:1–11:43)
    A. Solomon's Ascension to the Throne (1:1–3:1)
      1. His Anointing as King (1:1–53)

A. Beginning of Ahab's Reign (1 Kings 16:29–34)
B. Ahab's Contest with Elijah (17:1–19:21)
   1. Elijah's Prediction of Drought (17:1)
   2. God's Provision for Elijah (17:2–24)
   3. Elijah's Challenge to the Prophets of Baal (18:1–46)
     a. Arranging the meeting with Ahab (18:1–16)
     b. Meeting with Ahab and the Contest on Mount Carmel (18:17–46)
   4. Elijah's Failure and Renewal (19:1–21)
     a. Flight to Horeb (19:1–18)
     b. Appointment of Elisha (19:19–21)
C. Ahab's Early Wars with Syria (20:1–43)
D. Ahab's Desire for Naboth's Vineyard (21:1–29)
E. Ahab's Final Syrian War (22:1–40)
F. Jehoshaphat of Judah (22:41–50)
G. Ahaziah of Israel (1 Kings 22:51–2 Kings 1:18)
H. Exit Elijah, Enter Elisha (2:1–25)
 I. Joram and Jehoshaphat Against the Moabites (3:1–27)
 J. Elisha's Miracles (4:1–6:7)
K. Wars with Syria and Deliverance of Samaria (6:8–8:15)
L. Joram of Judah (8:16–24)
M. Ahaziah of Judah (8:25–29)
N. Jehu's Revolution (9:1–37)
IV. Renewed Hostilities Between the Kingdoms and the Fall of Samaria (2 Kings 10:1–17:41)
A. Jehu's Extermination of Princes and Priests (10:1–36)
B. Athaliah and the Accession of Joash (11:1–20)
C. Joash and the Temple Repairs (11:21–12:21)
D. Jehoahaz of Israel and Defeat by Syria (13:1–9)
E. Jehoash of Israel and Partial Recovery (13:10–25)
F. Amaziah of Judah (14:1–22)
G. Prosperity of the Two Kingdoms (14:23–15:7)
   1. Israel Under Jeroboam II (14:23–29)
   2. Judah Under Uzziah (15:1–7)
H. The Last Days of Israel (15:8–17:41)

Name

Kings was originally one book in the Hebrew Bible and formed a sequel to Samuel, which was also one book. The name comes from the Hebrew opening word (translated, "And the king") and from the contents, describing the history of the kings from David through the reigns of the kings of Israel and Judah. In the Septuagint (Greek translation of the Old Testament), Samuel and Kings were first divided and were called 1, 2, 3, 4 "Of the Kingdoms." The Latin Vulgate of Jerome (fifth century A.D.) used the title "Books of the Kings," for our 1, 2 Kings, and this terminology passed into English translations.

Authorship and Composition

The author of Kings is not named in Scripture, but according to the Jewish Talmud (*Baba Bathra* 14b), Jeremiah wrote the book. Some scholars have found this to be a very attractive theory, and it helps to explain the absence of Jeremiah from the book (on the assumption of his modesty) when he was active in Jerusalem during the latter part of the pre-exilic period. The epilogue on the release of Jehoiachin (2 Kings 25:27–39) indicates, however, a knowledge of affairs in Babylon, and that Jeremiah was carried off to Egypt (Jer. 43:6, 7) and presumably died there. Of course, Jeremiah could have written the book before he was taken to Egypt and someone else may have composed the epilogue after Jehoiachin's release about 561. In any case, Kings must have been completed by about 550 because there is no hint in the book of return from Babylon to Judah.

Regardless of who wrote the book, we must argue for a single creative authorship under the guidance of the Holy Spirit, rather than fragmenting the work into a collection of narratives and sources as higher critics have done. The account of the kings consists of a stereotyped framework, in which the date of accession of a king is related to the reigning year of the contemporary ruler of the opposite kingdom; the length of the reign is given; there is an evaluation of the character and conduct of the king; there is reference to a documentary source or annal from which more can be learned about the king; and mention of his death and his successor is included. Moreover, various phrases and terms recur from beginning to end; e.g., "now the rest of the acts of . . . are they not written," "as surely as the LORD lives," "evil in the sight of the LORD."

An assertion of single authorship does not require, however, that the writer worked without sources. In fact, he made extensive use of them. He mentions "the book of the acts of Solomon" (1 Kings 11:41), the "books of the chronicles of the kings of Israel" (17 times), and "the books of the chronicles of the kings of Judah" (15 times). Then presumably, he used sections of Isaiah 36–39 in 2 Kings 18–20. The various court or official records just noted would provide chronological references and information about public events, but they would not evaluate the character of the king and the quality of his administration. Such information had to come from another type of source. Evidently some of the prophets also penned accounts of official doings. A look at parallel passages in 2 Chronicles provides the clue. There it is clear that the sacred historian was looking at accounts of Shemaiah the prophet and Iddo the seer (2 Chron. 12:15); Iddo the prophet (2 Chron. 13:22); and Isaiah the prophet (2 Chron. 26:22; 32:32). Of course, the use of sources does not in any way detract from divine inspiration of the text. Inspiration does not require that the writer sit with a blank tablet and a blank mind, waiting for the Holy Spirit to produce the biblical book. It insists only that the Holy Spirit guided or superintended the writer in the choice of material and that the finished product is an appropriate and accurate statement of what God wanted said.

Chronology of the Kings

One of the greatest difficulties facing the reverent Bible student who believes in the accuracy of the biblical text is the chronology of the kings as presented in these books. Scholars used to conclude that there was no way to reconcile all the seemingly conflicting chronological references in the books of Kings and Chronicles and that certainly the Bible could not be depended on to provide the basis for a chronology of the kingdoms of Israel and Judah. For example, the length of time from Jeroboam I to Joram in Israel should be the same as the time from Rehoboam to Ahaziah in the Southern Kingdom. This is true because Rehoboam and Jeroboam began to reign at the same time, and Joram and Ahaziah met their deaths simultaneously at the hands of Jehu. However, when we add up the reigns of the kings in each line, we discover that the same period of time totals ninety-eight years for Israel and only ninety-five years for Judah. Several other problems could be noted.

Finally Edwin R. Thiele attacked these chronological difficulties in his doctoral dissertation at the University of Chicago. Ultimately the University of Chicago Press published his work under the title of *The Mysterious Numbers of the Hebrew Kings* in 1951. Zondervan produced a Revised Edition in 1983.

Thiele made a number of discoveries, of which the following are some of the most important. (1) Both Israel and Judah used coregencies, but in neither nation did interregna occur. (2) In the case of coregencies the years of the king were usually counted from the beginning of the coregency. (3) In Israel the regnal year began with the month Nisan (March–April), while in Judah it began with the month Tishri (September). (4) Two methods of reckoning were used for the Hebrew kings: the nonaccession-year and accession-year systems. In the nonaccession-year system, the year in which a king began to rule was counted as his first official year. In the accession-year system, the part of the year in which the king ruled when he first came to the throne was his accession year, not his first year. His first year was reckoned as beginning with the month Tishri, following his accession to the throne. (5) Judah used the accession-year system from Rehoboam to Jehoshaphat, nonaccession year dating from Jehoram to Joash, and accession-year reckoning again from Amaziah to Zedekiah. Israel used nonaccession year dating from Jeroboam to Jehoahaz and accession-year reckoning from Jehoash to Hoshea. (6) Israel and Judah, when computing the years of each other's kings, did so according to the system of reckoning then being used in their own countries, and not according to the system used by their neighbors.

Obviously this is a very technical study and the interested

student may consult Thiele's masterful work. Suffice it to say that Thiele has essentially resolved the problems of the chronology of the kings, though all scholars do not agree with him at every point. The following chart is adapted from Thiele's work.

Rulers of the Divided Kingdom

Israel		*Judah*	
Jeroboam I	930–909	Rehoboam	931–913
Nadab	909–908	Abijam(h)	913–910
Baasha	908–886	Asa	910–869
Elah	886–885		
Zimri	885		
Tibni	885–880		
Omri	885–874	Jehoshaphat	873–848
Ahab	874–853		
Ahaziah	853–852	Jehoram	853–841
Joram	852–841	Ahaziah	841
Jehu	841–814	Athaliah	841–835
Jehoahaz	814–798	Joash	835–796
Jehoash	798–782	Amaziah	796–767
Jeroboam II	793–753	Azariah (Uzziah)	792–740
Zechariah	753–752	Jotham	750–732
Shallum	752		
Menahem	752–742		
Pekahiah	742–740		
Pekah	752–732	Ahaz	735–715
Hoshea	732–723	Hezekiah	715–686
		Manasseh	696–642
		Amon	642–640
		Josiah	640–609
		Jehoahaz	609
		Jehoiakim	609–598
		Jehoiachin	597
		Zedekiah	597–586

For Further Study

1. Skim the books of 1, 2 Kings at one sitting and note what you think are the main divisions of the books. State the main points of your outline.

2. As you worked your way through these books, what major developments or personalities stood out in your thinking? Why?

3. What actions to be emulated or avoided caught your eye?

4. Did you discover any reasons why it would be worthwhile for you to pursue an in-depth study of these books?

Chapter 3

The Reign of Solomon
(1 Kings 1:1–11:43)

When the Hebrews came to Samuel, the prophet and judge, with a request for a king like the nations surrounding them (1 Sam. 8:5, 20), they got what they asked for. Like their neighbors, they had a man who collected a harem with the attendant harem intrigues and jealousies. Like their neighbors, they found themselves saddled with a man who sought to be a powerful potentate and who needed a standing army and war materiel to realize that dream. And like their neighbors, they discovered that their king launched grandiose building projects. Those military and civilian programs forced them to shoulder an increasing tax burden. Moreover, they discovered that their king, like the rulers around them, tended to welcome into the court and the kingdom the worship of foreign deities to whom princesses of the harem were devoted. There the God of Israel drew the line. He would tolerate no competition for His affections; He scored idolatry vehemently and even warned that in punishment the kingdom would be split because of Solomon's permission and support of idolatry.

These themes all surface in the first eleven chapters of 1 Kings. At the outset there is competition in the harem over the succession to the throne as the question arises over whether Adonijah or Solomon shall be king. Ambitious military and civilian projects had resulted in such a heavy tax burden that the northern tribes seceded from the kingdom over that issue after Solomon's death (1 Kings 12). Though Solomon started well and built for his God the great temple in Jerusalem, his political

33

marriages brought in many foreign deities that ultimately corrupted the worship of Israel and brought God's condemnation on himself and his kingdom.

A. Solomon's Ascension to the Throne (1:1–3:1)

1. His Anointing as King (1:1–53)

a. David's old age (1:1–4). David's condition set the stage for the momentous events to follow. He was "old, advanced in years."[1] His chronological age was about seventy (see 2 Sam. 5:4), which was old enough in a society where the average lifespan was probably not much over thirty-five. But his physiological age must have seemed much greater as a result of the rigors of warfare and the years of flight from Saul. This description of age is applied only to Joshua (Josh. 13:1; 23:1) and Abraham and Sarah (Gen. 18:11). In the latter case it is connected with persons who were childless, incapable of bearing children. Possibly the term implies that David had lost his sexual powers; at least he presumably no longer exercised them (v. 4). In fact, his body was so worn out that the courtiers of the bedchamber could not keep him warm at night even though they piled on the bedclothes. "Clothes" does not refer to clothing but blankets or covers (cf. 1 Sam. 19:13). The text does not say David was bedridden; it only indicates he was without normal body heat when in bed.

The officials of the bedchamber sought to solve the problem by finding a young woman to sleep with him to keep him warm and to act as his nurse. Modern westerners should look at this passage in terms of an oriental, polygamous society. And they should recognize that physicians did make such recommendations.[2] Their search led them to the village of Shunem, about seven miles southeast of Nazareth, a town where Elisha later brought a woman's son to life. She had to be beautiful to serve the king and she had to be a virgin (unattached to any man). She is named because of her connection with the Adonijah narrative

---

[1] Translations in this commentary are the author's unless otherwise specified. Translations may or may not be similar to those appearing in the various versions.

[2] Josephus, *Antiquities*, VII.14.3; Galen, *Methodus Medicus* 10.7.7 (second century A.D.), and medieval sources.

that follows. The observation that David did not cohabit with her is probably meant to emphasize that he was too destitute of energy to carry on the functions of government. In any case, the whole scene leads to the conclusion that there was a political vacuum in Israel. When an absolute monarch ceases to function, there is virtually no government at all and ambitious persons grow impatient to take power.

b. Adonijah's elevation (1:5–10). Such an ambitious person was Adonijah. Evidently he was David's eldest living son now that Amnon, Absalom, and probably Chileab had died. Though primogeniture had not been established for succession to the throne in Israel, it was common elsewhere in the Near East and in other aspects of Israelite society. Moreover, he was "very handsome" (v. 6) and presumably that made him somewhat popular. Then, while the first part of verse 6 is difficult in the Hebrew, it seems to indicate that David had neglected parental discipline and that Adonijah was a somewhat rebellious and willful young man. Adonijah announced, "I will be king" (v. 5). To bolster his image he procured chariots (state chariots, not war chariots) and horsemen and fifty runners (as a guard of honor), as Absalom had done before him (2 Sam. 15:1).

Also, he won the support of two of David's inner circle: Joab, who had served as his commander of the armed forces, and Abiathar the high priest. It is easy to understand why Joab joined Adonijah's cause; he had had a falling out with David over various matters, especially because he had killed Absalom. No doubt he hoped to gain influence with the new king if he helped him win the throne. Why Abiathar joined Adonijah is not clear, it may possibly have been out of jealousy of Zadok.

Adonijah began his usurpation, as Absalom had (2 Sam. 15:12), with a sacrifice and a common meal at which he was proclaimed king. Such a meal had the effect of uniting his followers in a joint venture. The feast took place at En-Rogel, the southern spring of the city, located where the valleys of the Kidron and Hinnon join, near the modern village of Silwan. Invited to the feast were all the king's sons except Solomon, the Judeans who were in the king's service, and Joab and Abiathar (v. 19). Specifically excluded was the Solomonic faction, including Nathan (the court prophet), Benaiah (captain of the king's

bodyguard, 2 Sam. 8:18; 23:20–23), Zadok (the priest), and
David's "mighty men." Either they were not invited or refused
to participate in Adonijah's coronation (cf. v. 26).

   c. Solomon's coronation (1:11–40). Jerusalem was a small
city of fewer than fifteen acres in David's day, and the plans of
Adonijah could not have been kept from the Solomonic faction
for very long. Nathan swung into action and staged a carefully
orchestrated drama involving the entrance of Bathsheba, his
own precisely timed entrance, the manipulated response of
David, and the coronation of Solomon itself. In implying that
Adonijah's coronation threatened the life of Bathsheba and
Solomon, Nathan was not merely concocting a threat for effect
(v. 12). It was perfectly consistent with the practices of the
times for a main contender for the throne and members of his
family to be executed (cf. v. 21). As a case in point, Adonijah lost
his life after Solomon's accession to the throne. That no Davidic
oath promising the throne to Solomon appears in Scripture
before this point (v. 13) has led some commentators to argue
that it was never made, and that Bathsheba and Nathan were
now putting the idea in the senile king's mind. There is only a
hint that at the birth of Solomon God showed some special favor
toward him (2 Sam. 12:24–25). Arguments from silence are
often dangerous and almost always inconclusive, and the
question must be left open.

   When Bathsheba came for her audience with David (vv.
15–21), she showed that she had a mind of her own. Instead of
politely asking questions, as Nathan had instructed her to do,
she turned the various points into declarative statements. Now
the king knew about the coronation of Adonijah and the parties
to the deed. The point is made that Abishag the Shunammite is
still ministering to David, and there is no hint that she was sent
out while Bathsheba or Nathan was conferring with the king.

   Just about the time Bathsheba finished her plea, Nathan
came along (vv. 22–27). Because he did not have the run of the
palace as the queen did, he was properly announced and
Bathsheba retired (v. 23). Unlike Bathsheba, Nathan was not the
least bit confrontational. He merely asked questions about
whether the king was aware of the coronation proceedings and
whether he really meant for Adonijah to be king. He did not

even refer to the promise made to Bathsheba that Solomon was to be king; that was a matter to be settled between the king and his wife. If there was any complaint, it was only that perhaps the king had failed to inform his servants of a plan for succession to the throne. In the process he was careful to point out, however, that he and Zadok and Benaiah had not been parties to the proceedings at En-Rogel. Having stated his case, Nathan retired.

Deeply stirred by these audiences and goaded by the urgency of a coronation ceremony in progress, David acted promptly. Though weak in body, the king demonstrated great strength of mind and will. First he called Bathsheba, who evidently had been waiting nearby to see how things would turn out (vv. 28–31). When addressed by the king, she need not kneel as a suppliant; she "stood" before David. He promised that "as surely as the LORD lives" (NIV), as certain as God's very existence, he would fulfill his promise that Solomon would succeed him on the throne. David's determination to keep a promise made intimates that he really had made the promise at an earlier time and that it was not merely a thought put into his mind by Bathsheba and Nathan on this occasion. The expression, "May my lord King David live forever" is usually taken as a conventional wish that God would grant a monarch long life. But in this case, as Bathsheba uttered it to a king who did not have long to live, De Vries thinks it involves a wish "that David's life power should live in his posterity."[3]

Next David laid careful plans to defuse the impact of Adonijah's actions. He called in Zadok, Nathan, and Benaiah, the ranking priest, prophet, and soldier loyal to him, and issued a series of commands: (1) "Take the servants of your lord," the total party loyal to him, including the Kerethites and Pelethites, the palace guards. (2) "Cause Solomon . . . to mount my own mule," evidence that David was turning authority over to Solomon. (3) "Take him to Gihon" (just outside the east wall of the city in the Kidron Valley) and let Zadok and Nathan anoint him there (Adonijah was not officially anointed). As there was no prophet in Adonijah's camp, Nathan's presence indicated divine choice of Solomon as king. (4) "Blow the ram's horn and cry,

[3] Simon J. DeVries, 1 Kings, Word Biblical Commentary, Vol. 13 (Waco, Tex.: Word Books, 1985), 16.

'Long live king Solomon,'" as a solemn proclamation after the anointing. (5) Accompany Solomon back into the city and place him on my throne where he is to be king over Israel and Judah.

Benaiah responded to the king's orders with great enthusiasm and expressed a wish that the rule of Solomon might be even greater than that of David—a wish for the prosperity of the monarchy. Then immediately the three stalwart supporters of the king, the Kerethites and Pelethites, and others hastened to do exactly as David had ordered. Zadok "took the horn of oil" (evidently the animal's horn that held holy anointing oil used for anointing priests and vessels of the sanctuary) "from the tent" (the tent David had set up for the ark of the covenant on Mount Zion, 2 Sam. 6:17) "and anointed Solomon." "All the people," both the official group and the spontaneous gathering, made a tremendous racket as they celebrated. "Piping with pipes" is a better rendering than "playing on flutes." This was no gentle sweetness of orchestral flutes, but pipes used as noisemakers. The din was so great that the earth seemed almost "to burst in pieces" (v. 40).

d. The surprise of Adonijah's party (1:41–53). Just as Adonijah's feast was coming to an end, the noise of Solomon's inaugural celebration reached the ears of his company. It was possible for them to hear but not see the inauguration because although less than seven hundred yards separated the two companies, there was a slight rise in the ground and a curve in the valley between them. When Joab, doughty military man that he was, heard the ear-splitting sound of the ram's horn, he knew that something very significant was happening and wondered out loud what it was. As the group stood there looking at each other and asking questions, Abiathar's son Jonathan came on the scene. Possibly he had been left behind as a spy to keep an eye on events at the palace. Adonijah invited him to speak, but no one was happy with his report. Jonathan gave a capsule summary of events exactly as they had occurred (vv. 43–48), adding the detail that David himself (while in his bed) had rejoiced in prayer to God because God had established the succession to kingship while David was still alive to see it: "today" (v. 48).

It was a good day's work for the loyalists. But the news of

the day's events spread terror among Adonijah's guests and they all fled, seeking to distance themselves from the traitor as fast as they could. Adonijah, left alone, took the one course of action he could as a good Hebrew. He fled to the tabernacle and claimed refuge by grasping the horns of the bronze altar in the tabernacle courtyard. Here one could claim protection until a matter had been investigated and settled (cf. Exod. 21:13, 14). Actually this practice was intended for an innocent man and there would have been no need for Solomon to spare a guilty man who fled there (cf. 1 Kings 2:31). A report of Adonijah's action was brought to Solomon with the plea that Adonijah not be executed. Solomon agreed on the condition that Adonijah behave himself in the future. Then Adonijah came and did homage to the newly enthroned king and Solomon sent him home in peace, not to a house arrest but as a release, with the expectation that he retire to private life.

2. His Father's Charge (2:1–12)

a. A personal charge (2:1–4). Perhaps some months had passed since the events of chapter one (1 Chron. 28, 29). Probably Solomon had assumed the day-to-day responsibilities of government. David grew weaker and recognized that his death was near, so he issued a twofold deathbed charge to his son: a personal charge and an administrative charge. The personal charge is similar in some respects to the one Moses gave Joshua (Josh. 1:6–9) and to the farewell God gave to Joshua (Deut. 31:23). To "show yourself a man" means following God's ways. Keeping the commandments of God would assure Solomon of personal success and dynastic perpetuity. God had doubtless decreed the Davidic covenant (2 Sam. 7), which had promised an eternal Davidic dynasty, an eternal throne, and an eternal kingdom. But David gave the unconditional covenant a negative twist. The implication is that though the covenant is perpetual, it does not necessarily promise that it will be visibly operative in every generation, regardless of the conduct of kings in the Davidic line.

b. An administrative charge (2:5–9). The question must be raised as to how this paragraph squares with the previous one. Was it just a "piece of oriental cruelty," as the critics often claim? Not necessarily. After all, both Joab and Shimei had committed acts worthy of the death penalty. Moreover, as both of them had been a problem or threat to David, they could also be to Solomon. Then, too, modern Americans need to remember that ancient Semitic governance prescribed the death penalty for many crimes that would not warrant the same treatment today. If David, in fact, erred in his judgment in this paragraph, it should be noted that inspiration of Scripture does not necessarily involve approval of the conduct of an individual; it only guarantees accurate reporting of what the person thought or did.

David turned Solomon's attention first to Joab, commander of the armed forces, who had often served David well. He had captured Jerusalem (2 Sam. 5) and Rabbah, capital of Ammon (2 Sam. 12), and had protected David at the beginning of Absalom's revolt (2 Sam. 14). He was David's agent in the manipulation of Uriah (2 Sam. 11) and had done much else for his master. But Joab was guilty of a double murder: of Abner (2 Sam. 3:22–27) and Amasa (2 Sam. 20:4–10). In both cases Joab had caused David great administrative and personal hurt ("did to me," v. 5). At the time David was unable to deal forcefully with Joab because of the unstable political and military situation and Joab's great clout with the army, and possibly because Joab knew too much about David's personal affairs (the Uriah tragedy, etc.). Joab had also killed Absalom and just recently had been involved in the Adonijah affair, but David passed over those and other failures of Joab. He concentrated only on his double murder and observed that the blood of his innocent victims still stained his clothing. "According to your wisdom" (practical intelligence of a political or legal sort), find a proper opportunity of punishing him and do not let him die a natural death.

Shimei, a Benjamite, had cursed David and had threatened his life at the time of Absalom's rebellion, but David had spared his life (2 Sam. 16:5–14; 19:22–23). Why the king now felt that judgment had to be executed against Shimei is not clear. Possibly David suffered from the superstitious belief that removal of the curse required removal of the one who had pronounced it. It has also been suggested that Shimei, as a

Benjamite from the neighborhood of King Saul, might strike at David's son as he had struck at David.

But David was not all negative. He wanted Solomon to show kindness to the sons of Barzillai, an aged man who had provided for David during his flight from Absalom and perhaps had saved him from starvation (2 Sam. 17:27–29). Barzillai had on that occasion declined David's invitation to take a place at court but had recommended a son for the position. David now wanted to make sure Solomon provided for the members of this loyal family.

c. **David's death (2:10–12).** Soon afterward David died and was buried in the City of David, not in his ancestral home of Bethlehem. The City of David was then the southeastern hill of Jerusalem, and the tombs of the kings were for a long time located in a recognizable place there. Thus, the traditional tomb of David shown to tourists on the southwestern hill can have no connection with the real tomb of David. David ruled for forty years (1010–970), seven years at Hebron and thirty-three years over all Israel, and died at the age of seventy (2 Sam. 5:4–5). Solomon sat on his father's throne—evidently at a young age. Josephus said he was fourteen at the time of his accession,[4] but various considerations point to his being older than that.

3. His Purge of Royal Enemies (2:13–46)

Critics are often cynical about Solomon's actions in this passage, considering him to have engaged in a callous, systematic elimination of all threats to his rule. They have him looking for pretexts to destroy all who might be dangerous to him. At this distance and on the basis of the limited amount of biblical material available, it is difficult to assess his actions. He did have good reasons for most of his actions, and he was young and inexperienced; supposedly, not much over twenty at the time. If he was too severe, perhaps his immaturity and insecurity led him to be more suspicious, condemnatory, and vengeful than he needed to be. After all, he had just survived his older brother's plot to take the throne. Moreover, the judicial mentality of the ancient Near East was not that of modern America, and the

---

[4]Josephus, *Antiquities*, VIII.7.8.

Bible was not available in every hotel room to influence public
and private conduct. In fact, even most of the Old Testament
had not yet been written, and few copies of what did exist were
available to the small percentage of the populace that could
read. Furthermore, Scripture does not varnish over or sanitize
the thinking and conduct of Solomon any more than it does
anyone else who strides across its pages. He comes across as a
flesh and blood personality, a real person with a real agenda.
Too often biblical heroes are so idealized and romanticized that
they become something in the popular mind that they never
were in real life. At any rate, Solomon did eliminate those who
posed any threat to him or those whom his father had urged him
to dispose of.

a. **Adonijah (2:13–25).**   Adonijah enlisted the help of
Bathsheba in winning for him the hand of David's nurse
Abishag. Evidently she was one of the most beautiful women in
the kingdom. Whether or not he knew Abishag had not had
sexual relations with David and was therefore only a nurse and,
in a sense, not a full-fledged member of the harem, is open to
question. Nor is it clear whether Adonijah was merely enamored
with Abishag or whether his request had some political over-
tones. The request could be construed as a claim on the throne,
as custom dictated that the royal harem belonged to the new
king (see 2 Sam. 3:6–11; 16:20–23). Solomon did interpret it as
a claim to the throne, and Adonijah had vaguely related his
request to Solomon's accession to the throne (vv. 15–16).
Solomon could easily consider Adonijah's action as a violation of
the prohibition against any political activity or insubordination
on Adonijah's part (1 Kings 1:52).

The reader must remember that David had just recently
died, the king was young and somewhat insecure, the entire
Adonijah faction was still alive and potentially threatening, and
a young adolescent coming of age had just entertained a request
from a mother who may have been somewhat domineering.
Evidently Bathsheba had touched a raw nerve, because Solo-
mon said she might as well have requested the kingdom for
Adonijah, Abiathar, and Joab (v. 22). Under the circumstances
Solomon's reaction was somewhat predictable; he ordered that
Adonijah be executed, and commissioned Benaiah as execu-

tioner. In the process he demonstrated some uneasiness over his control of the throne and a determination to establish that control firmly (v. 24). Whether Bathsheba passed on Adonijah's request to Solomon because she saw no great threat to Solomon's rule in it or because she had promised Adonijah and had to keep her promise, is not clear.

b. Abiathar (2:26–27). Having disposed of Adonijah, Solomon next moved against Abiathar the priest. He removed Abiathar from office and sent him back to private life in his home village of Anathoth, about three miles northeast of Jerusalem. Solomon deemed him worthy of death for participation in Adonijah's revolt, but both because of his high-priestly dignity and his faithful service to David from the time of his persecution at the hands of Saul through Absalom's rebellion, he simply banished Abiathar. The historian adds that this deposition from the priesthood was in fulfillment of the prophecy that Eli's line of priests, of which Abiathar was a member, would be cut off (1 Sam. 2:30–35).

c. Joab (2:28–35). When Joab heard what had happened to Adonijah and Abiathar, he evidently concluded that Solomon was now moving against all the principals in the abortive attempt to crown Adonijah. Joab, like Adonijah, fled to the "tent," probably the sanctuary at Gibeon, and grasped the horns of the bronze altar of sacrifice in the courtyard. As noted earlier, this was a place of refuge for those unjustly accused of a crime or those guilty of minor crimes or accidental manslaughter, but not for deliberate murder (Exod. 21:13–14). Therefore, Joab must have thought Solomon was after him for insurrection. But David in his charge to Solomon had mentioned only Joab's guilt for two deliberate murders, for which there was no protection. Solomon again dispatched Benaiah as executioner. When ordered to come outside the sanctuary, Joab declared, "I will die here." Benaiah then fell on him at the altar, a course of action that was possible because Joab did not come under the protection of the state or religion (Exod. 21:14). Joab was not completely dishonored, however, because he was buried "on his own land in the wilderness," probably in the wilderness of Judea near Bethlehem, in a tomb he had prepared there.

Thus Solomon removed any blood guiltiness that remained

on the king and his house—a guilt that existed because Joab had committed his crimes while dispensing official duties. Removal of such guilt eliminated a barrier to God's blessing on the Davidic dynasty (v. 33). The historian then added a postscript that with Joab's removal as general of the army, Benaiah was appointed to take his place, and with the deposition of Abiathar, Zadok now became chief priest.

d. Shimei (2:36–46). Then Solomon proceeded to deal with the last person mentioned in David's charge. He put Shimei on a short tether. He had to live in Jerusalem and not cross the Kidron, the border between the tribe of Judah and the tribe of Benjamin, the latter being the tribe from which Shimei came. Shimei happily agreed to the restrictions placed upon him and was fully aware of the dire consequences if he violated them. He must have lived well, with a staff of servants; if two ran away, presumably he had others. After three years, two of Shimei's servants ran away to Gath in Philistine territory some thirty miles southwest of Jerusalem. Shimei violated the restrictions placed on him by going to search for them and paid with his life.

One could go on interminably discussing how justified Solomon was in executing Shimei, again at the hands of Benaiah. The introduction to this section has dealt with the general question of Solomon's conduct. In this case Solomon may have shared some of the superstition of Near Easterners and may have felt that executing one who had levied a curse eliminated the curse on his house and himself. With the curse lifted, he could be more sure "King Solomon will be blessed" (v. 45). With the elimination of all the known threats to the throne, the historian could confidently announce: "the kingdom was established in Solomon's hands" (v. 46).

4. His Marriage (3:1)

Reference to Solomon's marriage at the beginning of chapter 3 seems out of order, and some would place it much later in the book. It may be appropriate, however, to think of this verse as the last one of chapter 2. Then, as the kingdom was established in Solomon's hands, he entered into a political alliance with the pharaoh of Egypt and married his daughter.

Which pharaoh this was cannot be certainly determined, but he must have been from the late Twenty-first Dynasty. Egypt evidently saw some advantage to a linkage with the rising fortunes of the Davidic dynasty. This was not Solomon's first marriage, for before he became king he had already married Naamah an Ammonitess and had had a son by her, the future king Rehoboam (compare 1 Kings 14:21 with 11:42–43). Probably the daughter of Pharaoh renounced her idolatry because there does not seem to have been any Egyptian idolatry in Israel in Solomon's day, and it seems that in 1 Kings 11:1 she is not included among the foreign wives who led him into idolatry during his later years. He brought the daughter of Pharaoh into the "City of David," the southeastern hill of Jerusalem, until he finished construction of the royal complex and the temple to the north of the old walled Jebusite city.

B. Solomon's Choice of Wisdom (1 Kings 3:2–28)

1. Solomon's Dream (3:2–15)

From the time of Israel's occupation of the land of Canaan the people were accustomed to worship at the high places and to offer sacrifices to God there. This practice was tolerated because the temple had not yet been built. The Philistines had evidently destroyed the worship center at Shiloh (1 Sam. 4; Jer. 7:12–14; 26:6–9), and during David's reign there was not even a single sanctuary; the ark of the covenant stood in a tabernacle in Jerusalem and the bronze altar of sacrifice was located at the high place at Gibeon, six miles northwest of Jerusalem. Later, after construction of the temple, the prophets and priests increasingly condemned the high places, and often they became centers of pagan worship. Solomon himself was known to sacrifice at the high places, but the sacred historian is careful to note that he "followed the precepts of his father David" (v. 3).

Near the beginning of his reign, Solomon held a kind of inaugural religious ceremony at Gibeon, which a large number of officials and clan leaders of all Israel attended (see 2 Chron. 1:1–13). Zadok was apparently the resident priest (1 Chron. 16:39). On that occasion Solomon offered "a thousand burnt offerings," either to be taken literally or to indicate a very large

number. At such sacrifices it was customary to burn only part of
the animal as an offering to God; the worshipers ate the rest in a
fellowship meal. The size of the crowd would have required a
very large number of sacrifices. In the context of this moment of
religious ecstasy and in response to this sacrifice to God for
blessing on his reign, God appeared to Solomon in a dream
during the night and said, "Ask for what you would like me to
give you."

The king responded first with thanksgiving, then with a
sense of inadequacy, and finally with his request. Solomon
thanked God for His great covenant love and favor to His
faithful, covenant-keeping servant David and then for extending
His kindness in putting Solomon on the throne. But he was
overwhelmed with his youth and inexperience and the multitude of the people to be governed. "Little child" (v. 7) is an
oriental figure of speech expressing humility; but he was young,
as noted earlier. The statement should be taken in conjunction
with what follows: "I do not know how to go out or come in,"
which is an idiom for "inexperienced in leadership." "A people
too numerous to be counted" (v. 8) shows that the Abrahamic
covenant was in the process of fulfillment (cf. Gen. 13:16).

Then Solomon made his request for a "discerning heart" or
"judicial wisdom" to "judge" or "govern your people," to
"judge between good and evil," or in equity and truth. God
congratulated Solomon and said that since he had not asked for
long life or wealth or victory in warfare but for "discerning
judgment," He would grant his request. He would give him a
"wise and discerning mind" such as never had been before nor
ever will be in the future. Unfortunately, except for a hint or two
such as what appears in the following account, there is no record
of Solomon's legal or juridical system or his social order.

Then the God of the "superabundantly above" granted
Solomon what he did not ask for: riches and honor greater than
that of all other contemporary kings. From what we know of the
rulers of contemporary Italy or Greece or Egypt or Assyria or
perhaps even China, for example, it seems that Solomon does
come out on top of the heap. It is hard to evaluate verse 14: a
promise of long life in return for obedience to God's statutes.
Solomon was obedient during the early part of his reign and

then became involved in idolatry. Though he ruled for forty years, his life may have been cut short for disobedience. He must have died when not much older than sixty.

A concluding thought on Solomon's wisdom is in order. His gift was for judicial wisdom or discerning judgment, not necessarily wisdom for all of life. He was not uniformly wise. For example, his lack of fiscal judgment or fiscal restraint left the kingdom virtually bankrupt at his death. His lack of wisdom in marital matters resulted in the collection of a harem of seven hundred wives and three hundred concubines with the attendant idolatry, financial burden to the state, and impossible condition for the conduct of proper family life. Having said this, however, we have to infer that the book of Proverbs and other biblical and non-biblical references do indicate that Solomon's wisdom was far-reaching. But possession of wisdom of a certain sort does not necessarily mean that one will have the courage or restraint or perseverance to pursue a wise course of action.

2. Solomon's Exercise of Wisdom (3:16–28)

The following incident is undoubtedly reported as a typical example to demonstrate that God had indeed imparted the promised wisdom. As in other ancient Near Eastern societies with an absolute monarchy and an inadequately developed legal system, the common people had open access to Solomon for the adjudication of all sorts of cases. The story is a familiar one. Two prostitutes gave birth to children three days apart. The one rolled over on her child in the night and killed it; then she substituted her dead child for her companion's live child. In the morning the victimized mother realized what had happened and a wrangle developed between the two women over ownership of the live child, each claiming it. Finally they took the matter to Solomon. With his perception of maternal instincts, he commanded that a sword be brought and the infant be divided and half given to each woman. The real mother was willing to give up the child rather than have it killed; the false claimant agreed to having the child divided so neither could have anything. Immediately Solomon perceived who was the real mother and awarded her custody. This judicial decision was a convincing demonstration to all the people that Solomon had received divine wisdom for the administration of justice (v. 28).

C. Solomon's Administration (1 Kings 4:1–34)

Though this section does not at first directly mention Solomon's wisdom, it does reflect his administrative skill. At the onset it speaks of his chief officials (4:1–6) and then it proceeds to detail his district organization (4:7–19) and his general prosperity (4:20–28). Finally there is a summary statement concerning his intellectual achievements (4:29–34).

1. His Chief Officials (4:1–6)

Solomon appointed eleven men as a kind of cabinet for administration of the state. Though delegation of authority is a mark of wisdom, he was not the first ruler in Israel to do so. In fact, the list of his father's right-hand men had similar functions, and even some of the names are the same (2 Sam. 8:16–18; 20:23–26). It is as easy to give Solomon credit for something David had inaugurated as it is to credit Augustus Caesar's administrative reforms with many programs launched by Julius Caesar.

The list seems simple enough, but identification of the individuals and their functions is another matter. Four of the eleven are called priests: Azariah, Zadok, Abiathar, and Zabud. Azariah (v. 2) is frequently thought (on the basis of 1 Chron. 6:8, 9) to be the grandson of Zadok the priest who had been involved in the anointing of Solomon ("son" often means grandson or descendant in Scripture). But if that is the case, Azariah could hardly have been old enough to function as high priest near the beginning of Solomon's reign. Moreover, Zadok seems clearly in the picture as high priest, as previous discussion in this commentary has shown. After such consideration, Keil makes him out to be the administrator of the kingdom or prime minister, and others argue for something similar.[5] Abiathar (v. 4) had been demoted from the priesthood at the outset of Solomon's reign (2:35) but presumably retained the title and

[5]C. F. Keil, "The Books of the Kings" in *Biblical Commentary on the Old Testament*, ed. by C. F. Keil and F. Delitzsch, 2nd ed. (Edinburgh: T. & T. Clark, n.d.), 44.

honor even though Solomon did not permit him to function. Zadok was clearly the high priest. Zabud, though of the priestly class (v. 5), did not function as one. He was "the king's friend," evidently a personal counselor. The NIV captures the intent: "personal advisor to the king."

Elihoreph and Ahijah are listed as secretaries. Apparently they had responsibilities connected with writing, and one should not think of them as holding such posts as secretary of state or secretary of the interior. Some have suggested that the one had the responsibility of keeping records or supervising the archives and the other handled the correspondence. Others think that one took care of domestic correspondence and the other foreign correspondence. Jehoshaphat is commonly identified as "recorder," as maintaining records of daily affairs in the kingdom. But secretaries do that. The idea of "herald" has been extracted from the Hebrew in recent years. So this person had the task of communicating between king and country and of taking charge of arranging royal ceremonies (including audiences). Benaiah's description as commander-in-chief of the forces is clear enough. Azariah (v. 5) was in charge of the regional or district governors to be named in verses 7–19. This was a new office instituted by Solomon after his more effective organization of the kingdom. Ahishar was "in charge of the palace"; the NEB has "comptroller of the household." Apparently he had charge of the household staff, functions of the household (preparations of meals, etc.), and the maintenance and cleaning of the palace structure. Adoniram supervised "forced labor," evidently for such purposes as fortification, building of the seaport at Ezion-geber, or the construction of roads and bridges.

Of course, these eleven were only a small part of the official family. Jones estimates that in the days of David and Solomon, upwards of 5,600 court officials and their dependents were on the public payroll in the Jerusalem area.[6]

2. His District Organization (4:7–19)

As the bureaucracy became large and expensive, Solomon found it necessary to make provision for such. He divided the

---

[6]Gwilym H. Jones, "1 and 2 Kings" in *New Century Bible Commentary* (Grand Rapids: Eerdmans, 1984), 1:133.

land into twelve districts, each under the supervision of a
district governor and each to provide food for the royal household for one month of the year. The twelve districts in number
equaled the twelve tribes of Israel, but the districts were not
coextensive with the old tribal regions, and Judah was exempted
from the obligation; so Israel did not refer to all Israel in this
passage. Judah's favored status accentuated tribal rivalries and
contributed to the split that occurred in Rehoboam's day.

The districts were as follows. (1) The hill country of
Ephraim (including Samaria, Shiloh, Bethel, etc.). (2) A section
of the Shephelah or foothills southeast of modern Tel Aviv. (3)
The central Sharon plain and Mount Carmel. (4) The coastal
region north of the third district. (5) The northern hill country,
including Megiddo, Taanach, and Dothan. (6) The old territory
of Bashan, northeast of the Sea of Galilee. (7) Gilead and
western Ammon. (8) The land of Naphtali, west of the Sea of
Galilee and north to Dan. (9) The land of Asher, to the west of
Naphtali. (10) Land southwest of the Sea of Galilee, including
Jezreel. (11) Benjamin, a narrow swath extending west from
Jericho about two-thirds of the way across western Palestine.
(12) The land of Gad, much of old Moab.

This organization and list must date to the latter half of
Solomon's reign because two of the governors were sons-in-law
of Solomon (vv. 11, 15), and the list does not include towns of
the plain of Acco transferred to Hiram of Tyre about the middle
of his reign (1 Kings 9:10–14). Why five of the names of
governors are missing and they are distinguished only as "son
of . . ." can only be conjectured.

3. His General Prosperity (4:20–28)

This passage portrays Solomon's kingdom as secure and
prosperous. Prosperity is defined first, in terms of a large
population: "as numerous as the sand by the sea" (v. 20), and
second, in terms of the fact that these people generally enjoyed
the basic comforts of life: "They ate, and drank, and lived
happily" (v. 20; the last expression appears only here in the Old
Testament). Israel experienced a wonderful security, a kind of
Pax Hebraica or Hebrew peace. Solomon dominated all the
lands from Tipsah (Gr., Thapsacus) at the bend of the Euphrates

in the north to land of Philistia in the west and the "border of Egypt" (the Wadi el-'Arish at the northern edge of the Sinai) in the south. The various subject peoples of these lands brought tribute, and Solomon generally enjoyed peace. Presumably the unrest in Edom and Syria that arose at the beginning of his reign (1 Kings 11:14–25) was not a serious threat to the well-being of the empire. At least from Dan to Beersheba, the traditional borders of Hebrew Palestine, Judah and Israel "dwelt in safety" (v. 25).

This security was made possible not only by the blessing of God but also by Solomon's fortifications and military preparedness. He kept 12,000 horses (v. 26; cf. 2 Chron. 1:14) in 4,000 "stalls" or "chariot parks," where three horses for each chariot were stabled together in pens. The figure of 40,000 stalls in the Hebrew of verse 26 must be a copyist's error and 4,000 has been adopted from the parallel passage in 2 Chronicles 9:25. Solomon maintained 1,400 chariots (2 Chron. 1:14) in several locations called "chariot cities" (2 Chron. 9:25; cf. 1 Kings 9:19).

The general peace and prosperity made it possible for the twelve district governors to maintain regular deliveries of barley (the ordinary food of horses in ancient Palestine) and straw for the horses and a large daily provision for the king's table (for the support of public officials). That provision included thirty kors of fine flour (if computed at the usual rate of 6.3 bushels to the kor, the total would be 189 bushels), sixty kors of ordinary flour (378 bushels), and a substantial list of domesticated and wild animals. Fruits and vegetables were not included in the tally.

4. His Intellectual Achievements (4:29–34)

As in chapter 3, the sacred historian emphasizes that "God gave Solomon wisdom." But the wisdom described here is of a more general sort than the judicial wisdom of 3:28. God's endowment of "wisdom," "discernment" or "insight," and "understanding" or "largeness of mind" was to be immeasurable "as the sands on the seashore." This "wisdom" (hokmah) involves an understanding of the basic issues of life, a proper discernment between good and evil, and a skill in performing business affairs and the handling of people.[7] "Discernment" or "insight" *(bînah)* concerns the ability to distinguish between truth and error, between the valid and invalid.[8] "Largeness of mind" probably refers to breadth of interests. Solomon's wisdom exceeded that of the "people" or "sons of the east" (usually a reference to the Arab tribes east of Israel and extending to the Euphrates) and of "Egypt" (known for its wisdom literature; e.g., of Ptah-hotep, ca. 2450 B.C.; and Amenemope, ca. 1000 B.C.).

Next, his wisdom is declared to be superior to that of several specific individuals who must have been highly regarded in Solomon's day. They are almost completely unknown now. Ethan the Ezrahite appears in the title of Psalm 89 and presumably he wrote that psalm; Ethan and Heman were musicians according to 1 Chronicles 15:19.

Then Solomon is credited with three thousand proverbs (short, pithy sayings setting forth truth in the form of simile or metaphor) and "a thousand and five" songs. Since canonical proverbs contain only eight hundred verses and the Song of Solomon a limited number of songs (in addition to Psalms 72 and 127), the great king must have been responsible for much that has not been preserved. The reference to his knowledge of botany and zoology may refer to his insights in those fields as revealed in his proverbs or to more scientific studies such as botanical or zoological classifications. The fame of Solomon's wisdom was so great that people came to "hear" it from his own lips. The coming of the queen of Sheba (1 Kings 10) is the only biblical example of such a visit. "All the kings of the earth" is hyperbole designed to describe a widespread practice.

D. Solomon's Construction of the Temple and His Palace (1 Kings 5:1–8:66)

1. Preparations for the Temple (5:1–18)

a. Solomon's agreement with Hiram (5:1–12). Now that the sacred historian has told the story of Solomon's establishment on his throne, the organization of his administration, and the stabilization of the kingdom, it is appropriate for him to proceed

---

[7] Gleason L. Archer, *A Survey of Old Testament Introduction,* rev. ed. (Chicago: Moody, 1974), 467.
[8] Ibid.

to an account of his building activities. Construction required architectural skill, materials, and craftsmen that Israel did not have. To fill those needs David had turned to Phoenicia and had established a virtual alliance with Hiram, king of Tyre (2 Sam. 5:11–12). With the death of David and the accession of Solomon to the throne, Hiram sent condolences to Solomon and best wishes for his administration; but especially he wanted to negotiate a treaty of alliance or trade with Solomon. Phoenicia was not a united state in those days but a collection of city-states under the domination of Tyre. The finest sailors of antiquity, the Phoenicians became the middlemen of the Near East during the first millennium B.C. In addition to trading the goods of other lands, they produced purple dye and fabrics, metal goods, and especially the much-sought-after cedars of Lebanon. Not only was it advantageous for their commercial ventures to have good relations with the Hebrews, but also the Phoenicians depended on Hebrew protection of their hinterland to the east.

Solomon jumped at the chance to meet his building needs (cf. 2 Chron. 2:3–15). Though his plan included construction of several buildings, his focus is on the temple here. He assumed that Hiram knew of David's earnest desire to build a temple for his God and the prohibition against it because David was a man of war. His son, who would be a man of peace, was to build it instead (2 Sam. 7). He assured Hiram that he was indeed firmly established on the throne, peace reigned in the kingdom, and no "disaster" or "misfortune" had befallen (such as a rebellion or pestilence or famine).

Solomon then made the proposal that Hiram provide him with cedar of Lebanon and that Hebrews work with Sidonians to complete the task. "Sidonian" must be understood as virtually synonymous with Phoenician. "None among us know how to cut timber . . ." refers to knowledge of which trees to cut, the time for cutting, the treatment of the wood, and transport of the huge logs from the mountains to the coast. Solomon offered to pay whatever wages Hiram set. Obviously this is all preliminary bargaining with no specific amount of timber mentioned and no exact amount of payment.

Hiram's response was enthusiastic; it was good business and good politics to have close relations with the Hebrews and a long-range business contract. Hiram's praise of Yahweh does not imply that he recognized Him as the only true God; undoubtedly he simply accepted Yahweh as the God of the Hebrews as Baal was his lord. He might as easily have said, "Praise be to the gods." He was respecting the religious sensitivities of the Hebrews and making a very diplomatic statement. Then Hiram got more specific: he would provide the needed "cedar" and "cypress" logs. His men would haul them down to the sea and bind them into rafts and float them to wherever Solomon specified. Then they would uncouple the logs and Solomon's men could transport them to Jerusalem. It turned out that Solomon wanted them delivered to Joppa (2 Chron. 2:15). From there they could be taken up the Yarkon River, just north of Joppa, and overland to Jerusalem. Tell Qasile (that has been partially excavated, ancient name unknown) near the mouth of the Yarkon, may have figured significantly in this venture.

In return Hiram requested wheat and olive oil for his royal court. So the two of them made a treaty (v. 12; cf. 2 Chron. 2:3–15), and Solomon annually provided Hiram with twenty thousand kors of wheat (about 126,000 bushels) and twenty kors or two hundred baths (1850–2100 gallons) of olive oil according to the Hebrew and twenty thousand baths (about 115,000 gallons) according to the Septuagint (the reading—or figure—adopted by the NIV).

b. The corvée in Israel (5:13–18). Corvée, or forced labor, was now introduced in Israel. Verse 13 mentions thirty thousand men conscripted from all Israel and divided into relays of ten thousand. Each man served one month in Lebanon and two months at home or "in his house," that is, in Solomon's temple; so the total service was three months a year. Apparently thirty thousand were called up at one time; on this relay plan a total of one hundred-twenty thousand would be needed in the course of a year. This passage should not be thought to conflict with 1 Kings 9:20–22, which says that only non-Israelites were conscripted. The forced labor here is temporary and did not involve serfdom; the forced labor in 9:20–22 is forced labor on slaves or aliens and may be taken as more permanent. Adoniram was in charge of the corvée (cf. 1 Kings 4:6).

In addition, Solomon had seventy thousand burden bearers

or porters and eighty thousand stonecutters working in the hills north of Jerusalem under the supervision of 3,300 (some manuscripts say 3,600) foremen. These were evidently all aliens, for 2 Chronicles 2:17 mentions a Solomonic census of aliens that turned up 153,600 of them, of which seventy thousand became burden bearers or carriers and eighty thousand stonecutters. Huge blocks of "choice stone" (v. 17) were cut for the foundations of the temple. Men of Gebal (v. 18), modern Byblos (about 25 miles north of Beirut), were among the master carpenters and masons employed in Jerusalem.

2. Construction of the Temple (6:1–38)

a. Time of construction (6:1). Solomon had established himself on his throne, had achieved a certain amount of internal organization, and had arranged a treaty with Hiram of Tyre that would assure him of the supplies and expertise required to build the temple and his administrative complex. Now it was time to begin construction. Solomon found himself in his fourth year. Based on Thiele's reckonings he would have started to rule in 970 and his fourth year would have been 967 or 966. The second month, Zif or Ziv, is equivalent to our April–May.

The historian adds an intriguing note, however, that the Exodus took place 480 years before the beginning of construction (as an alternative, the Septuagint gives 440 years). Taken literally, the date of the Exodus would be fixed at 1447/46 B.C. and some basis for figuring a chronology back to Abraham would be available. The matter is not that easily settled, however, and a great many put the Exodus in the thirteenth century, about 1275 B.C.[9] In becoming involved with the chronological issue of this verse we should not ignore the fact that placing the construction of the temple and the Exodus in close juxtaposition seems to put this project on a par with or especially relates it to the Exodus in some sense. The promise inaugurated in the freedom from Egypt would at last be realized in the building of the temple.

---

[9] For a discussion see Howard F. Vos, *An Introduction to Bible Archaeology*, rev. ed. (Chicago: Moody, 1983), 55–60; John J. Davis, *Moses and the Gods of Egypt* (Grand Rapids: Baker, 1971), 16–37.

b. General plan and measurements (6:2–10). The temple
was sixty cubits long, twenty cubits wide, and thirty cubits high,
double the dimensions of the tabernacle (Exod. 26:16, 18). If the
cubit is computed at its usual length of about eighteen inches,
the measurements were ninety feet long, thirty feet wide, and
forty-five feet high. Thus it was not a large structure—only the
size of a large house; its expense in time and materials resulted
not from size but care and exquisiteness of ornamentation. The
"portico" or "porch" in front of the temple extended across the
entire structure (20 cubits or 30 feet) and was ten cubits or
fifteen feet deep. What the windows were like (v. 4) is unclear.
The NIV considers them to be "clerestory windows," and they
probably were; but that does not really describe them. The JPS
and JB identify them as "latticed." Perhaps they were framed
with immovable latticework that would permit circulation of air
but would cut down the glare of bright light; small latticework
would prevent the entrance of birds. "Windows of narrow
lights" (KJV) may indicate windows of close or small latticework.

According to verses 5, 6, 8, 10, rooms were built around
three sides of the temple (excluding the entrance side). Constructed in three stories, they were entered on the "right" or
"south" side of the temple. Rooms on the lower floor were five
cubits broad on the inside; those on the middle level, six cubits;
and those on the upper level, seven cubits. Thus the builders
were making the walls successively thinner on the two upper
levels, creating ledges ("narrowed rests," KJV) on which ceiling
beams of cedar could be placed; the goal was to avoid cutting
holes in the temple wall for ceiling beams (v. 6). Access to the
upper floors was by a "winding" stairs, according to KJV, NASB,
and JPS, but the nature of the stairs is not clear in the Hebrew.
Evidently each of the three floors was five cubits high, giving a
total of fifteen cubits. So the height of the roof of the temple
proper was thirty cubits and the height of this service area
fifteen cubits plus (if one adds ceilings), and windows on the
side of the temple above the addition thus would be "clerestory" windows (v. 4, NIV).

There is a question of whether the "covering" with beams
and planks of cedar (v. 9) refers to roofing (so NIV) or paneling on
the inside of the stone work (so, e.g., JPS). It seems that roofing

("beams and planks") is in view in this general descriptive; paneling of the interior is mentioned later (vv. 16–18). To maintain the dignity and sanctity of this holy place during construction, stone was so carefully prepared in the quarries that it was not necessary to use heavy tools to dress it on location (v. 7).

c. **God's charge to Solomon (6:11–13).** Though some claim that this divine message to Solomon was designed to provide encouragement for him in the midst of a challenging under-taking, that may be debated. Solomon was concerned with building a house for God—with doing a great work for God. God, for His part, was more concerned with Solomon's walk (as He is with ours); so He sent a message to Solomon, evidently through an unnamed prophet, because He appeared directly to Solomon at Gibeon and not again until at the dedication of the temple (1 Kings 3:5; 9:2; 11:9).

God had unequivocally promised David that He would establish the throne of his kingdom forever (2 Sam. 7:13, evidently in the fullest sense in the rule of David's greater Son, Jesus Christ, in His eternal kingdom). Now He tells Solomon that if he will obey Him, He will fulfill that promise through Solomon. Later it turned out that his disobedience resulted in God's removing much of the kingdom from the control of his son Rehoboam. It is appropriate in this context for God to add another conditional promise, that if Solomon would obey, his nation would enjoy God's presence and protection. The reason that it was appropriate to add the promise was that God's presence was soon to fill the temple (1 Kings 8:10, 11) and especially dwell among them. With the passage of time, Solomon's disobedience, and later that of his people, would result in God's withdrawal of His presence from the temple (Ezek. 9:3; 10:4; 11:23) and its destruction along with that of the city of Jerusalem and the rest of the kingdom.

d. **Completion and ornamentation (6:14–38).** When Solomon had completed the exterior stone work, he turned his attention to the interior of the temple. The entire interior was lined with boards of cedar from floor to ceiling, and the floor was covered with planks of cypress; no stone was left exposed. To form the Holy of Holies, Solomon instructed that a wooden

screen be erected from floor to ceiling to partition off the rear
twenty cubits of the interior. That left a Holy Place forty cubits
long as a main hall. The interior surface was decorated with
"gourds" (oval ornaments) and "open flowers" (v. 18) and
cherubim and palm trees (v. 29) carved into the wall. There is
no indication as to the placement of all this decoration, but on
the basis of Ezekiel 41:17–18 and other Near Eastern decorative
motifs, Keil suggests the alteration of cherubim and palm trees,
with garlands of flowers above and a border of gourds below. A
single band or row could have run around the wall, but he thinks
a double or even triple band, located one above the other, was
more likely.[10]

Then Solomon ordered preparation of an "inner sanctuary"
or Holy of Holies. This was to be a cube: twenty cubits long,
twenty cubits wide, and twenty cubits high that was placed
behind the screen. That left ten cubits between it and the
ceiling. Some suggest that it was elevated on a platform, but
there is no evidence of that fact or of any steps needed to ascend
to it. Probably there was simply a loft above it. Within the Holy
of Holies stood two immense cherubim (winged creatures with
human faces), carved from olive wood and covered with gold.
These were ten cubits high (half the height of the room) and
each had a wingspan of ten cubits. When they were put in place
against the west (back) wall, their combined wingspan extended
across the entire wall, the wing of the one touching the north
wall and the wing of the other touching the south wall; and their
wings met in the center above the ark of the covenant. In front of
the inner sanctuary stood the altar of incense made of cedar
wood and covered with gold. In fact, the entire inner surface of
the temple is said to have been covered with gold (vv. 20–22,
30).

Verses 31–35 describe the doors, but the Hebrew is
extremely difficult and unclear. At the entrance to the Holy of
Holies there were doors of olive wood carved with cherubim,
palm trees and flowers to match the inner walls and they were
overlaid with gold, but the nature of the doors is uncertain.
Perhaps the Hebrew means to say that the doors and the

---

[10]Keil, *The Books of the Kings*, 80.

doorposts formed about a fifth part of the wall, or about four cubits (v. 31). In that case, the doors would each have been about one and one-half cubits wide and the doorposts about a half cubit. It seems that there was also a curtain (2 Chron. 3:14) and a gold chain (v. 21) across this doorway. The doors of the Holy Place are likewise hard to visualize. Verse 33 may indicate that they formed about a fourth part of the wall; with their frames they would then have been about five cubits wide and eight cubits high. Keil suggests that verse 34, describing two doors, "each having two leaves" (NIV) may be understood to indicate doors divided so that only the lower half (of about two cubits in width and four in height) need be opened for daily entrance of the priests into the Holy Place.[11] An alternate interpretation concludes that they were large doors with two smaller doors inserted in them. In any case, the doors were made of cypress wood and matched the doors of the Holy of Holies in carving and gold overlay.

The inner courtyard of the temple is described only in the most general terms (v. 36) as constructed of three rows of cut stone and a row of cedar beams. This would then be timbered masonry with the use of timber to alternate with every three rows of masonry to provide flexibility in the walls in the event of an earthquake. The size of the courtyard in not given, but if it was proportionate to the dimensions of the tabernacle courtyard, it must have been about one hundred-fifty feet wide by about four hundred feet long.

A concluding statement on the length of time required to build the temple puts laying of the foundation in the second month of the year and completion of the construction in the eighth month of the eleventh year—a total of seven and one-half years, but that is rounded off to seven years in verse 38.

3. Construction of Solomon's House (7:1–12)

Naturally, the sacred historian focused attention on the temple when describing the building activities of Solomon, and it is proper that he should do so, for the temple has held a very special place in the hearts of the Hebrew people ever since.

---

[11] Ibid., 83.

That feeling continues to the present, as evidenced by the almost delirious happiness of Jews at the Western Wall of the temple after the Six Day War in 1967 gave them access to the Old City once more; or as Sabbath prayers are observed at the Western Wall on any given week in the present. But a secular historian who tried to give a balanced account of the construction of Solomon might have chosen to throw the spotlight elsewhere. Perhaps on his fortress cities. Or on his seaport and navy. Or on his great palace complex, as the sacred historian now attempts to do. After all, it took him thirteen years to complete the palace complex (7:1) and seven and one-half years to build the temple, but evidently both projects were proceeding concurrently.

Actually, the discussion of palace construction is sandwiched in between a description of the erection of the temple and its furnishings. As Jones observes, "The combination of the Temple and the palace may suggest an ideological link between the divine sovereign on his throne and the Davidic king in his palace."[12] The buildings or functional structures in the royal complex are five in number, apparently introduced from south to north as one moves from the City of David toward the temple. They are: the House of the Forest of Lebanon, the hall of pillars, the throne room, a palace for Pharaoh's daughter, and a palace for Solomon. The whole was surrounded by a courtyard enclosed by a stone wall. Unfortunately detail is so sketchy as to prevent a clear picture of size, nature, and function of the structures.

The House of the Forest of Lebanon is so called because of the extensive use of cedar of Lebanon in the building; the exterior was built of stone, as was true of the rest of the constructions in the complex. The dimensions were about one hundred-fifty feet long, seventy-five feet wide and forty-five feet high. Its function evidently was to serve as a storehouse, and especially as an armory (1 Kings 10:17; Isa. 22:8). The upper part of the structure was supported on four rows of cedar pillars (so Hebrew text, preferable to the three rows of the Septuagint). Then, presumably, two rows stood against the side walls and

---

[12]Gwilym H. Jones, "1 and 2 Kings," in *New Century Bible Commentary* (Grand Rapids: Eerdmans, 1984), 1:173, cf. p.79.

two rows stood opposite them to form side aisles. The four rows then supported cedar beams that, in turn, supported chambers above them. The interpretation of the Hebrew adopted here is that verse 3 refers not to forty-five pillars but to forty-five chambers in three stories, fifteen to a story on each side of the building; thus the rooms would be about ten feet wide and useful for storage of armaments.

Visualization of the interior of the building based on this interpretation is as follows. There were side aisles formed by two rows of pillars supporting three stories of rooms on either of the long sides of the building. The central aisle was open to the roof beams, so there was a large assembly hall with a high ceiling in the middle. At either end of the hall were three rows of windows (v. 4) with latticework (see Hebrew; cf. 1 Kings 6:4). Three doors faced each other at either end of the structure (v. 5).

The hall of pillars (v. 6) may have been freestanding or, more likely, it was attached to an end of the House of the Forest of Lebanon; it was fifty cubits long as the previously mentioned structure was wide. Apparently it was an open portico. The last part of verse 6 is difficult to translate, but very possibly it refers to a columned porch placed in the middle of the portico, much as a propylaeum to some Greek temple or complex, such as the Acropolis at Athens.

Next, the writer mentions the throne hall or hall of judgment (v. 7), which probably was a separate freestanding structure, and may have been connected with the hall of pillars. The latter could provide plenty of space for persons to wait to see the king or to socialize after an audience with him. The building was paneled with cedar from floor to ceiling.

"Set farther back" (NIV, v. 8), or "in a court set back from the colonnade" (NEB), that is, in an inner courtyard, separated from the outer courtyard where the aforementioned structures stood, were Solomon's private apartments and a house for Pharaoh's daughter (cf. 3:1; 9:24). What is meant by the observation that these private dwellings were "similar in design" and whether to the hall of pillars or the throne hall is not clear. At least they were built of limestone and paneled with cedar, as the following summary indicates.

"All these structures," all the ones described in verses 2–8, were made of "choice" or "costly" stone "cut to size" in the quarry and carefully dressed, "trimmed with a saw" on both the inside and outside. This was true of the foundations and the upper courses of the buildings all the way to the eaves, and of the wall surrounding the courtyard. Foundation stones were sometimes eight or ten cubits long. Carefully dressed cedar beams supported the roofs; the wall surrounding the royal complex was constructed like the temple courtyard wall with three courses of cut stone and one of cedar beams to give greater ability to absorb the shock of an earthquake. Perhaps it would be useful to note that Palestinian limestone is quite soft when first quarried, and hardens with exposure.

4. Furnishing of the Temple (7:13–51)

a. The chief craftsman (7:13–14). The construction work of Solomon now proceeds with the furnishing of the temple. At Solomon's request (2 Chron. 2:7), Hiram, king of Tyre, sent a craftsman to Solomon to direct the work. Though he had the same name as the king, he was unrelated to him. His mother evidently was a Danite (2 Chron. 2:13) who had married into the tribe of Naphtali. When her husband died, she married again as a widow of a Naphtalite, a Tyrian, and bore him Hiram. He was "endowed with wisdom, understanding, and knowledge" (v. 14) in craftsmanship in bronze; but according to 2 Chronicles 2:14, he could work effectively in gold, silver, iron, and other mediums as well. No doubt he brought with him additional skilled craftsmen.

b. The bronze pillars (7:15–22). Hiram's first task was to cast two great bronze pillars to flank the entrance to the temple. These freestanding columns were twenty-seven feet high and with their capitals rose to a total height of over thirty-four feet. They were eighteen feet in circumference and about six feet in diameter with a hollow center; the metal itself was three inches thick. It is known that freestanding pillars stood in front of some Phoenician temples and held a fire that glowed at night, but what function these pillars were supposed to serve is unclear. The pillar on the south (left) was called Jachin, "He [Yahweh] establishes," and the one on the north (right) Boaz, "In Him

[Yahweh] is strength." At the minimum they were a witness to God's security and strength available to the Hebrews. The description of the capitals in verses 17–20 is very difficult in the Hebrew. Presumably they consisted of a kind of filigree, the upper part of which was sculpture in the form of flowering lilies and the lower part of cords braided together and draped in the form of festoons on which pomegranates hung.

c. The great sea (7:23–26). The next item to be described is the "sea of cast metal" (v. 23, NIV). This is the only time in the Old Testament that "sea" is used in a figurative sense. According to 2 Chronicles 4:6 the sea was for the priests to wash in. In view of the fact that it was seven and one-half feet high, either some means of siphoning off water was necessary or else a means of ascent was available. Possibly also this was a source of water for the lavers described below. This great bronze basin was fifteen feet from rim to rim and thirty feet in circumference. Of course, that figure is not quite mathematically accurate. The problem is usually solved by assuming that the figures are simply rounded off. Another possibility is that the diameter was measured from the outer rim, but the circumference around the inside of the basin (the thickness of the rim was about three inches). The sea rested on twelve bulls; their hindquarters toward the center and three of them facing each point of the compass. They may have been simply decorative or they may have represented the twelve tribes of Israel or something else; commentators do not agree on this point. The sea could hold two thousand baths. Computed at the usual rate of just under five gallons per bath, its capacity would have been a little less than ten thousand gallons. The NIV margin uses a slightly different equivalent for the bath and computes the contents at 11,500 gallons. For decoration there were two rows of gourds around the outside of it, "cast in one piece with it."

d. The ten lavers (7:27–39). Hiram also cast ten lavers for distribution of water for purification and for cleansing the altar and the court (2 Chron. 4:6). These consisted of two parts: the basins and the stands to put them on. The stands were about six feet square and four and one-half feet high and mounted on four wheels like chariot wheels. The stands consisted of four panels attached to uprights and the whole of the exterior was decorated with lions, bulls, cherubim, and wreaths. In the top of the stand was a circular band on which the laver itself could rest. The bronze lavers measured six feet across and each held forty baths or just over 190 gallons. Hiram put five of these stands on the south side of the temple and five on the north.

e. Summary of Hiram's work (7:40–47). The historian now summarizes the work of Hiram. He made the two pillars and their capitals, the ten stands and the lavers, the sea, and the twelve bulls, and "pots" (used for carrying away ashes from the altar), "shovels" or "scrapers" (for cleaning out the altar), and "sprinkling bowls" (for applying the blood for the sacrifice). All that Hiram made he cast from burnished bronze (polished to make it shine), and he cast his productions in clay molds in the "plains of the Jordan between Succoth and Zarethan." Succoth is usually identified with Deir 'Alla, on the east side of the Jordan Valley just north of the river Jabbok. Excavations there demonstrate that it was a center of metallurgy during the Hebrew monarchy. Deposits of metal slag and furnaces have been found. The clay in the region was of a superior kind for making molds, and a supply of charcoal was available nearby.

f. Summary of furnishings of gold (7:48–50). "Solomon made"; it is not necessary to conclude that Hiram was not also responsible for these gold furnishings. The king is noted as the initiator in verses 45, 46, and 47; and it is natural for the historian to continue to refer to him as initiator in verses 48–50. Of course, craftsmen did the work. The list includes the "golden altar" (table of incense made of cedar and overlaid with gold), the "table of the bread of the Presence" (likewise of cedar and overlaid with gold; there were ten of these as there were ten lampstands, 2 Chron. 4:8, 19), the "ten lampstands of pure gold," an assortment of gold dishes, wick trimmers and the like for use in the Holy Place, and "gold sockets for the doors" (probably not the sockets in the floor of the lintel but hinges or some other part of the door).

g. David's contribution (7:51). To all that Solomon provided was added what David had been collecting for the temple: gifts received, spoils of war, and personal contributions.

5. Dedication of the Temple (8:1–66)

a. Placing of the ark (8:1–9). At last the great day had arrived. The completed temple stood there in all its splendor, the exterior white limestone reflecting the brilliant rays of the sun and the interior gold surfaces displaying their richness in the muted light that shone through the latticed windows. The marvelous burnished bronze creations of Hiram of Tyre and his crew stood in place, as brightly polished as devoted priests could make them. The gold furniture reposed in all its pristine glory in the appropriate places. The treasury was filled with the precious service utensils that David and Solomon had collected. Only the ark of the covenant was lacking, and the Shekinah Glory of God had not yet filled the place. Nor had the prayers and sacrifices of dedication been offered.

To proceed to the dedication, Solomon called together the "elders of Israel" (the community chiefs), the "heads of the tribes," and the "princes of the fathers' houses," as representatives of all Israel to bring up the ark from the "City of David," where it was located in a tent only a few hundred yards to the south (2 Chron. 6:5–7). The time of this gala occasion was the month Ethanim (the earlier name for Tishri), the seventh month of the year (September–October), when the "Feast" (v. 2, of Tabernacles) was celebrated. Thus, eleven months had elapsed since the structure itself had been completed (1 Kings 6:38). Why Solomon waited so long must remain a matter of conjecture. Some think that the postponement was designed to make the dedication roughly coincide with the beginning of the new year. Or perhaps, even though the temple itself had been completed much earlier, the furniture and equipment were not. The leaders of Israel merely acted as an honor guard. The actual bearers of the ark and tent and furnishings were "priests and Levites," as the Law prescribed (Num. 4:5, 6, 15, 19, 20).

When the company arrived in the temple courtyard, they stopped and offered numerous sacrifices, no doubt as acts of thanksgiving and rejoicing; on this occasion the focus was not on penitence. Though the persons involved in actual performance of the sacrifices are not named, they could not have been the king and other laymen. Only the priests could offer sacrifices, and there is no indication anywhere in the dedication narrative that God was displeased with violations of prescribed procedure.

After the sacrifices the priests carried the ark into the Holy of Holies and set it beneath the protective wings of the cherubim. Verse 8 makes a curious reference to the carrying poles of the ark. Those two long poles, passed through rings on either side of the ark, were now left in place and were visible from the Holy Place. Then, evidently, the ark was placed across the entrance to the Holy of Holies behind a veil or curtain to protect it from the eyes of the curious and profane. But the poles were so long they stuck out slightly on either side of the curtain as continuous proof that the holy ark was still there.

At this point the historian adds a note that the ark contained nothing but the two stone tablets on which were inscribed the Ten Commandments—placed there by Moses at Mount Sinai. There is no necessary contradiction between verse 9 and Hebrews 9:4 that says the ark also contained a pot of manna and Aaron's rod that budded. The Hebrews passage evidently refers to the fully working tabernacle of the period of wilderness wanderings and Judges, not to the temple. Hundreds of years separated the days of Moses and Joshua from those of Solomon. During the interim the ark had suffered some rough treatment, even straying into Philistine hands for a time. Conceivably, the other two items had simply gotten lost over the years.

b. God's possession of His temple (8:10–13). "When the priests came out of the Holy of Holies, the cloud filled the temple" (v. 10), visible evidence that God Himself had taken up residence in the house. A similar phenomenon had occurred when the tabernacle was completed (Exod. 40:34–35). On that occasion Moses could not enter because of God's glory; on this occasion the priests could not perform because "the glory of Yahweh filled the house." The darkness of a cloud is often said to shroud the Deity (e.g., Exod. 24:15ff.; Ps. 97:2). It is appropriate that God should enfold Himself in a cloud, because unholy human beings cannot stand before the glory of the Lord, which is like a consuming fire (Exod. 24:17; Deut. 4:24; 9:3).

Isaiah experienced this consuming fire of God's holiness some two hundred years later and cried, "Woe is me! I am lost

[or 'ruined'] . . . my eyes have beheld . . . the LORD Almighty"
(Isa. 6:5). Contemporary Christianity with its "buddy, buddy"
approach to God has largely forgotten the sovereign glory and
holiness of God, so that being a Christian often seems to make
little difference in the way we live.

These priests could not perform when God was so evidently
present in His sanctuary, for human beings cannot stand this
degree of evidence of God's presence on a daily basis. There is
no mention of offerings of incense at this point, as there had
been sacrifices when the ark was brought in. Obviously this
cloud did not remain perpetually; nor did it need to. The
symbolical act of God's taking up His abode in His house had
occurred. The Presence was always there, however, and was
visible to the high priest when he entered the Holy of Holies on
the Day of Atonement. The Shekinah Glory was not removed
until just before the Babylonians destroyed the temple (Ezek.
9:3; 10:4; 11:23). It is encouraging to note that although God's
presence in holiness and majesty is a rebuke of human sin and
inadequacy, it is also evidence of God's power and grace
extended to His people.

While still facing the Holy of Holies, Solomon responded to
God who had come to take up His abode: "I have built for you a
stately house, a place for you to dwell forever" (v. 13). This was
a permanent dwelling compared with the tent of the tabernacle;
and though he really did not expect the temple to stand forever,
Solomon was thinking of the permanency of God's covenant to
dwell with His people forever. The congregation also responded, as 2 Chronicles 5:12–13 indicates.

c. Solomon's address to the people (8:14–21). Now the
king, who had been facing the Holy of Holies, turned around
and addressed the assembled crowd in the court. First he
praised God who had fulfilled His promise to his father David.
Then he introduced a historical summary. God, who in the
earlier centuries of Hebrew history had not chosen a place for
His abode, had ultimately chosen Jerusalem (see 2 Chron. 6:6)
and David to rule there. David had had it in his heart to build
the temple, and God had complimented him for it but had
denied him the privilege, saying that his son would do it
instead.

God has kept His word. Solomon now sits on the throne of Israel and has built the temple "for the name of Yahweh," i.e., where His presence and character would be evident. "A place for the ark" (v. 21) indicates especially a place for the throne of God, from which His glory would be manifested. From this center, too, would radiate "the covenant of Yahweh," evidently an allusion to the ark's containing the tablets inscribed with the Ten Commandments. Throughout the speech Solomon glorified God for His faithfulness and emphasized His sovereignty in the history of Israel, the choice of Jerusalem as the location of the temple, and the choice of the Davidic line to rule there and to build the temple.

d. Solomon's prayer for the people (8:22–53).

(1) For perpetuity of the line and kingdom (8:22–26).

Then Solomon "stood" before the altar and in the course of the prayer he knelt (as v. 54 indicates and as 2 Chron. 6:13 clearly states). The parallel account in Chronicles also mentions a bronze platform or pulpit that he ascended in the outer court. The fact that here Solomon and David (2 Sam. 6:14–20; 24:25), Hezekiah (2 Kings 19:14ff.), and other kings officiated in prayer and religious services showed they had some priestly privileges. An analysis of Solomon's prayer demonstrates the maturity of his theology and that of Israel at the time and argues against the critical view that Israel's theology was not highly developed until about 500 B.C. Critics are so obsessed with the evolutionary view of Israel's religion that they find it hard to take anything in the early history of Israel at face value, even though archaeological and historical evidence continues to mount in support of the authenticity of the Old Testament.

This prayer begins, as should any good prayer, with thanksgiving and praise to God. The praise in verses 23 and 24 is threefold: God is incomparable ("there is no God like You"); keeps His covenant; and has kept His promise to David. Both God's immanence and transcendence surface again and again in the prayer; Solomon starts with a reference to God "in heaven above and on earth below" (v. 23). After praise the king launches into petition for the perpetuity of his line and his kingdom (vv. 25–26). Clearly he is reminding God of the Davidic covenant (2 Sam. 7) that, in its fuller fulfillment, is unconditional. But Solomon recognizes that there is a condition in the near term: "if only your sons will be careful and will walk before me as you have done" (v. 25). Unfortunately, Solomon himself was to fail to meet the conditions; and most of his kingdom was to be wrenched from the hands of his son.

(2) **For presence and protection (8:27–30).** Solomon is desperately concerned for God's presence in the temple and among His people and for His protective watchcare as evidenced by His answers to their prayers. He clearly expresses God's infinity in these verses: heaven cannot contain Him, much less a temple on earth. Moreover, he expresses God's transcendence and immanence: heaven is His dwelling place (v. 30) and yet in a sense He dwells in the temple ("My name shall abide there," v. 29). Solomon begs this God who is everywhere present to "keep His eyes open upon this temple" constantly so as to hear the prayers directed toward it. The ground for answer of this request is that the name of God will be in the temple, that is, He will manifest His presence there. Three words for prayer appear in verse 28: "prayer" (intercession), "supplication" (entreaty or plea), and "cry" (a wailing or cry of petition).

(3) **For righteous judgment (8:31–32).** Solomon asks God to judge righteously in interpersonal disputes. This prayer especially refers to cases mentioned in such passages as Exodus 22:6–12, where a person accused of a fraud or injury to his neighbor's property is required to take an oath in the temple to swear to his innocence. Often, dishonest persons swore falsely, and Solomon is praying for God's vindication of the innocent in such cases.

(4) **For forgiveness of sin leading to defeat in battle (8:33–34).** Solomon prays that when Israel is defeated in battle because of its sin and some are carried away prisoner, God will restore the captives to their land in response to the prayers of the penitent of Israel. Clearly, this passage does not refer to the period of the Babylonian captivity, because the temple did not then exist and the few who remained in the land intermarried with pagans and developed a half-breed people with a half-breed faith.

(5) **For forgiveness of sin leading to famine and plague (8:35–40).** As God might bring defeat in warfare for national sin, so He might bring drought or pestilence or other plagues to stir His people to repentance. When they repent of their sins in the midst of such circumstances, Solomon again asks for national forgiveness and removal of the calamity. God, who alone knows the hearts of all, will be aware when those who cry for forgiveness are truly penitent. Solomon's declaration of God's omniscience in verse 39 is a remarkable statement for an Old Testament saint: "You alone know the hearts of all men."

(6) **For blessing on God-fearing foreigners (8:41–43).** This passage is absolutely remarkable. Solomon not only recognized that God did not live in Jerusalem alone or in the temple alone but was the omnipresent God of all the earth. Moreover, though God had a covenant relationship with the Hebrews, He was not their God alone but was the God of all peoples who would worship Him by faith. Thus he was far advanced beyond the narrow provincialism of a Jonah and others like him who thought of Yahweh as a kind of personal possession of the Hebrews and therefore they should have no interest in proclaiming Him to the nations. Solomon has a very magnaminous attitude toward the Gentiles and asks that God-fearers or proselytes among those who seek God's face in the temple may have their prayers answered, too. They will "know that the house I have built bears your name" (v. 43) when the Gentiles who pray toward it experience the working of the living God on their behalf.

(7) **For victory in battle (8:44–45).** Here Solomon prays for victory for Israel over her enemies whenever they are engaged in war by divine appointment ("wherever you send them," v. 44), not necessarily in all their conflicts. And he pleads for victory when they earnestly call on God for help.

(8) **For restoration after captivity (8:46–51).** Obviously Solomon refers here to captivity but not necessarily to the Babylonian captivity; it could refer to any captives carried off in battle at any time before that horrendous event. In any case, the Hebrews were carried off. They did repent while in captivity, and as they cried out to God, He did restore them. Prayer "toward the land" (v. 48) is what Daniel did while in Babylon

(Dan. 6:10). The fact that this passage does not allude to praying "toward the temple" but only "toward the land," gives support to the suggestion that this is a prophecy of the Babylonian captivity when the temple no longer existed.

(9) **For divine answer to prayer (8:52–53).** This last paragraph of Solomon's prayer is a kind of summary in which he petitions God to hear His people "whenever they call out" to Him. They were, after all, His chosen "inheritance"; to them God had been faithful in the past, and Solomon asks that that faithfulness shall continue. Throughout the prayer, confession and forsaking of sin are prerequisites for God's hearing His people's prayers.

e. Solomon's blessing of the people (8:54–61). After Solomon's prayer, he arose to pronounce his blessing on the people. First, he reminded them of God's goodness to them. Then he enunciated three special desires: (1) that God would be with his generation as He had been with their forefathers (v. 57); (2) that God would strengthen His people "to walk in all His ways" (v. 58); (3) that God would remember the requests Solomon had made "day and night" (v. 59). Again, remarkably, Solomon took a world view. All this blessing on the assembly of Israel was not primarily for their benefit but "to the end that all peoples of the earth may know that Yahweh is God" (v. 60). Finally, Solomon issued a reminder to the assembled crowd that God's blessing, and even God's reputation in the world, was contingent on their commitment or "loyalty" to Him.

f. Solomon's dedication of the temple (8:62–66). As the king finished speaking, "fire came down from heaven and consumed the burnt offering and the sacrifices, and the glory of the LORD filled the temple" (2 Chron. 7:1, NIV). Thus, God demonstrated His acceptance of the proceedings up to that point. Naturally, all the assembled throng were awestruck and they worshiped God. Yahweh's march from Sinai to the place of His earthly enthronement had reached a culmination (cf. Ps. 68).

Then began a round of sacrificial offerings in dedication of the temple; the sacred historian gives a total of 22,000 cattle and 120,000 sheep and goats. The number seems unbelievably large but thousands of priests were involved and many auxiliary altars must have been used (see v. 64). In dealing with these large numbers of sacrifices, several factors need to be kept in mind. First, the parallel passage in 2 Chronicles 7 gives the same numbers, so a discrepancy in transcription of numbers does not cast doubt on the totals noted here. Second, the dedication of the temple coincided with the Feast of Tabernacles, and the usual one-week feast was extended to two weeks (v. 65). Third, substantial numbers of Israelites from Hamath in the far north to the border of Egypt in the south (v. 65) were present in Jerusalem for all or part of the two weeks. These people had to be fed and it was customary to have fellowship meals after the sacrifices; parts of the animals were offered to God and the worshipers ate the rest. It can readily be seen, then, that the large number of sacrifices coincided with the need to feed crowds of pilgrims. At the end of the twofold celebration the people returned home thankful for all God had done and with a new sense of the divine destiny of king and country.

E. Solomon's Wealth and Glory (9:1–10:29)

1. His Covenant from God (9:1–9)

"When" Solomon had finished building the temple and his palace complex, God appeared to him a "second" time. The exact time of the appearance is problematical. It took seven and one-half years to finish the temple and it was completed in Solomon's eleventh year (1 Kings 6:38); it took thirteen years to construct the palace complex (1 Kings 7:1), and the two projects were somewhat contemporaneous. They were both completed by the middle of his reign, "at the end of twenty years" (1 Kings 9:10). Whether "all his desire" (v. 1) also included Solomon's seaport, navy, store cities, and other construction noted in chapter 9 is not clear. Verses 1 and 10 of chapter 9 are commonly joined, with verses 2–9 considered to be parenthetical.

It would be very easy to assume that the time referred to was in Solomon's twentieth year, but verse 3 seems to have reference to Solomon's prayer of dedication of the temple in his twelfth year. Perhaps that is only apparent because it stands in the truncated account of Solomon's reign right after his prayer of dedication. Solomon must have often repeated themes from the dedicatory prayer in his petitions to God. McNeely believes that the appearance came at the beginning of the second half of Solomon's reign when the kingdom was at the height of its glory but in danger of losing its tremendous drive and of becoming inert.[13] In any event, God appeared to Solomon a "second time," "as" He had done at Gibeon (1 Kings 3:5). The "as" could mean in the same manner, a dream-vision, or merely indicate that the revelation was direct instead of through a prophet.

The subject of the revelation is clearly the Davidic covenant. The kings will be known as David's sons and the throne as David's throne, never as Solomon's. In verses 3–5 the address is to Solomon, in the second person singular, and the tone is one of promise. In verses 6–9 the address is in the second person plural (Solomon, his descendants, Israel) and the approach is threatening. God assured Solomon that He had heard his prayer and that He would "always" dwell in the temple in a special sense. And He promised that if Solomon would walk before God in "integrity of heart" in his inner man and "uprightness" of conduct, he would always have a son on the throne of Israel.

The warning was a dire one, however. If Solomon or his sons conduct themselves in such a way as to reflect disobedience to God's word and turn aside to serve other gods, Yahweh will "sweep Israel off the land" and "reject" or "cast out of my presence this temple." As Israel wanders among the peoples of the earth, she will be the subject of mocking and spite. The temple, once "exalted" or "majestic," will, in its ruinous state, cause people to be astonished and to "hiss" or "whistle" in surprise. And foreigners will comment that God brought all this misfortune on them because of their idolatry (v. 9). Though Solomon had so much to influence him to walk in God-honoring ways, he himself would later lead his people down paths of idolatry (1 Kings 11:4–8). In retribution, ultimately the nation and the temple met destruction. The temple never again approximated the glory of Solomon's day; under Herod there was no such prolific use of gold.

---

[13]Richard I. McNeely, *First and Second Kings* (Chicago: Moody, 1978), 52.

2. His Building Projects Summarized (9:10–28)

Tremendous sums of money were needed to finance Solomon's building activities. Chapter 5 reported the basic financial agreement between Solomon and Hiram of Tyre, but that did not provide all the gold and bronze and other materials Solomon needed for the temple and other projects. Evidently cash-flow problems forced him to borrow large sums of money from Hiram. The gold obtained was 120 talents worth, a total of about four and one-half tons, according to the NIV margin (9:14). As surety, Solomon gave Hiram twenty towns in Galilee, apparently southeast of Tyre on the border between Israel and Phoenicia. The population was probably almost all pagan Canaanites, because Israelite people and lands could not have been alienated or separated from the Commonwealth of Israel in this way. Upon inspection of these towns, Hiram called them the "land of Cabul," which Keil argues originally meant "pawned land," but in time came to be twisted to mean "good for nothing."[14] Eventually Solomon seems to have repaid the loan and to have gotten the towns back (2 Chron. 8:2). Then he rebuilt them and repopulated them with Israelites.

Solomon accomplished much of his construction by means of forced or conscripted labor or the corvée (vv. 15, 20). This burden fell on non-Israelite peoples of the kingdom, descendants of ethnic groups that had been conquered but not exterminated. The Israelites, though they might be subjected to work temporarily on some project, were not reduced to slave labor. They served as soldiers and supervisors.

Solomon's construction projects were almost too numerous to itemize. They included the temple, the palace complex, supporting terraces on which buildings could be erected, the extension of the wall of Jerusalem northward to enclose the palace complex and the temple (more than doubling the enclosed area of the city), a string of fortresses and store cities (for horses and chariots and supplies for the army), a seaport, and merchant marine.

The system of fortresses was formidable. Hazor guarded a strategic point north of the Sea of Galilee; Megiddo stood at the

---

[14] Keil, *The Books of the Kings*, 141.

base of the Plain of Esdraelon; Beth-horon blocked the pass to Jerusalem by way of Aijalon; Baalath stood on the highway from Jerusalem to the port of Joppa; Gezer protected the main road and entrance to the valley of Sorek; Tamar on the southern border could defend caravans from Ezion-geber. No fortress stood east of Jerusalem, the valley of the Jordan being considered a sufficient barrier. Excavations at Hazor, Megiddo and Gezer reveal significant Solomonic construction at each place. Some have identified "Tadmor" (v. 18) with Palmyra in Syria, but arguments for placing it in Judah are quite compelling.

Though Joppa provided a port of sorts on the Mediterranean, Solomon established a much more effective port at Ezion-geber, near modern Eilat on the Red Sea. Hiram was happy to help build harbor facilities there, to help the Hebrews construct a merchant marine, and then to provide sailors to operate the fleet. It was to Hiram's advantage to be involved in that project because there was no Suez Canal in those days and no way across the Isthmus of Suez. Thus, luxury goods could be brought by ship to Ezion-geber from points east and south and thence by caravan overland to Phoenician centers for trans-shipment across the Mediterranean. An important port of call for Solomon's ships was the land of Ophir, but its location is not certain. Suggestions include the west coast of the Red Sea known as the land of Punt, Zimbabwe in East Africa, India, or more probably, South Arabia. The report that the fleet brought back four hundred talents of gold (v. 28; NIV margin, 16 tons) probably refers to the total from the several expeditions during the latter half of Solomon's reign.

There are three other incidental items of interest in this passage: (1) Solomon got Gezer as a wedding gift from his father-in-law, the king of Egypt, and then Solomon proceeded to rebuild it (v. 17). (2) Reference to Pharaoh's daughter's moving from the City of David to her residence in the royal complex (v. 24) may indicate that her house was the last part of the complex to be completed. This appears to be some sort of news item. (3) Perhaps to encourage termination of sacrifice on the high places and to bring greater respect for the central sanctuary (cf. 3:2), Solomon offered (or had offered, for he would not have intruded into the priest's office) burnt offerings and thank

offerings three times a year: probably at Passover, Feast of
Weeks, and Feast of Tabernacles.

3. His Visit from the Queen of Sheba (10:1–13)

The description of Solomon's wealth and glory now proceeds with an account of a visit from the queen of Sheba. In the
past, critics have tended to classify this narrative as legendary,
but in recent years they have increasingly come to accept it as
historical. Sheba was located in southwestern Arabia, in the
region of modern Yemen. Former doubt that a queen could have
ruled in Arabia has been severely blunted by discovery of
Assyrian records referring to five queens of Arabia during the
eighth and seventh centuries B.C. Though those inscriptions do
not have direct bearing on events as early as Solomon's day,
they do give greater plausibility to the account reported in this
chapter.

The reason given for the queen's visit was so that she could
test Solomon's wisdom and bask in his glory (v. 1), but that tells
only part of the story. Scripture is extremely selective in its
political and biographical accounts and rarely delves into
economic and social factors of a narrative. In this case it needs to
be noted that Sheba controlled the ports of southwest Arabia and
the trade routes between India and East Africa and the
Mediterranean. One can argue that on the one hand Solomon's
maritime and commercial activity in the Red Sea, along the east
coast of Africa, and in the Indian Ocean threatened Sheba's
economic well-being. On the other hand, it can be just as
cogently argued that Solomon's commercial successes and the
validity of his commercial agreements with Hiram of Tyre
depended on an effective working relationship with the Sabae-
ans. In any case, commentators now generally agree that the
queen's visit really had the character of a trade mission. Nelson
Glueck anticipated this point of view back in 1940 and com-
mented, "When one realizes what a terrifically hard journey it
must have been for the fair ruler of a rich part of southern
Arabia, to come by camel a distance of some 1200 miles or more
on her famous trip to Jerusalem to see Solomon, it is hard to

believe that she undertook the long and arduous journey merely to bask in the brilliance of the king of Jerusalem."[15]

Whatever the hidden agenda, Scripture says the queen came to test Solomon with "hard questions" (v. 1), the word used for the riddles posed by Samson in Judges 14. Tests of wit were common in ancient Oriental courts, and Josephus reported that Solomon and Hiram engaged in such repartee.[16] The queen arrived in Jerusalem with "a very large retinue," not a military force as the word commonly signifies, but a large company of attendants. "A very great caravan" (NIV) gives the intended sense. Of course, she brought rich gifts, both as a matter of protocol and to cement any agreements entered into. "Spices" probably came from the balsam tree, plentiful in southwest Arabia; and "gold and precious stones," not native to the region, would have been obtained by trade with East Africa and India. After the presentation of gifts the queen engaged in testing Solomon's wisdom. "All that she had in mind" in this context and at the beginning of this meeting, probably refers to riddles or questions with which she wished to test the king. As verse 3 indicates, Solomon was able to meet her effectively at every point; "explain" translates a Hebrew word that is almost a technical term for solving riddles.

The text next describes the queen's inner response to her observations at Solomon's court. The statement that she "saw all the wisdom" must refer to Solomon's judicial and administrative wisdom, as exemplified in his conduct of affairs. She was impressed by the palace complex which, with its high quality Palestinian limestone and cedar of Lebanon, must certainly have been far superior to anything she possessed or had seen in timber-starved Arabia. Then her woman's eye took special note of the "food" on his table, both the variety and the elegance of the table settings (cf. v. 21), the touch of class evident in the "seating of his courtiers," the quality of the attention and attire of the servants, "his wine service" (v. 21, in solid gold), "and his ascent by which he went up into the house of the LORD" (KJV), probably a reference to the great royal processional. Her

[15] Nelson Glueck, *The Other Side of Jordan* (New Haven, Conn.: American Schools of Oriental Research, 1940), 85.

[16] Josephus, *Antiquities*, VIII.5.3

response to all this was that she "was left breathless" in amazement.

Then the queen responded audibly to Solomon. She confessed that she had not believed what she had heard in her own country, but as a matter of fact, "not half had been told me." Some consider that the preferred reading for the first part of verse 8 is, "How happy your wives must be" (based on the Septuagint). "How happy, too, should be the officials who are able to enjoy your wisdom all the time." Verse 9 does not indicate that the queen of Sheba had become a worshiper of Yahweh. The statement is easily reconcilable with polytheism, recognizing the God of Israel on the level of the gods of other peoples—who presumably were also thought to have elevated their rulers to the throne. There is no record that she was prompted to sacrifice to Yahweh.

Probably near the end of her visit the queen presented magnificent gifts to Solomon. No doubt she had given him something near her time of arrival as a part of normal diplomatic protocol; now she gave him spices, precious stones, and "120 talents of gold," an incredible sum that the NIV margin makes equivalent to about four and one-half tons, rather much to carry across the desert on the backs of camels. We cannot be very sure about some of these computations.

Solomon responded by giving her "all her desire," which most interpret to involve especially a trade agreement, and that some interpret sexually. Ethiopian tradition makes Menelik, founder of the royal dynasty, to be a son of Solomon and the queen of Sheba. Emperor Haile Selassie of Ethiopia (whose tribal group migrated across the Red Sea from Arabia) considered himself to be a descendant of Solomon and kept chained lions, symbol of the house of Judah, near his throne (cf. 1 Kings 10:19–20). In addition, Solomon gave the queen gifts "out of his royal bounty" (v. 13); they must have been substantial.

Verses 11 and 12 are often thought to be entirely out of place here; they appear in exactly the same manner in 2 Chronicles 9:10, 11, however. The RSV makes a proper connection with the flow of information by inserting "moreover" and reads, "Moreover the fleet of Hiram ... " (actually of Hiram and Solomon, cf. 1 Kings 9:27–28). Perhaps the point is that a trade pact was, in fact, being negotiated that was important to the queen, Hiram, and Solomon. Presumably such a pact permitted Solomon's ships to use ports of Sheba at the entrance to the Red Sea. Moreover, all three of the signatories to the pact may have had their eyes on the gold of Ophir (v. 11; cf. 9:28; 10:22), and the queen of Sheba may have obtained much of what she had just given Solomon from that source. If so, these verses are very much in the mainstream of the narrative. "Almug wood" (vv. 11, 12), has been identified as sandalwood, pine, amber, and even red coral, with sandalwood being preferred. No one really knows what it was, but presumably it was a very fine wood used for musical instruments and for "steps" ("supports," NIV and NASB) for the temple and the royal palace.

4. His Trade and Riches (10:14–29)

These verses provide brief notes on Solomon's wealth and glory—on his income, his ceremonial shields, his throne, activities of his merchant marine, his international reputation, and his horse trading.

His annual income in gold is pegged at 666 talents, computed to weigh twenty-five tons, according to the NIV margin. From what sources that came is not clear. In addition he received income from "merchants" (foreign merchants active in Israel) and "traders" (domestic traders, perhaps employed by Solomon himself).[17] "Kings of the Arabs" (probably Arabian sheiks involved in trade and subject to various tariffs) and "governors" (not the same Hebrew word used for Solomon's district officers; perhaps administrators in other areas like Syria) also provided considerable revenues. In contemplating all this, plus income from gifts (v. 25), from the activities of the merchant marine, from the twelve districts noted earlier, and from other sources, one is impressed with the tremendous amount of revenue available to Solomon. It should be remembered, however, that this was not his personal income but revenues of the national treasury, to be used for national defense, the public payroll, capital improvements, ceremonial functions, sacrifices (e.g., 1 Kings 9:25), maintenance of the

---

[17]Jones, "1 and 2 Kings," 1:226, cf. pp. 60, 49.

merchant marine, and much more. Of course, Solomon's income would not have been so substantial during the early part of his reign. When he reached this plateau is not stated.

Solomon made two hundred large gold shields (Septuagint says three hundred) long enough to cover the whole body; and three hundred small gold shields, round and worn on the left arm. Evidently these were made of wood and covered with beaten gold. Each large shield required six hundred bekas of gold (about seven and one-half pounds); each small one required three minas of gold (about three and three-fourths pounds). Since gold is too soft a metal for military action, these shields must have been intended for ceremonial purposes. They were kept in the House of the Forest of Lebanon (the armory). There they hung for some twenty-five years until Shishak of Egypt carried them off in 926 B.C. (1 Kings 14:26).

Next, Solomon's magnificent throne is described. Visualizing it helps the modern reader to understand a little better why the queen of Sheba was almost speechless. The throne was made of wood and inlaid with ivory, and apparently the wooden parts not inlaid were covered with gold. Though there is some controversy over the nature of the back of it, the Hebrew text indicates it was "rounded" (v. 19), and there were arm rests. Six steps approached the throne, which apparently stood on a seventh level or dais. At either end of each of the six steps stood a lion, perhaps representing the twelve tribes of Israel. The lion seems to have been the symbol of the tribe of Judah and symbolized royal strength. Nothing is said about the composition of the lions.

Appended to the description of the throne is an observation that all of Solomon's drinking vessels (goblets) were of gold, as was also true of the various articles (purpose unspecified) in the House of the Forest of Lebanon. Some commentators consider this to be an exaggeration, but great commercial people such as the Minoans and Myceneans hundreds of years earlier had drinking vessels and many other objects of solid gold. The Persians after Solomon did also, and one may see these artifacts in the museums of Europe and Asia. Since these and other peoples had such possessions, there is no real reason why Solomon, too, could not have had them.

Perhaps to account not only for the wealth of Solomon but also for the large quantities of gold available to him, something is said about his merchant marine once more. The king had a "fleet of ships of Tarshish" (v. 22), large sea-going vessels that "once every three years" returned to port (Ezion-geber), probably moving very slowly from port to port and trading as they went. They brought back cargoes of gold, silver, ivory, apes, and another species that used to be identified as "peacocks" but now is thought to have been baboons. Where they went is not clear, certainly along the coasts of Arabia and Africa, and possibly into the Persian Gulf and as far as India. The Phoenicians were intrepid sailors, the greatest in antiquity; and Israelites, though agriculturalists, could learn the ways of the sea.

Verse 23 returns to the theme introduced in 4:34. Solomon's wisdom and wealth were noised abroad and the "whole earth," at least peoples from many places in the Near East, sought to visit him, as the queen of Sheba had done. The point is clearly made that Solomon's wisdom was a gift from God (cf. 3:28; 4:29). Verse 25 may be interpreted to mean that Solomon's fame was so great that a steady flow of visitors came every year and brought him presents. Or it may mean that people came year by year to bring their tribute. Following the latter interpretation, the KJV indicates that every man gave according to "a rate year by year" and the JPS states that each man gave "in the amount due each year." Actually, the Hebrew word may mean "tribute" or "present" and probably some came gladly and some grudgingly.

Verse 25 includes "horses" among the list of gifts, and that introduces the last topic, Solomon as a builder of a chariot corps and as a horse breeder and trader. Verse 26 says that Solomon "accumulated" or "assembled" or "built up" a force of fourteen hundred chariots and twelve thousand horses. The figures are reasonable in view of the fact that Ahab would field two thousand chariots against Shalmaneser III of Assyria at the battle of Qarqar a century later. Solomon's chariot cities are mentioned also in 9:19. Solomon imported his horses from Egypt and Kue or Cilicia (v. 28), the plain in southeast Asia Minor where the metropolis of Tarsus (the apostle Paul's home town) was to rise later. Probably the latter part of verse 28 should read, "the king's agents took delivery from them from

Cilicia at a fixed rate" (JB; JPS rendering is similar). Verse 29
indicates that the price ratio of horses to chariots was 4 to 1.
While Egypt bred horses and Solomon did, too, the best horses
came from Cilicia and the best chariots from Egypt. Solomon
stood in a good position to trans-ship Cilician horses to Egypt
and Egyptian chariots to the Hittites and the Syrians (Arame-
ans).[18] Of course, the Hittite Empire had ceased to exist shortly
after 1200 B.C. But Hittite city-states continued to exist in Syria
until the Assyrians destroyed the last of them in 709 B.C.
Solomon's trade mentioned here was with some of those city-
states. In passing, it may be noted that Uriah the Hittite, first
husband of Bathsheba, Solomon's mother, had come from one of
those city-states.

F. Solomon's Apostasy and Resultant Troubles (11:1–43)

1. Solomon's Apostasy (11:1–8)

The newness of the temple had hardly worn off when
Solomon began to drift away from both a commitment to the
central sanctuary and the God who especially manifested His
presence there. This resulted largely from his marriage to
idolatrous women.

The size of a harem of an ancient oriental ruler was often
considered to be an indication of his degree of greatness.
Solomon, who was supposed to be the most opulent ruler of his
generation, therefore might be expected to have a large harem.
Moreover, marriage alliances were commonly used to guarantee
peace with one's neighbors. Solomon seems to have employed
this means in part to maintain a *Pax Hebraica;* he enjoyed peace
with all his neighbors. Solomon's marriage to princesses from
Egypt, Moab, Ammon, Edom, Phoenicia, and the Hittite states
(v. 1) went a long way toward establishing his borders. Egypt
was located on the far south; Edom, Moab, and Ammon on the
east, the Phoenician city-states on the northwest, and the Hittite
city-states on the far north. If other princesses were daughters of
Arab sheiks and tribal chiefs located south of Judah and of the

---

[18] Y. Ikeda, "Solomon's Trade in Horses and Chariots," *Studies in the Period
of David and Solomon,* ed. T. Ishida, 1982, 215–38, shows that trading followed
the land route of the Orontes Valley, using store cities in Hamath as relay
stations.

city-states of inner Syria, then his marriage would ring Israel
proper with friendly border states and would help to cement the
subject states of some of them as part of the Hebrew Empire.

As plausible and defensible as all this might sound, Yahweh
condemned both the multiplication of wives and especially
intermarriage with pagan peoples because such practices would
lead to idolatry (Deut. 7:3–4; 17:17; cf. Exod. 34:15, 16). Some
think the number of Solomon's wives (700) and concubines
(300) is "fictitious" or "greatly exaggerated." If the Song of
Solomon 6:8 refers to Solomon, at that time he had sixty queens,
eighty concubines, and maidens without number. But even if
one has not a high view of the accuracy of Scripture, either in
the original autographs or the copies that have come down to us,
the total number of a thousand is not impossible. LaSor reports
that Chosroes II, king of Sassanid Persia (590–628 A.D.) had
between 3,012 concubines, and Mulai Ismail (ruler of Morocco
1672–1727) had 2,000 wives, 800 concubines, and hundreds of
sons and daughters.[19]

"In Solomon's old age, his wives swayed his heart to other
gods" (v. 4). What is meant by his "old age" is uncertain. He
died at about sixty; the process of apostasy must have set in as
his harem grew ever larger during the last half of his reign.
Actually he had married Naamah the Ammonitess and had
fathered by her Rehoboam the crown prince by about the age of
twenty (1 Kings 14:21). Possibly she had never really converted
to the religion of Yahweh. Solomon's heart "was not wholly
true" to Yahweh. Along with the worship in the temple, he
"followed after" (v. 5) the worship of foreign deities. The text
does not say he actually sacrificed to those gods, but he did
build high places to them to accommodate his wives and other
foreigners in the vicinity and thus involved himself in their
worship and influenced his son Rehoboam to do so later
(2 Chron. 12:1). Solomon especially made provision for Ashtoreth, Chemosh, and Molech. Ashtoreth, variously known as
Ishtar, Astarte, and Venus, was principally the goddess of sex
and war. Her name was altered from Astarte to Ashtoreth by
vocalizing with the vowels of the Hebrew word *bosheth*,

---

[19]William S. LaSor, "1 and 2 Kings," in *New Bible Commentary*, 3rd ed.
Edited by D. Guthrie and J. A. Motyer (Grand Rapids: Eerdmans, 1970), 335.

meaning "shame." Chemosh was the national god of Moab and was sometimes worshiped with child sacrifices; Molech or Moloch, an Ammonite deity, also could be worshiped with human sacrifice. "A height east of Jerusalem" (v. 7) was the Mount of Olives.

2. God's Announcement of Judgment (11:9–13)

It is interesting that the text does not mention any prophet's crossing Solomon to warn him of the danger of his ways as he slid into apostasy. Perhaps it was enough that God had made the point so specifically in a revelation to him after the completion of the temple (cf. 9:6–7). And of course, David had also spoken similarly in his charge to his son. Solomon knew God's expectation of him and was without excuse. Possibly Solomon's real failure was a trust in wisdom and wealth and international fame; it is a short step from one kind of idolatry to another.

God's patience with the waywardness of Solomon finally wore out and He sent His sentence of judgment to the king, probably through a prophet. Again the Davidic covenant is introduced. Solomon's failure to keep God's commandments and His covenant will now result in the kingdom's being torn away from him, but not in his lifetime (v. 12) nor in its entirety (v. 13). Solomon's unfaithfulness will not lead God to cancel His promise to David nor His choice of Jerusalem as His special abode. The Davidic dynasty and the city will continue. God's promise will be fulfilled through the tribe of Judah and ultimately through the Messiah, David's greater Son.

3. Solomon's Adversaries (11:14–40)

a. Hadad the Edomite (11:14–22). Inserting this narrative here implies that it was connected with God's anger against Solomon during the latter part of his reign. Actually it fits chronologically shortly after Solomon's accession to the throne. The subjugation of Edom occurred during the reign of David and under the generalship of Joab (2 Sam. 8:13ff.). According to the Septuagint translation of the passage, Joab slaughtered eighteen thousand Edomites. "Slew every male in Edom" must be taken to express intent rather than actual fact.

Prince Hadad escaped with some compatriots to Egypt, and

possibly a few others fled elsewhere. At the time Hadad was a "young man" and he got away with some of his father's officials to Midian, the region east of the Gulf of Aqaba and south of Edom. From there they went to Paran, probably the Wadi Feran in the Sinai peninsula, and some men from there joined them in a flight to Egypt. In Egypt the ruling pharaoh was kind to the young prince and gave him property and his wife's sister in marriage. Their son Genubath was brought up at the palace. At length word reached Egypt that both David and Joab had died, so Hadad assumed it was safe to go home again. Evidently the pharaoh gave him permission to return, and he became an "adversary" of Solomon (v. 14). Presumably Hadad, as heir to the throne but unable to occupy what was rightfully his, launched an underground independence movement. If he had lived another thirty years, by which time a new generation would have matured, he or his son might have been in a position to give Solomon some serious trouble.

b. Rezon, son of Eliada (11:23–25). David had been victorious in the north as elsewhere in his borderlands. He had defeated Hadadezer, king of Zobah, not far from Damascus (2 Sam. 8:3). At that point Rezon broke away from his master, Hadadezer, and became the leader of "a marauding band." Though David stationed forces in Damascus, eventually Rezon was able to capture the city and found a dynasty and a new Aramaic kingdom that caused Solomon trouble during his reign and was to become the most powerful Syrian state during the ninth and eighth centuries B.C.

c. Jeroboam, an Ephraimite (11:26–40). Now the spotlight falls on Jeroboam, who will eventually split the kingdom and become king of the Northern Kingdom. Jeroboam was the son of Nebat (otherwise unknown) from the town of Zeredah, commonly identified with a village about fifteen miles southwest of Nablus. His mother was the widow Zeruah. Jeroboam was in charge of some of Solomon's construction in Jerusalem, twenty years or more after the beginning of his reign. "Jeroboam was a man of rank" (v. 28) or property and was also an "industrious" worker; so Solomon put him in charge of the "forced labor of the house of Joseph" (over some or all of the northern tribes). The nature of his insubordination does not appear; perhaps it was brought on by Ahijah's prediction. Probably it was an attempted coup that led to Solomon's attempt to kill him. Jeroboam then fled to Egypt where he enjoyed the protection of Shishak I or Sheshonk I, founder of the Twenty-second Dynasty, about 945 B.C. The time of Jeroboam's flight must have been about 940 B.C., and he then stayed in Egypt until Solomon's death.

Verses 29–39 give an account of Jeroboam's encounter with the prophet Ahijah of Shiloh on the open road outside Jerusalem. As an act of prophetic symbolism Ahijah took off his outer cloak and tore it into twelve pieces, giving ten to Jeroboam and indicating that the kingdom would be split. He would rule the ten tribes and Solomon's son would rule one. Of course, ten plus one equals eleven. Perhaps Levi was omitted because it was without a territory of its own. As an alternate way of computing, some think that by this time the territory of Simeon, south of Judah, had been absorbed into Judah and virtually ceased to exist. Judah also evidently had absorbed part of the tribe of Benjamin. In any case, Ahijah gave the same reason for the rupture that the Lord had (earlier) spoken to Solomon (11:9–13). Moreover, he asserted that God would honor the Davidic covenant in a continuation of the kingdom of Judah and He would continue in a special sense to dwell in Jerusalem. Jeroboam was to be king over "Israel," evidently referring to the northern state. Then Ahijah made a promise to Jeroboam similar to that made to David and Solomon (v. 38), to build "a sure house" in return for faithfulness to God. Especially, Israel would serve as an irritant to the house of David (v. 39). "But not forever" makes it clear that the house of Jeroboam was not to be permanent as David's was to be.

4. Solomon's Death (11:41–43)

After a long reign of forty years (970–931 B.C.), Solomon walked off the stage of history and into the record books. Evidently he died a natural death. The formula is introduced here that will be used for each of the following kings. The source containing more information about the dead king appears with the usual question: "are they [other events of his reign] not written in . . . ."? "Over all Israel" is somewhat meaningful in this context because Solomon was the last king to rule all Israel.

Then the notice of the king's death and burial appears with a reference to his son Rehoboam's accession to the throne. After all the glory of Solomon's reign and the evil practices he introduced to lead God's people astray, the sacred historian ends the account of his life in a very prosaic fashion. It would not be appropriate to praise him; the effects of his evil ways would become abundantly clear during the reign of his successors.

For Further Study

1. What factors contributed to Solomon's greatness or provided potential for personal success?

2. What factors threatened Solomon's personal sucess/effectiveness or the success of his kingdom?

3. Write an imaginative piece on the character and ambitions of Bathsheba.

4. Write a newspaper account of Adonijah's elevation to the kingship, and Solomon's counter-elevation.

5. Briefly summarize Joab's service to David.

6. Write an imaginative piece that seeks to capture the thoughts and feelings of Adonijah, Joab, and Solomon toward the death of David.

7. Briefly describe the aspects of the greatness of Solomon's reign.

8. Draw a diagram/floor plan of Solomon's construction in Jerusalem to scale, with dimensions.

9. Detail Solomon's view of God as reflected in his prayer in 1 Kings 8:22–53.

Chapter 4

Division of the Monarchy and Hostility of the Kingdoms
(1 Kings 12:1–16:28)

The glories of Solomon were exacted from his people at great price. The tax burden and his great expenditures virtually bankrupted the kingdom. The size and nature of his harem also took a high toll morally and religiously as the cancer of moral degradation and religious apostasy ate away at the vitals of Israelite society. From the human standpoint, the financial burden became intolerable; most of the tribes would no longer endure it and broke away to form a separate kingdom. From the divine standpoint, apostasy had become intolerable and in judgment God drove wedges into the body politic and split the kingdom. The tale of this division and its aftermath now occupies the sacred historian.

A. Rupture of the Kingdom (12:1–24)

1. The Coronation Conference at Shechem (12:1–15)

Rehoboam had won prompt recognition as king in Judah after the death of Solomon, but that acclamation did not carry with it automatic acceptance by the northern tribes. Union of the state of Israel was more apparent than real. After Saul's acceptance in Benjamin and Judah, he had won approval by all Israel at Gilgal (1 Sam. 11:15). After David had ruled over Judah for seven and one-half years, he became the leader of the northern tribes too, following negotiations at Hebron (2 Sam. 5:1–3). Solomon in his administrative policies had treated the northern tribes differently and apparently more harshly than he treated Judah. Actually, the northern tribes had maintained a somewhat semi-independent status within the united kingdom of David and Solomon, and Rehoboam was now seeking their acceptance.

Shechem was a logical place to go to meet them. Here Joshua had made a covenant with Israel. The town stood between Mounts Gerizim and Ebal, the mountains of blessing and cursing. It drew significance, too, from the fact that Joseph's tomb was there, as was Jacob's well. "All Israel" (v. 1) can refer to the twelve tribes, but primary reference at this point must be to the northern tribes. Jeroboam learned "of it" while still in Egypt, probably of the death of Solomon, the accession of Rehoboam, and plans for what amounted to negotiations with the northern tribes. He knew God had picked him to rule over Israel, and evidently he had "returned from Egypt" (so RSV, NIV, Septuagint, and 2 Chron. 10:2); the Hebrew reading of verse 2 says he "remained in Egypt." Though the Septuagint omits Jeroboam from verse 3, the Hebrew text has the leaders of Israel sending for Jeroboam after he returned from Egypt, and involves him in the meeting with Rehoboam.

As the representatives of the northern tribes appeared before Rehoboam, they did not produce a long list of grievances, nor did they threaten secession. Presumably they wanted to remain in the union. They asked only that he would lighten the "hard" or "harsh labor" and "heavy yoke" (as that worn by working beasts) that Solomon had imposed on them. The forced labor and heavy taxation had been almost more than they could bear, or at least were willing to bear. Parenthetically, the modern reader is curious about how great the burden really was. They enjoyed a peace and prosperity Israel had never known before; both come at a price. It is easy to complain about the responsibility of maintaining government and to forget the benefits received from membership in the state. And could they possibly have been any better off under kings like Ahab or Jehu than under Solomon? Of course, it was common to expect ancient kings to offer some public benefit such as a release of political prisoners or reduction of taxes on their accession to the throne, and these people could hope for the best.

If Rehoboam had been willing to grant their request, they

probably would have accepted his leadership and gone home peaceably. But it would not do for a powerful and absolute monarch to appear to capitulate hastily to popular demand, so Rehoboam asked for a delay of three days to give him time for consultations and a decision about the matter. First, he asked some of his father's advisors what they would recommend. These experienced administrators responded that if "today" you will "serve them" and will speak to them "with kind words," they will serve you "always" (and might even accept the forced labor some day).

Then Rehoboam turned to the younger advisors "who had grown up with him." These were not necessarily very young, but only inexperienced in government. Rehoboam himself was forty-one at the time (1 Kings 14:21) and some of his advisors actually may have been older than he. They counseled him to be severe with the people, saying by comparison, "My little finger is thicker than my father's loins" (v. 10), and "My father flogged you with whips, and I will flog you with scorpions" (v. 11). Actually, though the versions have almost identical readings of the former statement, it is only a paraphrase of very difficult Hebrew; the phraseology preserves the intent of the hyperbole, however. "Scorpions" were whips with sharp pieces of metal attached to them, causing a very cruel kind of punishment.

Rehoboam decided to follow the advice of his circle. It was not a spur-of-the-moment course of action, however. He had three days to think it over. When he replied, one can almost hear the insolence in his voice. Why he could have done something so undiplomatic can be explained from a human standpoint as an effort to intimidate opponents and cow them into submission. From a divine standpoint, it was a result of God's working to bring about the rupture in the kingdom that God had predicted (v. 15).

2. The Rupture (12:16–20)

The response of the northern tribes was a decision to separate from the house of David. The phraseology of verse 16 is essentially the same as 2 Samuel 20:1. "To your tents, O Israel" is the equivalent of saying, "Let's go home." "Look now to your house," urges David to take care of his own house now that the other tribes have broken away. Verse 17 is hard to interpret but frequently is thought to say that Rehoboam's rule over Israelites living in the towns of Judah refers to Benjamites (northerners) living in and around Jerusalem.

Apparently Rehoboam had taken some officials of the court with him to Shechem. One of these was the commissioner of the corvée or forced labor, "Adoram" in the Hebrew and "Adoniram" in some of the versions (Adoniram was Solomon's commissioner of forced labor, 1 Kings 4:6; 5:14). After the hostile response, Rehoboam sent him out, possibly to placate these Israelites by showing them the difference between forced labor and the permanent slavery of non-Israelites. The crowd was now growing ugly, and stoned Adoram to death. Recognizing that his own life might now be in danger, Rehoboam jumped in his chariot and fled the scene.

The rupture was complete (v. 19). To finalize the matter, the assembly of Israelites (realizing that they had to have a government) called Jeroboam and made him king over Israel (the ten tribes). Though evidently he had had contact with many of them before Rehoboam's arrival, he seems to have gone off somewhere during Rehoboam's confrontation with the assembly at Shechem. Now he is brought back, and the prophecy of Ahijah is fulfilled.

3. Rehoboam's Effort to Resubjugate Israel (12:21–24)

As soon as Rehoboam got back to Jerusalem, he called out the entire army to try to force Israel back into union with Judah. The mention of Benjamin as joined with Judah (v. 21) is problematic. All the references to the split indicate that the southern kingdom would consist of Judah alone. The solution may lie in Judah's having used force to keep Benjamin in the kingdom, or better, that the part of Benjamin located in the environs of Jerusalem joined with Judah and the rest was absorbed into the Northern Kingdom. The reference to 180,000 men in Rehoboam's army (v. 21) is often thought to be totally unrealistic, but that is not necessarily the case. If this was thought to be the kind of emergency that required the service of every able-bodied male (even 16- or 17-year-olds) whether trained or not, such a force could be mustered.

Before the army could march, the prophet Shemaiah received word from God to stop Rehoboam (Shemaiah appears only here and in 2 Chron. 11:1–4; 12:5–8, 15), and he was able to persuade the king to disband his forces. Shemaiah argued against going to war with blood brothers and made the point that God was in the rupture. So now Solomon, Jeroboam, and Rehoboam have all received the word of God about the split. A biblical philosophy of history occasionally reveals God's direct working behind the scenes to bring about His purposes. Rehoboam had sufficient fear of God to know that if he disobeyed, God could strike him down in defeat. Apart from the clear indication of divine intervention, it is hard to tell who might have won the conflict. Judah had the advantage of the machinery of government and the organization of the army; Israel had the greater population resources and much of the chariotry and equipment that Solomon had stored in his fortress cities. Speed and surprise might have given the victory to Judah. The fact that God stopped a major pitched battle between the two kingdoms on this occasion does not indicate He would likewise intervene to prevent all the border skirmishes between them later on.

B. Jeroboam's Consolidation of Power and His Condemnation (12:25–14:20)

1. Jeroboam's Institution of Idolatry (12:25–33)

Of course, Jeroboam (930–909) had an immediate need to organize the government of the Northern Kingdom; he chose Shechem as his first capital and fortified it. Subsequently (when is not stated), he built up Penuel or Peniel (Tell edh-Dhahab) in the Jabbok Valley as a fortified center. Later yet, he used Tirzah (1 Kings 14:17) as a capital. It is hard to tell the degree to which each was a capital or merely an administrative center.

As Jeroboam tried to establish his power, he rightly recognized that the chief cohesive factor in the nation had been the worship of Yahweh and His covenant with Israel. He feared that as his subjects made pilgrimages to the temple in Jerusalem to participate in the various feasts, they would gradually revive a sense of loyalty to Jerusalem and the Davidic monarchy and would liquidate him. So "he took counsel with himself," or, "after giving thought to the matter" (v. 28, NEB; not "After seeking advice," NIV), the king devised a new religious arrangement. He had two calves or young bulls made (probably of wood and covered with gold) and installed in sanctuaries at the southern border town of Bethel (about ten miles north of Jerusalem) and the northern border town of Dan (in the foothills of Mount Hermon), and declared them to be their gods. At these worship centers he installed priests chosen from the non-Levitical elements in the population. Then he established a new religious festival on the fifteenth day of the eighth month. In addition, he built other shrines on high places. He himself offered sacrifices at Bethel.

Perhaps Jeroboam chose the calf because he was influenced toward bovine worship by his years in Egypt. Possibly he sought to establish a bridge between Yahweh worship and the Canaanite population; bulls were symbols of fertility gods among the Canaanites. To answer the question of how he could expect his subjects to shift from the traditional Yahweh worship without images, to sanctuaries with calves, the following may be observed. Various peoples of the ancient Near East portrayed their gods as sitting or standing enthroned on the back of an animal. In this case, Yahweh might be represented as invisibly enthroned on the back of the calf. In all the facets of his new religion, Jeroboam violated the clear requirements of Mosaic religion. Israel was never able to extricate itself from Jeroboam's false worship, and of all the subsequent kings of Israel it is said that they walked in the "ways of Jeroboam."

2. Jeroboam's Confrontation by a Man of God (13:1–34)

a. Confrontation at Bethel (13:1–10). "By" or "In" the efficacious power of the "word of Yahweh" (the NEB has "moved by the word"), a "man of God" or prophet came from Judah to Bethel to pronounce judgment on the false altar there. He did not come on just any day but one on which King Jeroboam himself was offering a sacrifice. "As" Jeroboam was standing "on" the top step or at the top of the ramp leading to the altar and was about to make his offering, the man of God made his pronouncement. It was a dramatic moment. With the king stood some of his courtiers and the priests of the new cult, and possibly a few townspeople. Out of respect for the deity, all were quiet. Then the man of God split the silence with his curse from Yahweh, not against the king but the altar itself and all the false worship it represented.

"A son named Josiah" was to be born to the house of David, and he would desecrate this altar by burning there the bones of priests who had offered sacrifices upon it, rendering it unusable. The prophecy was remarkable; only two kings, Josiah and Cyrus, are specifically named in predictive prophecy, which is usually more general in nature. This good king would not come on the scene for about three hundred years to conduct his religious reforms (see especially 2 Kings 23:15–20). And the man of God did not even hint at what would happen before Josiah's day: that the kingdom of Israel would fall to Assyria because of her apostasy, and then as Assyrian power weakened, it would be possible for Josiah to extend the authority of Judah northward and to destroy the idolatrous sanctuaries there.

Of course, anyone can utter a curse like that. To prove that his word was from God, the prophet declared that on that very day the "altar" would be "split apart" and the "ashes" of the sacrifices "poured out." Furious, Jeroboam stretched out his hand and pointed at the man of God and started to give the order to "Seize him." Before any soldiers could act, Jeroboam's hand froze in its outstretched position, paralyzed; and the altar "burst apart" and the "ashes scattered," as had been predicted. Jeroboam now acknowledged the power of God and asked the man of God to pray to "your God" for restoration; He was not the God of the idolatrous king. This the man of God did and the king was instantly healed. Then the king offered the man of God the hospitality of the palace, a meal, and a gift—perhaps to win some additional blessing from one with such power. The reasons for the invitation are not fully evident; they certainly did not include conversion to Yahweh worship. The man of God refused, citing God's specific command to him not to accept sustenance in Israel and to return home by a different road from the one on which he had come.

Laypersons and biblical critics alike often treat biblical

miracles as incidental happenings and debate their relative plausibility accordingly. But biblical miracles should not be treated as incidental. They have as their primary purpose the accreditation of God's message and messenger and the preservation of God's truth in the midst of especially apostate times. Thus, there were groups of miracles at strategic times in biblical history: in the days of Moses and Joshua to accredit God's message and messenger and to establish the Hebrew nation; in the midst of the deep apostasy of the Northern Kingdom to protect the truth of God from extinction (hence the miracles here and the seven miracles of Elijah and the fourteen of Elisha); in the days of the captivity (especially in connection with Daniel) for the same reason; in the days of Christ and the early church (again to accredit message and messenger) to support Christ's truth claims and to launch the new movement of God in the world; and in the end times as portrayed in the Revelation (once more to protect the message and program of God from destruction in times of dire apostasy).

It is interesting to note that performance of a miracle does not necessarily have anything to do with a person's spirituality; Abraham, Samuel, David and many other giants of faith are not reported to have performed any miracles. Moreover, for reasons noted above, miracles seem to have been reserved for pagan contexts; thus, there were miracles in the apostate kingdom of Ahab but rarely in Jerusalem where the temple and the priesthood were present.

b. Seduction of the man of God (13:11–32). The sacred historian now inserts a strange story that at first does not seem to contribute much to the Jeroboam narrative, but in retrospect does have significance. An "old prophet" (perhaps so designated because he was a member of the school of the prophets) was living in the environs of Bethel. When his sons gave him an account of the events in town that day, he was determined to meet this man of God. Finding him, he invited him to stay with him. But the man of God declined, citing the same reasons he had given Jeroboam. At this point the prophet lied to the man of God, asserting that he had had word through an angel countermanding God's clear directive. Why he lied is not clear; perhaps he merely wanted to know more about this remarkable man through whom the power of God was working. His motives may even have been good, but the apostasy that infected Jeroboam seems to have tainted the prophet, too. It was brazen disobedience to use subterfuge of this sort to persuade a believer to disobey the clearly revealed will of God.

The man of God capitulated and went home with the old prophet to eat. (His action serves as a warning to modern believers to avoid the advice of others if it directly conflicts with what we know in our hearts to be God's will for us.) Then while they were eating, God spoke to the old prophet; the means by which He did so is not reported. If the prophet had been jealous because God was not speaking to him as He was to this servant of God from Judah, now he had a divine message. He had the unpleasant task of delivering God's word of judgment to his guest for his disobedience to the word of God. The fact that the man's body would not be buried in the tomb of his fathers (v. 22) indicates that he would probably die a violent death away from home.

This was severe judgment but apparently was commensurate with his sin and the character of his ministry. His ministry had been to pronounce judgment on Jeroboam publicly for his disobedience to the word of God through Moses. Now judgment fell on him for his disobedience to the word of God, as he had publicly enunciated it to the king before a considerable company and to the prophet privately. What punishment the prophet suffered is not specified, and it need not be, because it is not germane to this narrative.

Probably Jeroboam's sacrifice had taken place in the morning and the meal at the prophet's house in the middle of the day or early afternoon. Then the man of God apparently wanted to get across the border before nightfall, so he went on his way. Not far outside Bethel a lion attacked him and killed him; then the narrative states twice that it did not eat him nor did it kill his donkey but only stood sentinel by his corpse and the donkey. This was indeed a supernatural judgment, and it reminds us that miracles are not necessarily always acts of great benefit but may also be designed for discipline or judgment.

The death scene of the man of God was so remarkable that word of it began to spread around Bethel and soon reached the ears of the old prophet. In a flash the prophet realized the identity of the dead man by the side of the road and he went out to retrieve the body. Remarkably, the lion did not bother the prophet, either, when he put the dead man on his donkey and went back to town. The prophet buried the man of God in his own family tomb and "mourned," perhaps over his own sin that contributed to the man's death, over the loss to Israel of such a godly man, and over the sorry state of affairs in the Northern Kingdom in general. He recognized that the judgment the man of God had leveled against the false worship of Israel would be executed (v. 32).

The death and burial of the man of God was not the end of the story. Three hundred years later when Josiah came to Bethel to extend his reform to the Northern Kingdom and to desecrate the altar of Jeroboam, "the men of the city" still identified the tomb of the man of God who had pronounced judgment against the altar (2 Kings 23:17). For all those years he had witnessed silently to the worship of Yahweh and against the apostasy of Jeroboam. "Though he is dead, he still speaks" (Heb. 11:4, NASB).

c. Subsequent actions of Jeroboam (13:33, 34). "After this incident, Jeroboam did not give up his evil ways." In spite of the prophetic pronouncement at Bethel, he did not turn from his evil ways but continued his cultic irregularities. This passage mentions only the appointment of priests for the high places, but it was symbolic or representative of his disregard for the Law of Moses and the commands of God. These verses must be placed alongside the summary in 1 Kings 12:25–33. To be sure, political, social, and international conditions all contributed to the destruction of Jeroboam's line and of his kingdom, but the root cause lay in the king's disobedience to the commands of a holy God and the willingness of his successors to walk in his steps.

3. Jeroboam's Condemnation (14:1–20)

"At that time," a reference to an indefinite time during the reign of Jeroboam, his son Abijah fell ill. Probably the time was fairly late in Jeroboam's reign because the judgment spelled out below was based on the continuing impact of his idolatry and because Ahijah, the prophet, was now old and blind. Presumably, Abijah was the crown prince but the text does not say so. In desperation over the seriousness of his son's condition, Jeroboam decided to appeal to the prophet Ahijah, who was now living in Shiloh, the ancient site of the tabernacle. Why he did so is not clear. Perhaps he did not really trust the prophets and priests of the new religion. Or perhaps he hoped that the prophet who had once predicted his elevation to the throne and had wished him well would give him another good message.

Of course, it was risky business to be making an appeal to Ahijah, for knowledge of it would undermine confidence in the state cult that was now an important prop of the government itself. So Jeroboam did not dare to go; and if he were well enough to travel, the son could not be brought for healing, either, because he would be recognized. Therefore, the king decided to send his wife, carefully disguised so neither the public nor the prophet would recognize her. If the prophet did know her at the outset, he might refuse her an audience. The queen went as a peasant woman and brought a gift commensurate with her supposed social and economic status, not that of royalty: "ten loaves of bread (flat and round like modern Arab bread), some sweet cakes, and a jar of honey." How the king and queen could expect a prophet of God to know the future and yet not be able to see through a disguise is somewhat incomprehensible. As a matter of fact, the all-knowing God of the universe told the blind prophet that the queen was coming and exactly what to say to her.

When the queen came in, Ahijah unmasked her immediately and informed her he had been sent with "a harsh message" or "bad news" for Jeroboam. Then he proceeded to remind her of what God had done for Jeroboam, what Jeroboam had not done or had done wrong, and on that basis what judgment God would impose. For His part, God had graciously elevated Jeroboam to the kingship at the expense of the unity of the Davidic empire. But He had done so on the condition of Jeroboam's faithfulness to Him (1 Kings 11:38). Jeroboam, for his part, had not been faithful to God as David had been in all his public policy. But worse, he had done more evil than all his "predecessors." Exactly what that means is not clear for

Jeroboam was the first of the line; it could refer to other kings who had ruled over Israel (Saul, David, Solomon) and it could even extend to the Judges, Joshua, and Moses. None of these leaders of God's people had made "other gods, idols of cast metal" (v. 9) and enjoined the people to worship them. To "cast" or "thrust" God "behind" one's "back" is to treat Him with scornful contempt and is the opposite of keeping God before the eyes and in the heart (cf. Ezek. 23:35; Neh. 9:26).

For Jeroboam's failure, God would bring "disaster" on his house. He would cut off "every male," "bond or free," perhaps meaning married or unmarried, and destroy every trace of the existence of his house with shameful and utter extermination as one "burns dung until it is gone." His descendants will go unburied; those who die in the city will be eaten by the scavenging dogs that run wild there, and those who die in the country will suffer the same fate from scavenging birds. In addition, God will raise up a king who will cut off Jeroboam's line (v. 14), a reference to Baasha (1 Kings 15:27) who conspired against Nadab, Jeroboam's son. Long range, Ahijah saw the whole Northern Kingdom going into captivity "beyond the River" (the Euphrates, v. 15) because of their capitulation to the sins of Jeroboam, and for making "sacred poles" or "Asherah idols" (v. 15). These were poles or stylized idols or trees representing the goddess Asherah, consort of Baal, the god of fertility. Thus Canaanite idolatry mixed with calf worship to bring the double condemnation of Yahweh.

Then specifically, in response to the queen's inquiry, Ahijah announced that her son would die as soon as she set foot in the city, that all Israel would mourn his death, and that he was the only one of Jeroboam's sons who would have an honorable burial. Then Jeroboam's wife left and went to Tirzah that was then serving as a capital, and all turned out as Ahijah had predicted. It is a characteristic of Scripture not to dramatize events or to play up emotional or human elements. Nothing is said here of the brokenhearted mother over the death of her son, the possible sorrow of Ahijah over the waywardness of Israel, or the consternation of Jeroboam on hearing of the judgment pronounced against him. If the Bible were a purely human book, as is often asserted, no doubt these emotional and dramatic elements would frequently be inserted.

Under divine guidance the author of the books of Kings has selected information about Jeroboam that especially underscores his spiritual apostasy. Other information about his military involvements and political administration were available in the "annals of the kings of Israel," records kept in the national archives. The writer refers to these annals in describing the reigns of nearly all the kings of Israel. Jeroboam ruled for twenty-two years (contemporary with the seventeen of Rehoboam, the three of Abijah, and two years of Asa's reign in Judah), and his son Nadab succeeded him. He must have had considerable charisma and leadership qualities to have endured so long in such a difficult position. Various hints indicate the truncation of Israelite territory during Jeroboam's reign, however. An Aramaean kingdom with its capital at Damascus became independent in the north and Moab apparently shed Israelite control in the east. Abijah of Judah managed to take a border area in the south.

C. Wars Between Israel and Judah (14:21–16:28)

During the reigns of several kings of Israel and Judah there was armed conflict between the two states, and that fact is used here as an organizing factor. Although Rehoboam had disbanded his troops and dropped his plans to resubjugate the north on orders of Shemaiah the prophet (1 Kings 12:22–24), there was "continual warfare" between him and Jeroboam, presumably in the nature of border skirmishes.

1. Rehoboam of Judah (14:21–31)

Rehoboam (931–913) had come on the scene earlier, taking the throne after the death of his father Solomon, but the appearance of Jeroboam and the split of the kingdom had interrupted discussion of his reign. The few verses here must be supplemented with 2 Chronicles 10–12. Actually Rehoboam started well. During the first three years of his rule, he led the kingdom in ways of righteousness. But then a rapid declension set in, and high places and groves began to appear everywhere. At those high places stood "sacred stones" representing the male deity, and "sacred pillars" (of wood) or "Asherah pillars," representing the female deity. There were also "male cult prostitutes" so that when sacrifice was offered, sexual relations formed part of the rite (cf. Hos. 4:14) on the belief that through magic symbolism fertility could be secured for human and animal reproduction and for crops. "Abominable practices" (v. 24) refers to Canaanite cultic rites.

In punishment for Judean apostasy, God sent against the land a massive Egyptian invasion under the leadership of Shishak (Sheshonk I, 945–924 B.C.). Coming during Rehoboam's fifth year, probably 926 B.C., this invasion wrought havoc not only in Judah, but also in the Northern Kingdom and even Transjordan, as Shishak's inscriptions on a wall at the Temple of Karnak in Luxor show. Interestingly, Shishak did not include Jerusalem in the list of towns he took or sacked; so the impression one gets is that Shishak's price for sparing Jerusalem was so high that all the treasures of temple and palace had to be plundered to pay the ransom. Especially, all the gold ceremonial shields that Solomon had commissioned to be made were surrendered and burnished bronze shields put in their place. When God made it clear to Rehoboam that this punishment had come because of idolatry (2 Chron. 12:5), the king and many of the leaders of the nation confessed their sins and God spared them. Subsequently, Rehoboam fortified at least fifteen cities to the south and west of Jerusalem to prevent a recurrence of Egyptian inroads. As noted, Rehoboam was involved in constant military confrontation with Israel.

The text indicates (v. 21) that Rehoboam was forty-one when he became king, so he was born just before Solomon became king. He reigned seventeen years in Jerusalem and was buried in the City of David—in the tombs of the kings in the southeastern part of the city. Twice (vv. 21, 31) the point is made that his mother was Naamah an Ammonitess, but it is not clear that she influenced him to allow or encourage pagan cultic practices in the kingdom. Following the example of his father, he had a large harem of eighteen wives and sixty concubines and fathered twenty-eight sons and sixty daughters (2 Chron. 11:21). His favorite wife was Maacah, and her oldest son, Abijah, became the next king. Additional events of the king's reign are said to be recorded in the Annals of the Kings of Judah, a source that the sacred historian also used in composing nearly all of the other statements about Judean kings in 1 and 2 Kings.

2. Abijah(m) of Judah (15:1-8)

Abijah's brief three-year reign (913–910) began in the eighteenth year of Jeroboam. His mother, Maacah, was a daughter of Abishalom, a shortened form of Absalom, usually identified with the son of David; hence Maacah was David's granddaughter. But, truthfully, there is no compelling reason for identifying Abishalom with David's son Absalom. As his father had done, Abijah fell into idolatry. In fact, conditions were so bad that God would have brought an end to Abijah's line if it had not been for His covenant with David. In this case when reference is made to David's keeping God's commands, the exception of his handling of Uriah the Hittite is mentioned (v. 5). That Abijah's "heart was not wholly with Yahweh" does not mean that he forsook Yahweh altogether. In his "pretty speech" on a mountain not far from Bethel (2 Chron. 13:4–12) he scored Israel for its idolatry and bragged that by comparison Judah's public policy adhered to Mosaic religious requirements.

Abijah made this speech in the midst of conflict with Israel, and this points up the fact that like his father he engaged in continual warfare with his neighbor to the north. Scripture mentions only one major battle with Jeroboam. This must have been an all-out effort at conquest, for 800,000 men of Israel were pitted against 400,000 men of Judah (2 Chron. 13:2), evidently just about all the able-bodied males of both kingdoms (cf. 2 Sam. 24:9). Though the forces of Israel had trapped those of Judah and threatened to annihilate them, supernatural intervention wrought great destruction in the Israelite host and led to Judah's occupation of some border territory in Israel. Conceivably, Abijah was faithful to God before the battle and was not hypocritical in the speech he made, but then fell into idolatry later and suffered a shortening of his reign for his sin. Conversely, he may have fallen into idolatry before the battle; and then as a result of repentance and the public declaration of policy noted above, he may have enjoyed God's intervention in winning the struggle.

Like his father, Abijah fell into idolatry, engaged in warfare with Israel, practiced polygamy (had 14 wives and 38 children, 2 Chron. 13:21), and was buried in the royal cemetery in the City of David.

3. Asa of Judah (15:9–24)

For David's sake God gave Abijah a "lamp in Jerusalem" (15:4). Though this expression refers merely to a representative of the Davidic dynasty in Jerusalem, the lamp in this case was to burn more brightly than most. Asa (910–869) was a good king (15:11) and staged massive reforms in the kingdom; he was one of the four good kings of Judah to do so. Actually God evaluated eight of the nineteen kings of Judah as good, even though some of their deeds were evil.

Asa was the son of Abijah and he began to reign near the end of Jeroboam's reign—in his twentieth year. His "mother's name" is given as Maacah; undoubtedly she is to be understood as his "grandmother" (so NEB and NIV). Asa was probably still quite young and Maacah remained at the court as queen mother. Asa was destined to reign for forty-one years. During the first ten years of his reign he enjoyed peace (2 Chron. 14:1) and he began his reform measures, removing foreign altars in high places and smashing sacred pillars at cult centers (2 Chron. 14:2–5).

Asa also built up the army and his defenses. All his efforts were not enough, however, to meet the mighty Egyptian onslaught that came during his fifteenth year (ca. 895 B.C.). When the Ethiopian Zerah, apparently commander under Osorkon I, invaded the land, his force was so overwhelming that Asa ran to God for help and God gave a great victory (2 Chron. 14:9–15). On the heels of the victory, Azariah the prophet called on Asa to remember the source of his strength and to serve God faithfully (2 Chron. 15:1–7). Asa responded with a renewal of the covenant and a great sacrifice (probably made possible in part by spoils of the victory). Then he brought to the temple additional booty from the victory and presumably some of the spoils of his father's victory over Israel (1 Kings 15:15). Following all that, Asa proceeded in earnest with his reform, expelling "male cult prostitutes" and even deposing Maacah from her position at court because she maintained an Asherah shrine; the shrine statue he burned in the Kidron Valley (between Jerusalem and the Mount of Olives on the east, (1 Kings 15:12, 13; 2 Chron. 15:16).

After Asa's great victory over the Egyptians, people began streaming south from Israel because they saw God was with him. Baasha, who was now king of Israel, decided to build his own "Berlin Wall" to keep these people from going to Judah, and he decided to fortify Ramah, only about five miles north of Jerusalem (2 Chron. 16:1; 1 Kings 15:17). At that point, only approximately a year after his great victory over the Egyptians and in the midst of his reform moves,[1] Asa had a strange lapse of faith. Instead of depending on God to see him through the new emergency, he stripped the treasuries of the temple and palace and sent a large donative to Benhadad, king of Aram in Damascus, requesting a renewal of a treaty that their fathers had had and a breaking of the non-aggression pact Aram now had with Israel (1 Kings 15:19). There is no record of such a treaty between Abijah and Aram, but there is no reason to doubt it.

Asa's diplomatic initiatives were successful and Benhadad prepared to attack Israel's north. When Baasha heard about "this" (v. 21) threat to his northern border, he naturally stopped work on fortifying Ramah and rushed back to his capital at Tirzah (northeast of Nablus) to prepare to meet Benhadad in the field. Benhadad conquered several towns in the far north around Dan and in the Galilee region. Meanwhile, Asa issued an order to the militia and those subject to forced labor to engage in their own construction at the border with Israel. In effect, he moved the border a few miles north and used materials Baasha had gathered at Ramah to fortify Mizpah (some 15 miles north of Jerusalem) and Geba (about 6 miles northeast of Jerusalem).

For Asa's lapse of faith the prophet Hanani brought judgment down on the king, predicting that "from now on you will be at war." Not accepting God's rebuke, Asa flew into a rage and clapped the prophet into jail and then brutally suppressed some of his other opposition (2 Chron. 16:9–10). True to the prophet's word, from then on Asa and Baasha were at each

---

[1]Thiele, *Mysterious Numbers of the Hebrew Kings*, 84–85.

other's throats (1 Kings 15:16). The disease from which Asa suffered in his old age (15:23) cannot be identified with certainty; suggestions include gout, dropsy, a form of gangrene, or vascular disease.

4. Nadab of Israel (15:25–32)

During his short two years of rule (909–908), Nadab followed the precedent of his father in causing Israel to sin by fostering the calf worship at Dan and Bethel. While he was besieging Gibbethon (Tell el-Melat, 3 miles west of Gezer), a Philistine city, one of the officers of his own army, Baasha, rebelled against him, killed him, and took the throne. With his death the dynasty of Jeroboam I came to an end as Ahijah had predicted (1 Kings 14:7–16). Moreover, as Ahijah had foretold, Baasha exterminated Jeroboam's entire family.

5. Baasha of Israel (15:33–16:7)

Baasha ascended the throne in the third year of Asa and reigned for twenty-four years (908–886), the third longest reign in the Northern Kingdom. He ruled from Tirzah, which he seems to have made the capital; previously it had served only as one of the palace centers. Tirzah is now usually identified with northern Tell el-Far 'ah, about seven miles northeast of Nablus and Shechem. Since his reign was simultaneous with much of Asa's, some events of it have already been recounted. God's having lifted him up "from the dust" (16:2) implies that he had a lowly origin. The brevity of the biblical treatment of Baasha has prompted some to conclude that he was relatively insignificant. That may be true but the purpose of biblical history is not necessarily to summarize important developments; it seeks to teach moral and spiritual truth. McNeely well observes, " . . . the scriptural principle seems to be that a life lived out of fellowship with God is of little importance."[2] That Baasha's life was so lived is clear from the condemnation the prophet Jehu (not to be confused with the king) brought against him (16:2–4). He "followed in the footsteps of Jeroboam" (in personal apostasy) and "led my people Israel to sin" (by example and

---

[2]McNeely, *First and Second Kings*, 77.

official sponsorship of calf worship); therefore his fate was to be identical to that of Jeroboam: his line would be obliterated. Provoking God to anger against Israel (v. 2) should not be ignored. God was building a case against His people; their continued idolatry put them in increasing danger of national destruction and captivity. Moreover, God held Baasha responsible for destroying the house of Jeroboam (v. 7) because he had evidently done so merely to advance his own cause instead of as God's executioner.

6. Elah of Israel (16:8–14)

Baasha's son Elah ruled for less than two years (886–885) after his father died. The sacred historian found nothing good to say for him. In fact, while the army was off fighting at Gibbethon (v. 15), he was "drinking himself drunk" in the house of Arza, the official in charge of crown lands of Tirzah (v. 9). In the middle of this brief and uncomplimentary statement about Elah, Zimri, commander of half of the chariotry, dashed in from the wings, assassinated the king, and took the throne for himself. Immediately he also massacred all Elah's relatives and friends (his official circle) so there would be no one left to seek revenge (as family members of ancient Semites were wont to do). Zimri's action may have been a result of personal ambition or of the army's discontent with the rule of Elah. But whatever the reason, it fulfilled Jehu's prophecy (vv. 12–13); and though Elah does not seem to have been an exemplary ruler, his demise is not attributed to administrative failure so much as to sin against God.

7. Zimri of Israel (16:15–20)

From a divine standpoint, the woes of Israel rose primarily from the apostasy of king and people. Dynasties were short-lived because of the moral and spiritual failures of the monarchs. From a human standpoint, Israel's internal troubles can be partly explained by the fact that it was a collection of ten tribes with their individual agendas and their jealousies. There were political and social factions and rivals for the throne. By comparison, Judah, as essentially a one-tribe kingdom, was naturally a more cohesive unit.

When Zimri assassinated Elah and took the throne, he apparently unleashed some of the pent-up ambitions that had been simmering just below the surface. Omri and Tibni now suddenly appeared on the scene and plunged the kingdom into civil strife until Omri finally won out. Omri as "commander of the army" (v. 16) was made king as soon as word of Zimri's action arrived at Gibbethon, which the army was besieging. Zimri had been commander of only half of the chariot corps, but Omri was commander of the infantry; his acceptance by "all Israel" (v. 16) must mean by the standing army and such representatives of the tribes as were present at Gibbethon. It would have taken a day for a messenger to bring news of what happened at the capital to the front. Then it would have taken the army four to five days to break off the siege at Gibbethon and return to Tirzah. When Zimri saw that the "city was taken" or that it could not hold out, he shut himself up in the "keep" or "citadel of the royal palace" and committed suicide by setting it on fire. The reference in verse 19 to his dying under the judgment of God because of this sin and his causing Israel to sin cannot refer to his short reign of seven days but must indicate that he, like the rest of the kings of Israel, walked in the steps of Jeroboam; he was of the same bent, and his administration would have been as bad as the rest of them.

8. Omri of Israel (16:21–28)

Verses 21 and 22 barely lift the curtain enough to give the reader a glimpse of what was going on in the Northern Kingdom. Omri and Tibni were having it out, each claiming to be king. It is not clear what constituency supported each, and all the speculation of scholars need not be recounted. The struggle must have been titanic, and what tipped the balance in favor of Omri eventually was the degree to which he controlled the army. Both Omri and Tibni put forward their claim to the throne at the death of Zimri, in the twenty-seventh year of Asa, king of Judah (885 B.C.). But Omri did not really establish his rule until the thirty-first year of Asa's rule (v. 29, 880 B.C.), indicating that there were over four years of civil war. At that time Tibni "died"; probably Omri dispatched him.

Because the sacred historian evaluated Omri as "worse than

all his predecessors" in promoting idolatry (v. 25), he considers him unworthy of much attention. All he reports about Omri's reign is that he bought the hill of Samaria, built a city on it, established it as the permanent capital of the Northern Kingdom, and was the first of the kings of Israel to be buried there. The choice of Samaria as the administrative center of the kingdom was a wise move. It was an easily defensible site some three to four hundred feet high and was surrounded by a rich agricultural hinterland. It had access to the coastal plain to the west, to Megiddo and the plain of Jezreel to the north, and to the line of communication along the Jordan Valley to the east.

But Omri did much more than establish a new capital. After he achieved internal stability, he began to look outward, conquering Moab and possibly making an alliance with King Ethbaal of Tyre. At least he married his son Ahab to Jezebel, daughter of Ethbaal. Moreover, he strengthened his kingdom so much that for generations thereafter kings of Assyria referred to Israel as the "land of Omri." He established a dynasty that was to last through three additional kings (Ahab, Ahaziah, and Jehoram). Another hint of his greatness is the reference in Micah 6:16 to "the statutes of Omri," an indication that he may have engaged in legal reform or a major codification of law. The text says that he ruled twelve years (885–874), six in Tirzah, before he moved the capital (v. 23). Those twelve years included the period of civil war with Tibni, and the first four years in Tirzah were a period when his hold was very tenuous indeed. Though the sacred historian did not choose to talk about Omri's greatness, he did allude to "the things he achieved," that could be learned about in the "annals of the kings of Israel" (v. 27).

For Further Study

1. Using a little imagination, develop a character study/ analysis of Rehoboam.

2. With the help of a Bible dictionary, study calf/bull worship in Egypt and Canaan to see the influences Jeroboam may have succumbed to in developing his new religion.

3. Write a newspaper account of the story of the "man of God" and the "old prophet" for the *Bethel Gazette*.

4. Write an imaginative soliloquy depicting the thoughts of

Jeroboam's queen from the time of Jeroboam's decision to send her to Ahijah until the death of her son.

5. Try to list the factors that contributed to the difficulties of the Northern Kingdom.

6. Can you identify any signs of greatness or success in the Northern Kingdom culturally, economically, politically, or militarily? Some of this information becomes more evident from subsequent studies in *1, 2 Kings*.

Chapter 5

Peace and Alliance Between the Two Kingdoms
(1 Kings 16:29–2 Kings 9:37)

During the days of the house of Omri, the former animosity between the two Hebrew kingdoms gave way to a time of peace between them, and possibly even a treaty. If there was not a formal treaty, at least there was a military alliance between Jehoshaphat of Judah and Ahab of Israel, and Ahab's daughter Athaliah was married to Jehoshaphat's son Jehoram. Then on the death of Jehoram, Athaliah actually ruled the kingdom of Judah for a time. These better relations may have been good for both kingdoms economically and politically, but they were very harmful to Judah religiously because of the importation of Baal worship from the north.

A. Beginning of Ahab's Reign (1 Kings 16:29–34)

Naturally the Bible is more interested in religious history than it is in political or economic or social history. Therefore the focus of attention in describing Ahab's reign is on the introduction of Baal worship into Israel, the determination of at least the queen to wipe Yahwism from the face of the earth, and Yahwism's counterattack in the person and work of Elijah and later Elisha.

For his religious shortcomings Ahab was roundly condemned, and the Bible reader often gets the impression that Ahab was a terribly incompetent monarch. But that does not seem to be a fair assessment. Excavations demonstrate the extent and quality of his construction at Samaria and Megiddo and Hazor, and the Scripture itself states that he built cities for the people (1 Kings 22:39). Moreover, Ahab appears to have been an effective military leader. On two occasions he defeated Aramaean forces (1 Kings 20:1–34). Then in 853 B.C. he joined a coalition of kings from Syria and Palestine that sought to turn back the advance of Shalmaneser III of Assyria at Qarqar on the Orontes. To that effort he contributed two thousand chariots and ten thousand men.[1] That number of chariots shows something of the wealth and power of Israel at the time; Solomon had kept only fourteen hundred chariots in his military establishment.

The account of Ahab's reign opens with the usual formula: a son of Omri, he began his reign in the thirty-eighth year of Asa, king of Judah, and reigned in Samaria over Israel for twenty-two years (874–853). But the usual formula concluding a king's reign does not appear until 22:39, 40, most of the intervening text being given over to the ministry of Elijah and his contest with the king. Ahab was more "displeasing to Yahweh" than "all who preceded him." That went for his father Omri, too, of whom the same epitaph was written (v. 25).

Then the sacred historian proceeded to detail the basis for that displeasure. First, "the least that he did" (v. 31, JB) was to follow the sinful example of Jeroboam. But he also married Jezebel. In those days of contract marriages, Ahab could hardly be held responsible for a marriage his father had arranged. But the verse (with its phraseology "took as wife") implies either that Ahab persuaded his father to make the arrangements, or, once they were made, he wholeheartedly approved of the marriage and endorsed Jezebel's religious policies. "Ethbaal, king of the Sidonians" (v. 31) was Ithobaal, king of Tyre; "Sidonians" must be regarded as a synonym for Phoenicians. Sidon's leadership among the Phoenician states had given way to that of Tyre. Ithobaal was an ardent worshiper of Baal, and his daughter was, too. When she came to Samaria, Ahab, like Solomon before him, made religious provision for his foreign wife. He built a temple for Baal in Samaria and an altar in the temple for sacrifice to the god, the Baal-Melqart of Tyre. Though originally this temple was probably for the use of Jezebel and any servants she may have brought with her from Phoenicia, it

---

[1] James B. Pritchard, ed., *Ancient Near Eastern Texts Relating to the Old Testament*, 2nd ed. (Princeton: Princeton University Press, 1955), 278–79.

seems to have become the center of the state cult. The "Asherah" (v. 33) was a plain pole or a stylistically carved pole that served as an image or symbol of the mother goddess of the Canaanite fertility cult.

Exactly how verse 34 fits in this context is not clear. Of course, Hiel's refortification of Jericho could qualify it as one of the cities built or rebuilt by Ahab (1 Kings 22:39). And in this context, where the worship of Yahweh was being squeezed out, it was significant to note that the word of Yahweh was still powerful: the prediction in Joshua 6:26 that anyone rebuilding Jericho would fall under a divine curse had been fulfilled. The verse may also fit if Hiel's loss of his two sons, as indicated here, involved pagan sacrifice of children and their burial as foundation sacrifices. If so, the wider implication of religious slippage in Ahab's day is underscored. But the former, common interpretation of the death of these two children as infant/foundation sacrifices is frequently challenged today. Perhaps they only died during the building project and their deaths were interpreted as fulfillment of the curse.

B. Ahab's Contest with Elijah (17:1–19:21)

1. Elijah's Prediction of Drought (17:1)

As Ahab's apostasy bit ever deeper into the very fabric of Israelite life and threatened to extinguish the flickering light of Yahwism, stalwart Elijah appeared on the scene. Coming from backward Gilead across the Jordan and dressed only in camel's hair clothing (2 Kings 1:8), he joined battle with king and queen and the sophisticated religionists at the court. Elijah simply bursts on the biblical stage without any introduction. The argument of some commentators that he must have developed quite a reputation before this in order for Ahab to take him seriously has merit, but there is nevertheless no record of his earlier activities.

His later reputation is firmly established, however. He did lead the fight effectively against Baal worship in Israel. Much later, John the Baptist, the forerunner of Christ, was to come in the spirit and power of Elijah (Luke 1:17). Elijah as the representative of the prophets was to join Moses as representative of the Law in giving witness to Jesus on the Mount of Transfiguration (Matt. 17:3; Luke 9:30–31). Elijah means "Yahweh is God" and that fact exemplified his mission, which was to show that Yahweh is indeed God (1 Kings 18:39) and He alone.

Whether Elijah burst in on Ahab at the palace or met him on the way is not clear, but he did have a personal encounter with the king, during which he made his dire predictions that "there will neither be dew nor rain these years, except at my order." The duration of the drought is not specified; Luke 4:25 and James 5:17 give the figure of three and one-half years. The inclusion of dew along with the rain is very important because in the hills of Palestine the dew falls between 100 and 180 nights per year and is a significant supplement to the rain. Elijah's pronouncement was a slap in the face of Baal who was supposed to be a rain god and god of fertility. If Elijah's order was necessary for rain to fall again, Ahab would be especially interested in finding him as the drought wore on.

2. God's Provision for Elijah (17:2–24)

a. By the ravens (17:2–7). God told Elijah to go eastward, out of the jurisdiction of Ahab, east of the Jordan, and hide himself by the Wadi Cherith (Kerith). The traditional identification of this brook with the Wadi Qelt near Jericho and his hideout with the monastery of Elijah located there cannot be accepted, because it is west of the Jordan. About all one can say concerning the identification of the stream is that it was probably one of the many seasonal rivulets that flowed into the Jordan from the east. The brook would provide him with water and ravens would bring him "bread" (a general word for food) and meat every morning and evening. It is remarkable that almost everything said about Elijah in Scripture involves the element of the miraculous.

But lest modern believers conclude that their lives are basically geared to the non-miraculous, they should remember that their faith is based on the miracles of the incarnation and resurrection, their Bible has become available by the miracle of inspiration, their salvation has been wrought through the miracle of substitutionary atonement, and their living of the Christian life is possible only through the indwelling Holy

Spirit, who empowers and teaches and guides. Scores of other miracles relate to their general well-being every day.

The Wadi Kerith, like other wadis, was a stream that flowed only during the rainy season, or at least did not flow all year long. When Elijah's water supply ran out, God directed him to go to Zarephath in Phoenicia, ancient Sarepta, excavated by James B. Pritchard, 1969–74. It is located about nine miles south of Sidon.[2]

b. By the widow of Zarephath (17:8–24). At Zarephath he was to meet a widow who would provide for him. That promise was remarkable indeed because poor widows usually ran out of food first during a famine. When Elijah got to Zarephath he had to discover who it was that God had arranged to care for him. By the town gate he saw a woman gathering "dry material" with which to build a fire, and he decided to pose a test.

First he asked her for a drink of water, which does not seem like much unless we are in a drought-stricken land. Her response was positive, indicating she might be the hospitable one who would care for him. He decided to test her further by asking for a scrap of bread. Then she blurted out her true plight: I have "nothing baked," but only "a handful of meal in a jar" and a "little [olive] oil in a jug." She was going to go home and fix that for herself and her son and then they would starve because that was all she had, and there was no hope of getting more. The woman had recognized that Elijah was an Israelite and uttered the statement, "as truly as Yahweh your God lives." To be sure she called Yahweh Elijah's God, but there is a hint of respect for Him, if not faith, in her voice. Then Elijah put the woman to the test again, asking that first she fix him something and promising that Yahweh would indeed provide for them all until the drought was over.

The woman passed the test and went off to do Elijah's bidding (cf. Luke 4:26). And God for His part kept the promise; there was always enough for the woman "and her household" or "family" (v. 15). It is not necessary to conclude from this that the woman had servants or was fairly well off as the "mistress of the house" (v. 17). The house may have been very tiny indeed

---

[2]James B. Pritchard, *Recovering Sarepta, A Phoenician City* (Princeton: Princeton University Press, 1978).

with a chamber or just a little sleeping place on the flat roof (v. 19), and though the passage does not say so, possibly a destitute sister or cousin or some other starving relative had moved in with her. Some translations substitute "son" for "household" in verse 15.

After some time the woman's son grew ill and apparently died. Commentators argue that he may have fallen into a coma or some other condition short of death; but both the woman and Elijah believed he was dead, and the language of verses 18, 20, 21, and 22 presupposes death. Immediately the woman's response was that Elijah as a man of God reproved sin in her life by his very presence and the conduct of his life and that because of her sin God had taken her son (v. 18).

Elijah now showed his tremendous faith; he did not accept what appeared to be inevitable. Though no one in Israel or in Phoenicia had ever known of anyone coming back from the dead, Elijah took the child to his little room on the roof and laid the boy on his bedroll on the floor. Then three times he agonized in prayer to God, begging for the child's life and for the woman to be spared this tragedy. If this was indeed her only son, his death meant the end of the family line and the loss of someone to support her when she grew old. Each time Elijah prayed, he "stretched himself upon the child" (v. 21), mouth to mouth, eyes to eyes, and hands to hands. God heard the prophet's cry, and the "child's soul returned to him" (v. 22), indicating restoration to life.

Then Elijah carried the boy down the outside stairway and "into the house" and returned him to his grieving mother. The text does not say whether the boy was almost instantly healed or whether he required a period of convalescence. But it does record the mother's response, which indicates the two main reasons for miracles in the Bible: accreditation of God's messenger ("I know you are a man of God") and accreditation of the message ("the word of Yahweh is truly in your mouth"). We do not have a report of what impact this miracle had on the people of Zarephath or what kind of witness for Yahweh this woman or her son may have been in later years. It had no value for Israel, for they were not present. It did help to strengthen the faith of the woman, however, and especially the faith of Elijah, who needed spiritual underpinning as he faced Ahab and Jezebel and all the prophets of Baal.

3. Elijah's Challenge to the Prophets of Baal (18:1–46)

a. Arranging the meeting with Ahab (18:1–16). At length God announced that the drought was coming to an end and directed Elijah to return to Ahab. The directive came "in the third year"; if that refers to the famine, it indicates that the famine did not last much more than two years. But Luke 4:25 and James 5:17 clearly state that the famine was three and one-half years in duration. Keil resolves the difficulty by concluding that 1 Kings 18:1 refers to the time Elijah spent with the widow at Zarephath, and thus the time since he had last received marching orders from God.[3] Elijah hastened to obey.

Next comes an aside about what was going on in Samaria. It is difficult to know whether to translate verse 2, "the famine was particularly severe in Samaria" (JB), i.e., worse than elsewhere under the judgment of God, or whether the famine was simply "at its height" (NEB). In any case, fodder for mules and horses (needed as dray animals and for defense) had now been exhausted, and Ahab proposed to the chief steward of crown properties that he and the king canvass the "springs" and "valleys" (places where water drained from the hills) to find grass. The chief steward, Obadiah by name (not the "minor" writing prophet), was a devout follower of Yahweh, and he had hidden one hundred prophets and was providing them with food and water—quite a task when shortages were so severe. This detail helps to document God's statement to Elijah that there were seven thousand who had not bowed the knee to Baal (19:18). God always strengthens a remnant of His own to stand for Him under pressure, whether in Israel during the days of Ahab and Jezebel, in Kenya during the Mau Mau uprising, in China during the Cultural Revolution, or in all the other difficult places of the world.

While Obadiah was engaged in his search, Elijah suddenly appeared to him. Whether Obadiah recognized the prophet from a previous meeting (about which nothing is known) or from his

---

[3] Keil, *The Books of the Kings*, 241.

appearance is an open question. Elijah then requested an audience with the king, to which Obadiah objected. Again, whether he did so because he feared for the prophet's safety or because he believed the prophet would disappear and the king would slay him in a rage, must be treated as an open question. At least Obadiah made a great deal of the fear for his own life, mentioning three times that Ahab would kill him if Elijah disappeared (vv. 9, 12, 14). Evidently Ahab's search for Elijah had been intense, and he had inquired about him in all of the surrounding kingdoms and city-states. If Elijah were to be almost within his grasp now and to elude him again, he would kill the steward for letting Elijah slip through his fingers.

But Elijah assured Obadiah that he would indeed face Ahab that day. "Lord of Hosts" (v. 15, first of five appearances in the book) is susceptible to various interpretations but probably indicates that Yahweh was the all-powerful One. Elijah seemingly means to say that because he serves a God of much power, he is confident that God is able to handle the meeting with Ahab and the terrible apostasy in Israel. Obadiah bowed to the wishes of Elijah and went off to arrange the audience.

b. Meeting with Ahab and the contest on Mount Carmel (18:17–46). Where Ahab and Elijah met is not indicated, nor is there a record of any polite court protocol; probably there was not any. There is no reason why the king should not have immediately attacked the prophet as soon as he was ushered in. After all, the king had been tramping around looking for grazing land and probably was hot and tired. So he blurted out, "You troubler of Israel" (v. 17). A "troubler" or "scourge" was one who brought a certain ritual disability; in this case Elijah had brought the wrath of Baal on Israel in withholding rain, the giving of which was Baal's province (as rain god and god of fertility) according to Canaanite belief. Then Elijah threw the charge back in the teeth of the king. It was, after all, Baal worship, apostasy from Yahweh worship, that had brought the punishment of Yahweh upon them. "Baals" (v. 18) in the plural refers to the various local shrines or manifestation of Baal (meaning "lord").

What was developing in the conversation was a debate over which was the true god, Baal or Yahweh; so Elijah proposed a test. Call representatives from among the people of Israel to meet on Mount Carmel, a mountain ridge rising just south of Haifa Bay and standing close to Phoenician territory. A pagan worship center stood there; it was not really Yahweh territory. Also to come were the 450 prophets of Baal (the male deity) and the 400 prophets of Asherah (Baal's female consort), Jezebel's subsidized religious establishment. Apparently Ahab liked the idea and probably was so naïve as to think his side would win any contest. The fact that the four hundred prophets of Asherah were not heard from again has led some commentators to conclude that this inclusion is not a genuine part of the text, but Keil argues that they found a way to evade Ahab's command and did not participate.[4]

The day agreed-to arrived and the group assembled, probably at the traditional site of the contest, the Muhraka, in the southeast part of the mountain. From there one can descend to the Brook Kishon. Near there, water was available on the mountain itself to meet the requirements of the sacrifice. The Hebrew of the question Elijah put to the people (v. 21) is difficult and is rendered variously. An appealing translation is, "How long will you go hobbling on two crutches?"—i.e., depending on both Yahweh and Baal, combining Baalism and Yahwism in a syncretistic approach. Make your choice, he advised. Then Elijah proceeded with the proposal for the test. Elijah did not literally believe, "I am the only prophet of Yahweh." He knew of one hundred hiding in caves. He was at that moment the only prophet of Yahweh publicly operating in Israel to face the 450 prophets of Baal, and he would now make an agreement with them. He proposed getting two bulls for sacrifice and preparing one for Baal and the other for Yahweh. Then the sacrifices were to be readied but the sacrificial fires not ignited. The devotees of each god were to call on their deity and the one who answered by kindling the fire was to be recognized as God. All agreed to the contest.

Elijah let the prophets of Baal make their sacrifice first, then they could not claim he had left them with an inferior bull or that he had in any other way put them at a disadvantage.

---

[4] Ibid., 244.

Moreover, he believed they would not be able to get their sacrificial fire lit and that he could achieve a dramatic effect with Yahweh's intervention. All morning the prophets of Baal called on their god and engaged in a ritual dance around the altar. Nothing happened and Elijah began to taunt them sarcastically: "perhaps he is preoccupied" or "deep in thought"; "busy" or "engaged" (literally, relieving himself); "on a journey"; "asleep." In short, he is not god and is unable to act. They shouted louder and slashed themselves in a more intense attempt to draw their god's attention to gain his favor. They "raved on" until time for the evening sacrifice (about 3:00 P.M.) but there was no response.

Finally Elijah felt it was his turn and he called for the attention of the people. On the ruins of an old Israelite altar he placed twelve stones—one for each of the twelve tribes—symbolizing the continuing unity of Israel under the covenant in the mind of God. Then he dug a trench around the altar and had water poured over the sacrifice and the wood three times until everything was thoroughly soaked and the trench itself was filled with water. By this means he sought to demonstrate that no trickery was possible; a real miracle would have to take place. (The significance of the two measures of seeds eludes us.) Then instead of all the frenzied calling, ritual dance, and laceration, Elijah prayed a simple prayer that Yahweh would prove that He was God and that He would accredit His messenger. The fire fell and consumed the sacrifice, the wood, and even the water in the trench. The effect on the people was the desired one: "They fell on their faces and cried, 'Yahweh is God.'"

With the people on his side, Elijah commanded that they seize the prophets of Baal, take them down to the Kishon Valley, and kill them there. This command fulfilled the law that condemned false prophets to death (Deut. 13:5), and was retribution for Jezebel's killing of the prophets of Yahweh. There is no record of Ahab's opposition to the execution, nor is there any indication of how he really felt about Yahweh's miraculous demonstration of Himself.

After the sacrifice, Elijah now appropriately prayed that God would send rain. Baal, the rain god, had been proven powerless and could not now be given credit for breaking the drought. Elijah sent Ahab off to celebrate the end of the drought, and he climbed to the top of Mount Carmel to pray for rain. A total of seven times he sent his servant to go look toward the Mediterranean, from which direction rainstorms came. Finally the servant saw a small cloud coming from the sea and Elijah sent word to Ahab to hurry and hitch up his chariot and drive to Jezreel before his chariot got mired in the muddy roads. Elijah ran before Ahab, perhaps as a loyal outrunner, receiving supernatural stamina for the race. The distance was some seventeen to twenty miles to Jezreel, the winter capital, about halfway between the traditional spot on Mount Carmel and the Jordan River. Of course, the chariot had to run on the road but Elijah could travel cross-country and take a more direct route. Moreover, the chariot would be increasingly slowed by muddy tracks. Perhaps Elijah's race was in part for the purpose of presenting the account of Yahweh's victory in the presence of and with the corroboration of the king.

4. Elijah's Failure and Renewal (19:1–21)

a. Flight to Horeb (19:1–18). From the heights of triumph Elijah suddenly plunged into the depths of despair. On the previous day he had taken on Ahab, the prophets of Baal, and an ambivalent public had seen God win a tremendous victory. Now he quailed before the queen who had threatened to kill him within the next twenty-four hours. In a way it seems almost irrelevant to ask whether Jezebel could have made good on her threat, considering the support of the populace for Elijah and a certain impression made on Ahab by the events on Mount Carmel. Of course, given the character of the queen, we must assume that she could have hired one or more assassins to do her dirty work. She was not the kind to let anything stand in the way of getting what she wanted. Elijah did not have the strength to face the kind of virulent fury that this vicious queen displayed; he "was afraid and ran."[5] Modern psychologists and physicians

---

[5] Ronald B. Allen, "Elijah, the Broken Prophet," *Journal of the Evangelical Theological Society*, 22:3 (1979), 193–202, argues the Hebrew means "saw" (NASB and NIV margins), and that Elijah was heartbroken that Jezebel had not capitulated, not scared to death.

would observe that he was so totally drained by the emotional strain of the previous day and his cross-country run that he simply did not have the stamina to stand up to a lesser challenge the next morning.

Elijah was still apparently in Jezreel when he received the threat from Jezebel. He "fled for his life" south through Israel and Judah, to the southern outpost of Judah, Beersheba— perhaps a journey of one hundred miles. At Beersheba he left his servant and went another day's journey (perhaps 15 miles) out into the Negev. There he sat under a broom tree, a bush with white flowers that grows to a height of some twelve feet in the wadis of that region, and prayed "that he might die." Having escaped from the long arm of Jezebel, he now asks God to be his executioner. "I am no better than my ancestors" probably means that as they served God in their day and endured their quota of pain, so had he, and he deserved no longer life than they. Now totally exhausted, Elijah can look only on the dark side of things; he falls asleep, not wishing to wake up in the morning.

Gracious and gentle, God did not lecture Elijah nor argue with him. He let the prophet sleep for a while and then sent an angel with food and water that Elijah consumed, and then he went back to sleep. Again the angel awakened him. This can be interpreted as the same angel that awakened him before or "the Angel of Yahweh," the second Person of the Godhead, as some believe. The food provided was truly miraculous because in its strength Elijah traveled "forty days and forty nights" as he wended his way toward Horeb at the tip of the Sinai Peninsula. His pace was not so frantic now; he took forty days to cover some two hundred miles. Finally he arrived at the "mountain of God" and went into "the cave" to spend the night. Presumably, this was the same cave where God had appeared to Moses (Exod. 33:12ff.).

As Elijah spent the night in the cave, God asked him, "What are you doing here, Elijah?" This could be merely an opportunity for Elijah to express his feelings, or rebuke in the sense of who gave him permission to be here; in other instances God had specifically directed him to go where he went. In either case, the answer would have been about the same. He was having something of a "pity party." He underscored his zeal for

Yahweh, but in spite of that saw only the total failure of the
Israelites in their rejection of God's covenant and in their
persecution of the prophets. In fact, he felt all alone in serving
God—and he was running for his life. In looking on the dark
side of things, he ignored God's victory over the prophets of
Baal on Mount Carmel and Obadiah's stand for God and his
protection of known prophets. Apparently, Elijah sensed failure
and wanted greater results of his zeal for God. His statement
implied criticism of God's failure to act in response to His
prophet's ministry; there was a lack of visible fruit for his labor.

Again God did not lecture his servant but merely gave him a
demonstration of His ways. First He caused a terrible tempest to
come crashing down on the mountain—so fierce that it even
smashed rocks, and then an earthquake, and then a fire. But
though Yahweh might sometimes use those modes of revelation,
He was not in any of those terrible phenomena on this occasion.
He spoke instead in the "still small voice" (KJV) or a "voice of
fine silence,"[6] or "the sound of gentle quietness."[7] It is
impossible to render the Hebrew effectively into English. What
the words mean to convey is that an awesome stillness confronted Elijah, one that the presence of Yahweh so dramatically
filled that it seemed almost to touch or speak. Actually, there
was no sound at all; and "still small voice," though often used in
sermons and hymns, does not really convey the meaning of the
original text.

At the evident presence of God, Elijah "covered his face
with his cloak" in breathless wonder. The message of this whole
demonstration seems to be that Elijah should not expect
spectacular revelations of Yahweh for the near term but communication of Himself in the quiet ordinary course of daily life or
quiet working behind the scenes.

After the great demonstration on the mountain, God again
asked Elijah what he was doing there, and the prophet replied
in language identical to his earlier response (v. 14, cf. v. 10).
Perhaps he was saying, "I understand what You are telling me,
but I still feel the same about myself as I did before." And
perhaps from what follows, God was saying, "I have other things

---

[6]A. Graeme Auld, *I and II Kings* (Philadelphia: Westminster, 1986), 117.
[7]LaSor, "1 and 2 Kings," 345.

for you to do now, and we shall take care of your feelings about yourself later."

The task for Elijah was threefold: to anoint Hazael in Damascus, to anoint Jehu king of Israel, and to anoint Elisha of Abel Meholah as his successor. God mentioned Hazael and Jehu first because they were to be His instruments of judgment on the royal family and the people of Israel for their idolatry. Actually, God was to appoint those two indirectly through Elijah, for it was his successor, Elisha, who would deliver God's word to them; and anointing should be taken in a rather general sense. Elisha did anoint Jehu but merely announced to Hazael that he would be king; Elijah consecrated Elisha for his office, but actual anointing probably did not take place.

And then to mollify the prophet's feelings about the degree of spiritual life left in the kingdom, Yahweh told him that there were seven thousand who had not capitulated to Baalism. The number may be taken literally or as symbolic of a substantial number of several thousand. Fortified by a new vision of God and armed with new instructions from Yahweh of Hosts, Elijah descended from the mountain of God to do battle with the forces of idolatry in the hills and valleys of Israel.

b. Appointment of Elisha (19:19–21). His first task was to find Elisha, however. He went to Abel Meholah in the Jordan Valley, about halfway between the Dead Sea and the Sea of Galilee, and found him plowing. The fact that twelve yoke of oxen were involved in the endeavor implies a considerable tract of land and therefore a family of considerable wealth. Elisha's plowing with the twelfth yoke probably means that his workmen and other members of his family were plowing with the other eleven. Elijah's throwing his "mantle" or "cloak" around Elisha was a sign or symbol of the call to prophetic office and of the passing of the power and authority of the office to him (cf. 2 Kings 2:13–14).

Elisha did not resist the call but immediately ran after Elijah. How his heart was prepared for this major step is not even hinted at, but his ready response is further evidence that there was some spiritual life left in Israel. Elisha asked that he might first go and say a proper goodbye to his mother and father. The absence of any mention of a wife indicates he was not

married, and the lack of any remonstrance with him on the part
of his family implies their support of his entering the service of
Yahweh. There is no hint as to whether he was the oldest son or
the only son.

Elijah's response to Elisha's request is difficult to interpret:
"What have I done to you?" Evidently it implies permission.
The NEB translates, "Go back; what have I done to prevent you?"
Gray's translation is perhaps better: "Go, but (remember) what I
have done to you."[8] Elijah was reminding him of the uncompro-
mising nature of the call. Then Elisha killed the oxen and
burned the plowing equipment to cook the meat, signifying a
complete break with his former life, and served the meat at a
farewell dinner for relatives and friends. Having said his
goodbyes, he set out to follow Elijah.

C. Ahab's Early Wars with Syria (20:1–43)

1. The Victory at Samaria (20:1–21)

The spotlight now turns from internal and religious matters
to the foreign affairs of Israel. The exact time of these Syrian
attacks is not clear, but it must have been several years before
the great battle of Qarqar in 853 B.C., when Ahab and Syria were
allied against Shalmaneser III of Assyria. The Syrian king, Ben-
Hadad, was probably the son of the Ben-Hadad who had
attacked Baasha of Israel on the urging of Asa some years earlier
(cf. 15:18, 20; 20:34). As king in Damascus, Ben-Hadad II had
achieved a certain hegemony in Syria and was able to command
the support of numerous other city-states in times of war; on this
occasion thirty-two of these petty kings were allied with him.

As Ben-Hadad besieged Samaria, he demanded silver and
gold and the king's wives and children, which Ahab interpreted
as tribute and hostages as a price of peace. To this he agreed. (In
asking for Ahab's wives and children, Ben-Hadad also may have
been seeking legitimate succession to the throne or a kind of
feudal suzerainty over Ahab.) But then Ben-Hadad required
more, the right to loot the city (v. 6), which is tantamount to a
demand for unconditional surrender. This time Ahab called the
"elders," probably the influential leaders of the capital, and they

---

[8]John Gray, *I & II Kings*, 2nd ed. (Philadelphia: Westminster, 1970), 413.

and the "people" (probably especially the citizen army) counseled resistance. Ahab then responded that the first demand he
would still meet but not the second. Seeing some weakness in
Ahab, Ben-Hadad then tried intimidation by threatening, in
effect, to pulverize the city of Samaria (v. 10). This time Ahab
replied with a proverb that is only four words in the Hebrew but
is approximately paraphrased in the NIV: "One who puts on his
armor should not boast like the one who takes it off." Perhaps a
contemporary parallel is: "Don't count your chickens before
they are hatched." This retort arrived from the Israelite side
while the Syrian kings were drinking in their "booths" (made of
branches and leaves), and it apparently inflamed them. Ben-
Hadad ordered his army to set themselves in battle array.

Meanwhile, an unnamed prophet of Yahweh came to Ahab,
again an evidence that Elijah was not the only one left to serve
Yahweh in Israel. The fact that he was able to operate openly
and that the king would listen to him may be some evidence of a
positive effect of Elijah's ministry and of abated persecution of
followers of Yahweh. The reason for God's intervention on this
occasion is not to be interpreted as blessing on an idolatrous
society but a further effort to get Israel to recognize the true
God.

Ahab did not reject the offered help and even accepted the
specific instructions for battle arrangements. "Aids of the district
governors," (232 young men who must have acted as a kind of
commando force recruited by the district governors, possibly
governors of the districts established by Solomon) were to lead
the attack. They were to be followed by the standing army of
seven thousand then bivouacked in the city. The time set for
attack was "noon," during lunch and siesta time, when the
officers would be drinking in their booths and the rank and file
would be "at ease."

As Ahab implemented the plan, Ben-Hadad's scouts reported the advance of the small band of Israelites and did not know
how to interpret what they were doing. He gave the order to
take them alive. When the commandos came out swinging, they
caught the Syrian army completely off guard. And when the
Israelite army advanced rapidly, they routed the Syrians totally.
What contributed to the victory was the Israelite capture of

horses and chariots, which they then used against the Syrians in
the final stages of the battle (the intent of v. 21). Ben-Hadad and
some of his chief officers and associates managed to get away.

2. The Victory at Aphek (20:22–34)

After the victory at Samaria, "the prophet," presumably the
same one who had come to Ahab before that victory, warned that
the following spring Ben-Hadad would attack again and necessary preparations should be made for the conflict. Meanwhile, in
the Syrian camp an agonizing reappraisal was taking place.
Since the Israelites had won in the hills, where the chariots and
cavalry of the Syrian states had been ineffective, Ben-Hadad's
advisors concluded that Yahweh was a god of the hills and that
they should seek another engagement in the plain. For such a
battle it would be necessary to rebuild the cavalry and chariot
corps, with which the Syrians could clearly have the advantage.
Moreover, since the generalship of numerous kings leading
their ethnic bands into battle had created a disunified military
posture, Ben-Hadad's advisors recommended a reorganized
army with regional contingents led by professional military men
(vv. 24–25). Ben-Hadad adopted these recommendations.

In the following spring the Syrian forces elected to fight at
Aphek, where they thought they would have a definite advantage. There were five Apheks; the battle probably took place
either at the one in the plain of Esdraelon or the one east of the
Sea of Galilee and commanding the road to Damascus. There
are good arguments for both, and it is difficult to determine
which is meant. At whichever site it was, the two armies spread
out in the plain, the Syrians with a vast multitude and the
Israelites with what looked like "two herds of goats" (v. 27).
Apparently Ahab had formed his army into two companies in
accord with his battle strategy. Into this hopeless situation
walked the "man of God," presumably the prophet who had
previously warned Ahab of the Syrian return. He said in effect
that because the Syrians thought Yahweh was powerful in the
hills only, He was bound to give the Israelites victory to prove
His omnipotence to the Syrians; and the Israelites who had
been so idolatrous would know that Yahweh truly was God.

For seven days the two armies took each other's measure

and worked on battle strategies. Perhaps the Syrians sought omens from their gods. Finally on the day of the battle the Israelites reportedly killed one hundred thousand foot soldiers, and the collapsing wall of Aphek supposedly killed another twenty-seven thousand. Nothing is said of the battle strategy or how God gave the victory. Even the most reverent student of Scripture has difficulty with battle statistics; the transmission of numbers is one of the greatest problems in Scripture. The numbers seem much too large. In the great battle of Qarqar in 853 B.C., in which eleven kings of greater Syria massed their forces against Shalmaneser III of Assyria, they put only about sixty-three thousand men in the field, of which twenty thousand were from the kingdom of Damascus and ten thousand from Israel. Moreover, while a collapsing wall of one of the small towns of Palestine might have killed a few thousand, twenty-seven thousand seems excessive. For present purposes it is enough to say that a vast Syrian army massed against Israel, whose forces seemed puny by comparison. God gave Israel a great victory, with heavy casualties on the Syrian side both on the battlefield and as a result of a collapsing wall in Aphek.

Ben-Hadad escaped into an "inner chamber" (a room within a room) in the town with a few of his officials. Finally his attendants proposed that they go to Ahab and plead for Ben-Hadad's life. They wore sackcloth (a coarse black material) around their waists as a sign of mourning and penitence, and ropes around their heads as a sign of subjection or willingness to act as porters to the victor. When they pleaded for Ben-Hadad's life, Ahab referred to him as a "brother," which they took to be a good omen. Shortly Ahab received the Syrian up into his chariot, an act of acceptance, and made a treaty with him. This involved Ben-Hadad's return of the cities that his father had taken from Baasha (Ahab's "father" or predecessor, 1 Kings 15:20), Israelite trade privileges in Damascus, and Syrian trade privileges in Samaria.

The reader wonders what is going on here and how Ahab could have been so generous when his victory was so complete. The explanation is simple: Assyrian power loomed on the eastern horizon, and Ahab believed he needed Syrian power as a buffer against the Assyrians and as an ally if open warfare should erupt. Within very few years, perhaps only two or three, the two kings were fighting side by side against the Assyrians.

3. Judgment on Ahab (20:35–43)

One of the young men in the schools of the prophets received an assignment from Yahweh to pronounce judgment on Ahab. He solicited a real wound from a companion so he could symbolically deliver his judgment. Then he disguised himself as a wounded soldier and stood by the road waiting for Ahab to pass by. When the king came, he called to him and told a fictitious story of how he had been assigned to guard a prisoner; and if the prisoner should be missing he was to answer with his own life or pay a talent of silver as punishment. The prophet reported that his prisoner had escaped and he presumably interceded with Ahab to save him from his punishment. But the king said he had pronounced his own sentence on himself and refused to help him.

Then, as in Nathan's story to David (2 Sam. 12:1–7), the prophet virtually said, "You are the man." He took off his disguise and the king recognized him as a prophet. Then he told Ahab that because he had let Ben-Hadad get away and had not obeyed God's order to execute the Syrian king (an order that the prophet must have given before the victory at Aphek), he would forfeit his own life in exchange for Ben-Hadad's. Ahab went back to Samaria "dispirited and angry" at himself and the prophet. Ahab thought he knew better than Yahweh how to handle the international situation, but his disobedience was to be very costly. Plausible courses of action may not always be God's choices for us.

D. Ahab's Desire for Naboth's Vineyard (21:1–29)

If the text is in chronological order, Ahab was relaxing after the Syrian wars and was attending to purely personal matters. At this point he was especially interested in obtaining a garden spot near the winter palace at Jezreel (usually identified with Zer'in, west of Beth-Shan at the eastern edge of the plain of Esdraelon); Naboth currently owned the land and had planted a vineyard there. Ahab's course of action was forthright enough. He offered to buy the land outright or exchange it for another even better plot. Apparently Naboth personally preferred not to sell the property, but more important to his response to Ahab was a religious and sociological reason. The Mosaic Law forbade his disposal of a paternal inheritance (Lev. 25:23–28; Num. 36:7ff.), and ancient Semitic records of Syria and Mesopotamia show how carefully family estates were protected. Ahab went home (to Samaria) "dispirited and angry" (cf. 20:43) and childishly lay on his "couch" (which Gray suggests may have been his couch used for eating),[9] turned his face toward the wall, and refused to eat, probably hoping to rouse his attendants to devise some way of gratifying his wishes.

When Jezebel found Ahab pouting, she pried from him the reason and then responded, "You, are you really king in Israel?" Then she told him to pull himself together because she would get the land for him. It may be argued that Jezebel was a brazen woman or simply that she had come from a despotic royal background in which the king had the absolute authority to do exactly as he wished and to take what he wanted for himself without regard to the rights of the citizens. Jezebel then sent a letter to the "elders" and "nobles" or "notables" of Jezreel, ordering them, in effect, to stage a kangaroo court to find Naboth guilty of blaspheming God and the king. And since the former was punishable by stoning to death (Lev. 24:16), they were to execute him. She was careful to be sure that the legal requirement of two (false) witnesses was observed (Deut. 17:6; 19:15). Of course, she made the order official by using the king's seal.

The elders of Jezreel fulfilled the command promptly, showing their degree of corruption and fear of the monarchy. Presumably the order included stoning Naboth's sons (2 Kings 9:26); otherwise, with their father dead, they would have inherited the property and Ahab still could not get his way. Legally, the sons could have been implicated in a plot against the king. Then the elders notified Jezebel of their action. "As soon as" (v. 15) she got the message, she informed Ahab, and he

---

[9] Gray, *I & II Kings*, 439. On such couches the diner reclined and ate with his right hand while propping himself up on his left hand. This was the practice of many ancient peoples of Near Eastern and Mediterranean lands and was certainly the manner of dining in several New Testament scenes (e.g., Matt. 26:7).

promptly went off to Jezreel to take possession of Naboth's vineyard.

While Jezebel and Ahab were moving rapidly, so was God. He sent Elijah to confront Ahab in the very act of taking possession of Naboth's property. As Ahab walked among the grapevines, suddenly Elijah appeared before him with a question from God: "Have you murdered and taken possession?" Then he went on to pronounce divine condemnation: "In the place where the dogs licked up Naboth's blood they will lick up yours" (v. 19). This prophecy was mitigated somewhat after Ahab's repentance (vv. 27–29). Instead of dying some ignominious death and having the dogs lick up his blood in Jezreel, he died in battle and was honorably buried in Samaria. But the dogs did lick up his blood as it was washed from his chariot (1 Kings 22:38). The corpse of his son, Jehoram, was cast onto Naboth's land, however (2 Kings 9:25–26).

"Have you found me, O my enemy?" queried the king, almost as if he felt like a hunted man. This time Elijah was not the "troubler of Israel" but an "enemy." Just as Elijah had turned the tables on Ahab before, he did so again when he said in effect that Ahab had made himself God's enemy because he had sold himself to do evil (v. 20). That is, he had made himself a slave of evil or had given himself to evil to the extent that he had no will of his own. Thus he had sacrificed his principles to get what he wanted. Elijah then announced to Ahab the extermination of his house as the dynasties of Jeroboam and Baasha had been cut off.

For Jezebel was reserved a more ignominious fate: "Dogs shall devour Jezebel by the wall of Jezreel." The same fate would befall Ahab's descendants. In ancient Palestinian cities dogs were not kept as house pets but ran wild in the streets as scavengers. Always hungry, they rapidly devoured anything edible. Then the historian inserted an editorial comment concerning Ahab's ungodly conduct that had brought such woe on himself and his house (vv. 25–26).

This volley of condemnation stunned Ahab into true contrition. In penitence he "tore his clothes," put on sackcloth and fasted and "walked about subdued," as one in deep trouble. For this sincere humiliation before Him, Yahweh postponed the fulfillment of the judgment against him until the days of his son Jehoram, but Jezebel, of course, showed no such repentance and suffered the full quota of her judgment herself.

E. Ahab's Final Syrian War (22:1-40)

1. Alliance with Jehoshaphat (22:1-4)

"For three years" (v. 1) there had been peace between Syria and Israel. The treaty between the two powers (20:34) had held through the joint effort to confront Shalmaneser III at Qarqar in 853. But apparently within months after the battle of Qarqar, Israel and Syria fell· to scrapping again. In this same general period—the exact time is not clear—Ahab and Jehoshaphat of Judah had made a treaty and cemented it with the marriage of Ahab's daughter Athaliah to Jehoshaphat's son Jehoram. "In the third year" (v. 2, reminding the reader that parts of years were counted as years, cf. v. 1, "three years") the kings of Israel and Judah had a conference in which they agreed to go to war against Syria. The language of verse 4, "I am as you are . . . ," does not necessarily imply that Judah was a vassal to Israel or even a weaker member of a free alliance. But at least Jehoshaphat was agreeing to honor the provisions of the alliance. Ahab's concern was to liberate Ramoth Gilead, an important city on the eastern caravan route, which Ben-Hadad had not returned when he restored the northern towns to Israel. Scholars argue over three or four possible locations for the ancient site, and it cannot be established with certainty.

2. The Counsel of Ahab's Prophets (22:5-12)

Though he was willing to accompany Ahab to war, Jehoshaphat requested that first they inquire of God to determine His will in the matter. Ahab then called in the prophets, about four hundred in number. These were prophets of the state cult, not of Baal. On the public payroll, they were viewed as agents of the community in its effort to influence God, and they said what they were paid to say or what they thought they should say. Knowing that the king wanted to retake Ramoth Gilead, they all urged him to do so and promised God's blessing on the effort. In fact, one of them, Zedekiah, produced iron horns, which by means of imitative magic, were to symbolize the way in which the Israelites would gore the Syrians. Such prophets could provide moral support for an intended action.

Jehoshaphat subscribed to an entirely different view of the prophetic office: that the prophet should speak what Yahweh told him to speak. He evidently saw through the charade produced by these false prophets, and sought for one or some who would appear to proclaim God's message, at whatever cost to themselves. Ahab knew of such a prophet, Micaiah by name, but he was unhappy with him because the prophet had often crossed him, declaring God's will to be diametrically opposed to the king's. In spite of that, Ahab agreed to call Micaiah, a further documentation that Elijah was certainly not the only prophet or layperson faithful to Yahweh in Israel. While the two kings waited, they sat enthroned at the gate of Samaria; apparently there was a large threshing floor just outside the gate. A similar place for such a throne with supports for a canopy over it has turned up in excavations at the gate of ancient Dan (dating to the end of the tenth century B.C.).

3. Micaiah's Prophecy (22:13–28)

As the king's messenger came to fetch Micaiah, he informed him of the issue at hand, what the other prophets were saying, and the advisability of agreeing with them. When Micaiah arrived, Ahab asked him about the course of action they should take, and Micaiah joined the other prophets in approval of the attack on Syria. Ahab recognized what Micaiah was doing and then asked him for the truth. "How many times" (v. 16) sounds good when uttered before Jehoshaphat, as if he always sought the truth, but he may never have made the point before.

Then Micaiah prophesied that Israel would be shepherd-less; with their king dead the army would simply break up and the war would be over; each one would go home "in peace." Micaiah next described a heavenly court scene (cf. Job 1–2; Isa. 6; Ezek. 1) in which God sought a volunteer angel to put a lying spirit in the mouth of the prophets to lure Ahab into battle to his destruction. Zedekiah countered with the claim that the lying spirit was the one who spoke through Micaiah, not the four hundred prophets. Micaiah replied that they would know who spoke the truth when the Israelite army was defeated and they would be forced to hide in a "room inside a room," some citadel or keep (v. 25; cf. 1 Kings 20:30).

Ahab chose to believe the other prophets and ordered that Micaiah be thrown into prison and fed with the prison diet of bread and water until he returned safely. He was put in the care of Amon, the mayor of the city, and Joash, "the king's son," probably a title for a highly trusted police officer in charge of prisoners, rather than an actual son of the king. Micaiah's parting word provides a test of all prophets whether they speak from the Lord or not: do their words come true?

4. The Battle of Ramoth Gilead (22:29–38)

Ignoring the warning of Micaiah, Ahab proceeded with his attack on Ramoth Gilead. Why Jehoshaphat, who was one of the good kings of Judah and a faithful worshiper of Yahweh, did not protest after the true prophet's warning is unknown. In order to prevent the prophecy from being fulfilled, Ahab went into battle disguised, but the king of Judah wore his royal uniform. Unknown to the kings of Israel and Judah, Ben-Hadad gave the order to his thirty-two chariot commanders (possibly contingents from the city-states of Syria) to attack the king of Israel only. The reason may be threefold: (1) anger against Ahab for breaking the treaty with Syria; (2) recognition that if the king died or were captured, the army would cease to fight; (3) the desire to kill the king only so the army might remain intact to join him in future warfare against Assyria. The Syrians made straight for Jehoshaphat, thinking he was Ahab; somehow he showed them he was not the king of Israel, and they stopped attacking him.

But a bowman shooting at random hit Ahab in the joints of his armor (perhaps between the breastplate and the abdomen and thigh armor) and mortally wounded him; thus the prophecy was "accidentally" fulfilled. Ahab bravely stayed in the battle all day, propped up in his chariot and gradually bleeding to death. Finally at sunset he died and the news spread through the army. As usually happened in such cases, the siege of Ramoth Gilead ended and the army disbanded. The Syrians did not pursue their advantage because the limited objective of successfully defending the city had been achieved. Moreover, as noted, they may have wanted Israel as an ally against Assyria. Ahab's body was buried in Samaria, but his chariot was washed in some pool outside the city that was probably used for washing clothes and watering animals (and "where prostitutes bathed"), and the dogs licked up his blood there. The pools inside the city were cisterns containing a limited water supply for the necessities of life. Thus was fulfilled the prophecy against Ahab (20:42; 21:19, 21). He must have died very late in the year 853 B.C.

5. Summary on Ahab (22:39–40)

As was true with all the kings of Israel and Judah, information concerning their reigns was very selective and fulfilled a religious purpose. Of course, Ahab was portrayed as the most evil of the kings of Israel. But he must have had many abilities, some military prowess, and considerable fiscal success. He built up the capital at Samaria and his ivory palace there (so-called for the tremendous amount of ivory inlay in furniture and possibly in wall panels). Excavations at the site turned up quantities of carved ivory decorations. He also fortified other centers (v. 39), among which were Hazor and Megiddo, as excavations show. His son Ahaziah succeeded him as king.

F. Jehoshaphat of Judah (22:41–50)

Jehoshaphat of Judah has already been introduced in connection with the Syrian war that was almost disastrous for him. The alliance with Israel had involved the marriage of Ahab's daughter Athaliah to Jehoshaphat's son Jehoram. This passage mentions a second joint venture between Jehoshaphat and Ahab's son Ahaziah: the building of a merchant marine at Ezion-geber, which was wrecked before it even set sail for Ophir (vv. 48–49). Jehoshaphat's third joint venture with Israel, during Joram's reign, involved attack on Moab and again was almost disastrous (2 Kings 3).

In spite of his unholy alliance, Jehoshaphat was a good king, one of Judah's eight good kings and one of its four reformers. He removed the high places according to 2 Chronicles 17:6, but not according to 1 Kings 22:43 and 2 Chronicles 20:33. This must indicate either that he removed some of the more important ones but did not fully clear the country of them, or that he removed them once but the people restored them and he did not remove them a second time. He did eliminate the rest of the male shrine prostitutes, however (22:46). His ordering of the teaching of the Law of Moses throughout Judah, the fortification of the kingdom, and improvement of the legal structure are topics treated in 2 Chronicles 17–20.

He began his reign in 872 at the age of thirty-five as coregent with his father Asa and ruled for twenty-five years until 848. His son Jehoram began coregency with him in 853.

G. Ahaziah of Israel (1 Kings 22:51–2 Kings 1:18)

When Ahab was killed in the battle of Ramoth Gilead, his son Ahaziah took the throne and ruled for "two years" (22:51), officially 853–852, but the total time was only about a year. The assessment of his reign was that he followed the example of his father and mother, both in worshiping Baal and in participating in the calf worship of Jeroboam. Therefore he incurred the wrath and judgment of God.

After the death of Ahab, Moab revolted (2 Kings 1:1), unsuccessfully at first during the short reign of Ahaziah and the early years of Joram. But near the end of Joram's reign Moab gained its independence. King Mesha of Moab recorded his version of the struggle, on what is known as the Moabite Stone.[10] Evidently verse 1 of 2 Kings belongs to the historical note at the end of 1 Kings. The Elijah narrative that occupies the rest of chapter 1 may also belong there; the present division of the books originated with the Septuagint, probably in the second century B.C.

As the book opens, Ahaziah lies in his bed, severely injured as a result of a fall at the palace. The second floor apparently had open balconies or terraces faced with flimsy lattice work designed to cut the glare of the sun but not to impede the flow of air. Ahaziah had fallen through some of this lattice work "from the balcony" (v. 2, JB). As he writhed in agony, he decided to appeal to the Baal of Ekron to learn whether he would recover. Baal-zebub means "lord of the flies" (because of his supposed power over flies he was thought to be able to send or protect

---

[10] See D. Winton Thomas, ed., *Documents from Old Testament Times* (New York: Harper & Row, 1958), 195–98.

against diseases). Ekron was the northernmost of the Philistine cities, now identified with Khirbet Muqanna (Tel Miqneh), about ten miles southeast of Jaffa. (Trude Dothan and Seymour Gitin have been excavating there in recent years.)

"The angel of Yahweh" sent Elijah to intercept Ahaziah's envoys. This messenger is virtually indistinguishable from Yahweh Himself and often is identified as the Second Person of the Trinity. The angel instructed Elijah to ask if Ahaziah went off to Philistia to consult a god because there was none in Israel. The real reason, more than likely, was that inquiry of a faithful prophet of Yahweh often brought answers Ahaziah did not like to hear. Elijah was now to condemn religious syncretism and to predict the death of the king.

Of course, the king's messengers did not need long to complete the shortened trip, and surprised the king by their early return. They explained that they had met a man who had sent them back to the king with a message of death. Naturally the king was curious about the identity of this "man." The descriptive that he was a "hairy man" could have referred to his long hair and beard (a Nazirite), but usually is taken to describe his clothing: a rough, shaggy cloak (possibly made of sheepskin, goatskin, or camel skin) with a leather belt at the waist (an anticipation of the dress of John the Baptist, Mal. 4:5; Matt. 3:4).

The king knew immediately that the one who had pronounced his doom was Elijah and sent a "captain" (a professional soldier who had won distinction) and his company of fifty men to arrest the prophet. When the band found Elijah on a hill, the captain ordered Elijah in the name of the king to come down. Then two judicial miracles occurred in which two companies of soldiers were wiped out. In dealing with the question of the morality of these acts, one must remember that God performed the miracle, not Elijah, and that the reason for the judgment apparently was contempt for the prophetic office in the person of Elijah and of Yahweh who had accredited him as His servant.[11]

The third captain demonstrated respect for Yahweh and His representative and begged for mercy. This time God told Elijah

---

[11]Keil, *The Books of the Kings*, 287.

to go with the soldiers and not to be afraid, probably because the hearts of the soldiers and of the king himself had been softened by the previous judgments. Elijah accompanied the troop and repeated the word that God had sent the king through his messengers earlier. So the king died, too young to have a son, and his brother Joram (Jehoram) ascended the throne.

H. Exit Elijah, Enter Elisha (2:1–25)

1. Elijah's Translation (2:1–11)

The charge is sometimes leveled that Elijah's flight from Jezebel after the victory on Mount Carmel greatly compromised his ministry in Israel and weakened his impact thereafter. But that does not seem to have been the case. After his meeting with God on Mount Horeb, he went back to active service. He met both Ahab and his son Ahaziah and pronounced judgment on both. And especially he attended to the guilds or associations of the prophets ("sons of the prophets"), a prophetic movement that arose during the Omride dynasty, in the days of Elijah and Elisha, and then disappeared thereafter (see 1 Kings 20:35; 2 Kings 2:3, 4, 6, 15; 5:22; 6:1; 9:1). These young men were significant for the maintenance of the truth and worship of Yahweh when Baal threatened to abolish it altogether. Now, before his departure, Elijah sought to encourage these guilds or chapters he may have been instrumental in helping to found. Also, of course, Elijah had been involved in the preparation of his successor Elisha.

As God was about to translate Elijah, He was apparently preparing all parties for that momentous event. Elijah himself had been specifically told (2:3, 5) and members of the prophetic guilds had also learned of it (2:3, 5). Apparently God had informed all of these parties independently and sought to strengthen their faith.

The story opens with Elijah and Elisha leaving Gilgal for Bethel. The Gilgal in question evidently is not the one in the Jordan Valley but one in the hills of Ephraim. Scholars argue over its exact location, but perhaps it was Jiljiliyeh, some seven miles northwest of Bethel. Elijah encouraged Elisha to stay behind in Gilgal, perhaps because he wanted to go to meet God alone, or else to test the faithfulness of Elisha. Elisha met the test but he probably also sought whatever blessing Elijah might pronounce upon him. So the two went to Bethel, the main cult center of Israel, just ten miles north of Jerusalem. There, in the very headquarters of apostasy, were "sons of the prophets" or apprentices who had attached themselves to prophets for training in the revealed word of God. One should not forget that prophets in both the Old and New Testaments were primarily forthtellers or preachers of the Word of God; prediction was only a secondary ministry. The fact that groups of preachers existed implies listeners and supporters, for someone had to provide the freewill offerings that sustained these prophets.

The question as to whether Elisha knew Yahweh was going to take his master or mentor "from over your head" today may be taken both figuratively and literally. Figuratively, it implies the lifting of supervision or governance or instruction; literally, it indicates carrying Elijah into the skies. His answer, "be quiet," may imply that Elisha did not want them to add to his sorrow or uneasiness in talking about it, or that he wanted to avoid creating problems for Elijah, or even that he did not want to let Elijah know that they all knew about it. At Bethel Elijah again tested Elisha by asking him to remain there while he went to Jericho. Again came the pledge of fidelity.

In Jericho occurred a repeat performance of Elisha's experience with the prophets at Bethel. Possibly these prophets were from the cult center at Gilgal, halfway between Jericho and the Jordan River. Elijah told Elisha to stay behind while he went on to the Jordan. For a third time Elisha made a pledge of faithfulness. The two of them went on alone. The excitement heightened. As they paused by the riverside, fifty men from the sons of the prophets (probably from the group at Gilgal) stood at a distance looking on. Then Elijah took his "cloak" or "mantle" and rolled it up to use it as a kind of stick or wand (similar to Moses' rod at the Red Sea, Exod. 14:16), to part the waters to enable them to cross on dry ground.

After they had crossed over, Elijah finally referred to his imminent departure and asked what he could do for Elisha as a parting blessing. Elisha's response was to ask for a "double share" of Elijah's spirit. What he was asking for was not to excel his master but to receive the double portion of the eldest son as inheritance rights under Hebrew law (Deut. 21:17). That is, he was asking to be the true heir and successor of Elijah. By way of answer, Elijah laid down a condition: "If you see me as I am taken," i.e., if he had the courage to face Elijah's translation. His status as a successor depended on his ability "to see and comprehend the spiritual world."[12] Then as they walked along and talked, suddenly a fiery chariot and horses, symbols of Yahweh's power, separated them and a whirlwind caught Elijah up into heaven.

2. Introduction of Elisha (2:12–25)

As he stood there alone, gazing into the sky, Elisha exclaimed, "My father! My father!" in respect and dependency. And then he called Elijah "the chariotry of Israel and its horsemen," that is, he represented the divine forces that were Israel's true defense. The chariot as the greatest weapon then known was symbolic of God's supreme power, and Elijah was the instrument through which God's power was operative in Israel. Then Elisha tore his clothes in sincere grief at Elijah's departure and over his own unworthiness. Next he picked up Elijah's cloak as a tangible symbol of his inheritance, i.e., that he was the true heir and successor of Elijah, and used it to part the waters as Elijah had done. His posing of the question, "Where is Yahweh, the God of Elijah?" was a prayer that God would show forth His great power to and through his obedient servant. It was not an impertinent exclamation.

Elisha's action convinced the prophets who were watching that "the spirit of Elijah" did indeed rest on Elisha and they bowed in respect. They did not realize, however, that Elijah had gone into the very presence of God; presumably they had not seen the chariots or the whirlwind. These "able-bodied men" wanted to form search parties and comb the area to look for Elijah. Elisha tried to tell them it was no use but they "kept pressing him" until he "had no heart" to refuse them. After searching for three days, they were convinced that Elijah was indeed gone and that Elisha was God's leader among them.

---

[12] Jones, Gwilym H. "1 and 2 Kings," 385.

Next appear two miracles designed to confirm Elisha's prophetic office. The first involved purification of the spring that served as the main water supply for Jericho. This is identified today as 'Ain es-Sultan or Elisha's Spring, the wonderful gushing spring at the foot of the mound on which stood ancient Jericho. The spring rendered the land "unfruitful" or "unproductive." Elisha engaged in a ritual of purification. First he called for a "new bowl," symbolically uncontaminated, and filled it with salt that was then used as a symbol of purifying from a curse. In the name and by the power of Yahweh, he said, "I purify this water" (v. 21, NEB). One should not look for special properties in the salt; God performed the miracle.

The second miracle involves something of a moral problem. On the face of it, the account tells of boys taunting Elisha, and his calling down a curse on them that was followed by bears attacking them. In more complete form, the prophet was going to Bethel which was, of course, especially the cult center of Israel. Apparently, as he was walking along near Bethel, though the town is not named, a gang began to jeer at him. Though some translations call them "children" or "boys," they were really young men. They called him "baldhead," which could not refer to baldness because his head would have been covered and they would not have known whether he was bald. Moreover, he lived fifty years after this time (2 Kings 13:14) and probably was not bald then. Some commentators conclude that "baldhead" was a taunt generated by the kind of hairstyle prophets wore. "Go on up" (v. 23) is meaningless to us, but Constable thinks it was a taunt that he should go to heaven as Elijah had reportedly done.[13]

If this was an organized demonstration by dozens of young men against the chief prophet of Yahweh, it was a serious matter. If, in addition, they were prophets of Baal or prophets connected with calf worship or were somehow connected with the official cult and represented opposition of the cult to Yahweh, their taunts were doubly serious. The text does not indicate why this confrontation was so reprehensible. At any

[13] Thomas L. Constable, "1 and 2 Kings," *The Bible Knowledge Commentary: Old Testament.* Edited by John F. Walvoord and Roy B. Zuck (Wheaton, Ill.: Victor Books, 1985), 541.

rate, Elisha called down a curse on the gang, and two bears came out of the woods and mauled forty-two of them—the text either to be taken literally or as an indication of a large indefinite number, as some think.

It should be remembered that Elisha could not perform this miracle; God did. Elisha did not even appear to have made the curse specific. If God did this, then there must have been reasons for judgment that do not readily appear on the surface. In any case, the miracle served to accredit God's messenger and to bring respect for the sanctity of his person. Thereafter Elisha went to Mount Carmel, possibly to commemorate Elijah's great victory there, and then returned to Samaria to be at the hub of national affairs.

I. Joram and Jehoshaphat Against the Moabites (3:1–27)

1. Joram's Reign (3:1–3)

Joram (Jehoram), son of Ahab, became king of Israel because his brother Ahaziah died without an heir. Joram ascended the throne in the eighteenth year of Jehoshaphat (852) and ruled for twelve years. Like all the other kings of Israel before him, he walked in the steps of Jeroboam, subscribing to the calf worship at Dan and Bethel. But he was not very supportive of Baal worship and destroyed a stone pillar of Baal that his father had erected (v. 2). Probably the pillar had a bas (low) relief of Baal and possibly an inscription. Since Jehu also destroyed a pillar of Baal (2 Kings 10:26), the question must be raised whether there were two and Joram's efforts were half-hearted or whether Jezebel managed to have a new one erected later. Jezebel lived as queen mother all during the reign of Joram (2 Kings 9:30), and it is very doubtful that much reform could have taken place as long as she lived.

2. Moabite Revolt (3:4–5)

Moab had been subject to Israel during the days of the Omride dynasty and paid tribute in kind in terms of the basic economy of the area: the raising of sheep and production of wool. Moab "used to pay" or "supply" (v. 4) probably on an annual basis, "regularly" (NEB), a very substantial sum; but what that was is not exactly clear. A common translation is that it involved one hundred thousand lambs and wool of one hundred thousand rams. But it is possible to refer "wool" to both clauses and to read with the NEB, "the wool of a hundred thousand lambs and a hundred thousand rams." Such a rendering seems preferable because the former translation seems to exact rather extortionate tribute. In any case, Moab rebelled against Israel after Ahab died. Ahab died late in 853 B.C. and Ahaziah had lasted little over a year before succumbing to the injuries sustained in his fall. Presumably near the end of Ahaziah's reign, probably during the weeks when he was lying in bed, Mesha king of Moab rebelled (see 2 Kings 1:1). So Joram inherited the revolt and now proceeded to squelch it.

3. Attack Against Moab (3:6–9a)

Joram mobilized his forces and then sought to utilize the alliance with Judah to give him success. So Jehoshaphat entered into his third cooperative venture with Israel. This one, like the others, did not end well. One reason for Joram's desire to have Judah's help in the fight is that Moab had highly fortified its northern frontier and it would therefore be advantageous to attack from the south. Joram and Jehoshaphat agreed to attack through the "wilderness of Edom," to the southeast of the most heavily fortified areas of Moab. It was possible to march through Edom at the time because Judah controlled it. The "king of Edom" (v. 9) was not a sovereign ruler of the state but some kind of puppet under the domination of Jehoshaphat. The line of march was south from Samaria through Jerusalem, Hebron, and Arad, and the south around the southern end of the Dead Sea and eastward in a circuitous route through the wilderness of Edom.

4. The Water Problem (3:9b–20)

This "circuitous march of seven days" exhausted the water supply of the combined armies and they were reduced to desperate straits. The reaction of Joram to the situation was to blame God for getting them into this predicament. The only simple explanation for such a charge is that he had consulted the court prophets of Israel before embarking on this expedition as his father Ahab had earlier (1 Kings 22), and that they had encouraged him to proceed and to believe he would win the conflict. But as in 1 Kings 22, the godly Jehoshaphat asked if there was a prophet of Yahweh of whom they could inquire to discover how to deal with the situation.

An attendant of the king of Israel informed them that Elisha was nearby, "who used to pour water on the hands of Elijah," i.e., to act as his personal servant. It is not strange that Elisha should have been referred to in this way, because his inheritance of Elijah's mantle must have occurred very recently; he had not yet established himself in his own right. Elisha presumably was present because of God's prompting; he was certainly not a kind of unofficial chaplain to the forces.

Desperate, the three kings "went down" to see him, evidently descending from the headquarters on a height to the wadi where he was located and where the men and the animals probably were bivouacked. The exchange between Elisha and Joram was very testy. First Elisha asked, "Why have you come to me?" Why not go to the court prophets of Israel? Then Joram again blamed Yahweh for getting them into this mess. Elisha countered that he would not even give Joram the time of day if the good king Jehoshaphat were not involved in their apparent catastrophe.

Agreeing to respond to their request, Elisha ordered, "Bring me a minstrel" or "one who can play the lyre." Elisha's dependence on musically induced prophetic ecstasy in this case does not prove that he received revelations in this way on other occasions, or that other prophets did, either. This is the only time that the Bible says music was connected with a prophet's reception of a divine revelation.

The exact intent of the divine oracle (v. 16) is not clear. Translators and commentators divide on whether we are to understand the Hebrew as an imperative ("make pools," dig pools and trenches to trap the water), a finite verb ("I will make pools"), or an impersonal construction ("pools will form"). Of course, the result is the same; in the wadi or dry streambed would be an abundance of water for the army and all their animals. They would see "neither wind nor rain"; so evidently a flash flood was involved—rain in the west with water flowing eastward down the wadi, a common occurrence in the region. The miracle in this case was the timing, not the means of supplying the water.

Provision of water was an "easy thing" for God to do; He would also give the allied forces victory over the Moabites, and they would engage in a scorched earth policy. Verses 18 and 19 are the prophet's summary of God's oracle, and verse 20 reports the fulfillment of the prediction. The next morning at dawn (the time for sacrifice) water "came suddenly from the direction of Edom" (from the tableland to the west), and the "land was covered") presumably not just the floor of the wadi, usually thought to be the Wadi Hesi or the Brook Zered).

5. Hebrew Victory (3:21–25)

Moabite intelligence had informed them of the approach of the allied forces, and hasty total mobilization occurred. "Young and old" in an emergency might include boys as young as eleven or twelve (compare present Iranian practice in the Iran-Iraq War). The army was stationed at the border. When the Moabites woke in the morning, they saw a misleading sight. Water, which had not been there the night before, appeared red under the combined effects of sun's rays, red soil, and red sandstone. The allied forces were moving about in some confusion to get out of the way of the rising or collecting water. The Moabites interpreted the confused movements as conflicts between allies and the redness as a coloring of the water by blood of men and animals. They concluded that all they had to do was advance on the enemy and plunder their camp. When the Moabites attacked, they were completely surprised and put to rout. Subsequently the allied forces ranged over the country-side engaging in a scorched-earth policy. Finally only one major city, Kir Hareseth, the capital, was left.

6. Hebrew Withdrawal (3:26–27)

As the three kings besieged the Moabite capital, King Mesha tried to break through "to the king of Edom," apparently believing that if he could breach the Edomite section of the line he might win a victory. That effort failed; and finally in desperation he sacrificed his son, the crown prince, to his god

Chemosh, on the city wall in an effort to appease his anger and win his favor.

That "a great wrath came upon Israel" is hard to explain or interpret. It certainly does not mean that powerless Chemosh had the capacity to bring down punishment on the kings. Nor does it appear that Yahweh had any special reason to discipline the army. The most natural explanation is that the tide of battle turned at that point. Such a change of events could have occurred because the sacrifice so inspired the Moabites with a conviction that they would win that they fought with an indescribable fury. This infusion of spirit may have been coupled with the belief of Edomites, pagan Israelites, and even many from Judah that Chemosh should be effective in his own land, especially after a sacrifice like that; and their morale snapped. In any case, the Hebrew expeditionary force withdrew after their earlier victories.

J. Elisha's Miracles (4:1–6:7)

Breaking into the historical narrative at this point is a series of miracles performed in connection with the ministry of Elisha. Undoubtedly they appear here because they occurred during this general time period. They show that spiritual light had not gone out in the land; there were always the seven thousand who had not bowed the knee to Baal. God continued to accredit His message and His messenger by means of mighty works. More-over, these miracles show how God sometimes works with the humble folk of society even when many of the leaders generally repudiate Him.

1. Elisha and the Widow (4:1–7)

The series begins with an account of a widow in desperate straits who comes to Elisha for relief. Her creditors are about to foreclose and even to seize her two children to reduce them to debt slavery. Her husband had been a member of the prophetic guild and he "revered Yahweh" (v. 1). This account demonstrates that one should not envision the "sons of the prophets" as all fairly young celibates who spent their time in religious exercises and lived off the largess of others. Here was one of them who was married, had a family, and evidently worked to support his family and accumulate a meager estate. Today some might call him a "tentmaker," i.e., he engaged in a trade to support himself while he performed the work of God.

This woman evidenced a faith in God and sought to fulfill the conditions for a miracle when Elisha presented them. He did not need to declare and demonstrate in the name of Yahweh to engender faith, as was commonly the case in the performance of miracles, because she already had faith and quietly understood that God was going to meet her need. As we are tempted to speculate on how many jars the woman accumulated, we remind ourselves that God is sometimes limited in working on our behalf by our lack of faith and the paucity of means we put at His disposal. This miracle illustrates God's care for those (and the families of those) who give themselves to Him in professional Christian service. Behind the widow's plea in this account is the fact that Hebrew law permitted the selling of a wife and children into slavery to settle a debt (Exod. 21:7; Neh. 5:5, 8; Amos 2:6; 8:6) but permitted their freedom in the year of jubilee (Lev. 25:39ff.). Although the miracle especially bolstered the faith of the widow and her children, it also spoke to all the widow's friends and acquaintances from whom she had borrowed jars.

2. Elisha and the Shunammite Woman (4:8–37)

In this account attention shifts from a widow woman with children to a childless married woman, and from a woman with nothing to one with some means, compared with other members of her community. Again the woman seems to be a person of faith. The picture one gets of Elisha in this whole section of the book is that he is quietly serving God, engaging in personal devotional exercises on Mount Carmel, encouraging the faithful, training the sons of the prophets, enjoying a little influence at court (e.g., 4:13), not waging a high-profile religious campaign, and apparently at ease in many sectors of society (e.g., the poor widow, the moderately well-fixed Shunammite, and possibly the court).

Once when Elisha passed through Shunem (some seven miles east of Megiddo and near Jezreel) a "prominent" or "wealthy" woman showed him hospitality. This became habitual for her whenever he came through. After several of his visits, she suggested to her husband that they construct for him "a small walled upper room," a permanent structure on the flat roof as opposed to open booths of branches or covered with vines. This "prophet's chamber" was furnished with a "bed" (probably a bedroll like a sleeping bag), a "chair" (probably without a back), a "table" (maybe only a cloth that could be spread on the floor), and a "lamp" (an open clay saucer with a pinched lip in which a wick was placed and in which olive oil was burned).

After enjoying this hospitality for a while, Elisha sought to reciprocate his hostess's kindness. He offered to speak on her behalf to the "king" or "commander of the army." Either Elisha was now enjoying better relations with a slightly reformed Joram or his successor Jehu, who exterminated the house of Ahab. In referring to the king and commander of the army, he must have had in mind some reduction of a military or economic levy for her husband's district. But the woman must have thought of the offer in slightly different terms and said she was quite content to stay among her people, thus expressing rural independence. After she broke off the conversation, Elisha learned from his servant Gehazi that the woman had no children and her husband was getting old. Then somehow on divine authority Elisha was able to promise his hostess that about that time the following year she would have a son. She urged him not "to excite delusive hopes," but she did indeed have a son about a year later.

When the child was perhaps four or five, he developed a terrible headache while he was out in the field one morning with his father at harvest time. His father had a servant take the boy to his mother, and he sat on her lap until noon and died. During the hours of anguish the Shunammite must have anticipated the boy's death and must have formulated a plan. As soon as he died she laid him on the prophet's bed and closed the door. Possibly that was meant as a reproach to the prophet, but it was also a practical move. If she left him in his own bed or somewhere else downstairs, a servant or the father would see him there; probably they would not think to look in the prophet's chamber.

Then she asked her husband for a servant and a donkey to

go to Elisha; it is interesting that she knew where to find him. Her husband did not know why she had to go then because it was not a "new moon or a sabbath." Various reasons are given for his response, but perhaps the best suggestion is that the appropriate or usual time for consulting a prophet for oracular guidance was at such times. Her only answer was, "Shalom," that in this case may be translated, "All is well," or as one might say today, "It's okay." She was trying to be as vague as possible to avoid telling him what had happened so he would not treat the death as final and start the usual oriental lamentations. If he did, she would not be able to go off to see the prophet. She had the donkey saddled and urged her servant to prod the beast to its utmost speed all the way; presumably he rode on a second donkey alongside hers, but both of them could have ridden on the same one. The distance to that part of Carmel where Elisha was must have been fifteen miles or more.

When Elisha saw the Shunammite in the distance, he sent Gehazi to inquire of her welfare. But she answered him, "Shalom," perhaps meaning to imply, "All will be well." With Gehazi she would be noncommittal; her business was with Elisha. When she reached the prophet, she grasped his feet as a sign of obeisance and respect and in deep distress. Elisha did not know what was wrong (v. 27) and that is not surprising. Prophets were not omniscient and knew only what God told them about situations requiring superhuman knowledge. Then the disturbed mother poured out her story, rebuking the prophet for giving her a son and deceiving her in this way; it would have been better if he had not been born.

Elisha ordered Gehazi to run back to Shunem with his staff, not stopping to greet people along the way. It was appropriate to issue such instructions because ancient oriental greetings were elaborate and time consuming. Why Elisha sent Gehazi is not exactly clear but may be guessed. The presence of the prophet's staff was a kind of guarantee that Elisha was on the way. Moreover, by the time Gehazi could arrive, or soon thereafter, the boy's death might be discovered. Gehazi was himself to try to revive the boy, and, should such efforts be made, he might stave off burial plans until Elisha arrived.

Meanwhile, the boy's mother refused to leave Elisha, and

he accompanied her back to Shunem. No time lapses are indicated. If the Shunammite left her home about noon, she and Elisha might have returned by four or five. Harvesters would still have been in the fields. Apparently the boy had not yet been discovered. At length Elisha and the mother arrived and Elisha prayed for the boy's resuscitation, engaging in the same action as Elijah had in 1 Kings 17:21: contact of mouth, eyes, and hands. Finally the boy sneezed seven times and then began to breath normally. Elisha restored him to his mother and the fame of the power of Yahweh and His prophet spread to nearby Jezreel and to Samaria and elsewhere, demonstrating the greatness of Yahweh as compared with the powerlessness of Baal and/or the state cult of Israel.

3. Elisha and the Poisoned Stew (4:38–41)

Elisha went to Gilgal during a famine; which Gilgal is not certain, but probably the one in the Jordan Valley. While the prophetic guild "was sitting with him," i.e., probably while he was teaching them, it was necessary to feed them. So he ordered that food be prepared. Since the food supply was not adequate to meet the situation, one of the group went out into the fields to gather wild herbs. Though he found some wild gourds that were unfamiliar to him, he pulled up the skirt of his robe and filled it with them. When they were put in the stew, some of the group recognized the taste of the gourds (now usually identified with *Citrullus colocynthus*) that were known to have powerful laxative properties and to be fatal if taken in substantial quantity. To counteract the effect of the "poison in the pot," Elisha symbolically threw in some good meal, and a miracle of purification of the food took place.

4. Elisha and the Multiplication of Bread (4:42–44)

How this account relates to the previous one is not certain. Perhaps the scene is still Gilgal and the group being fed is still the school of the prophets. The famine may have been slightly broken by the ingathering of a new harvest. It is surprising that this bread from the "first fruits" should have been brought to Elisha at all, because such offerings belonged to God and were for the special use of the priests (Lev. 23:20). With the

disruption of the Levitical establishment in Israel, the devout
may have thought it appropriate to make the offering to Elisha's
following as true priests of Yahweh, or it may have been made to
prophets as well as to priests.

In any case, a "man" (evidently a devout worshiper of
Yahweh) from Baal Shalishah (usually thought to be located in
the Sharon plain some fifteen miles north of Joppa) sent twenty
barley cakes (flat bread like pancakes) and some fresh grain from
the first fruits of the harvest. Elisha commanded that this food be
set before the assembled company. His servant (presumably
Gehazi) complained that the supply was not enough to feed one
hundred men (evidently the size of the prophetic guild at that
place at that time). Elisha repeated the command with the
implication that a miracle of multiplication was about to take
place. Gehazi as a servant should obey, and by now he had seen
enough miraculous power flowing through Elisha to have the
faith to act. There was enough for all with some left over, "as
Yahweh had said." The lesson for us is that tremendous power
resides in the Word of the Lord.

5. Elisha and Naaman the Leper (5:1–27)

The story of Naaman is a marvelous but sobering account, of
Yahweh who is not a tribal or ethnic God but a universal and
omnipotent deity, of Naaman who is a haughty but humbled
general who becomes a believer in Yahweh, of Naaman's loyal
and dedicated staff who see him through a crisis, of Elisha
whose selfless service saves a king and heals an enemy general,
and of Gehazi whose cupidity proves to be his total undoing.

a. Naaman's leprosy (5:1–7). Naaman was the commander-
in-chief of the king of Aram or Syria with its capital in
Damascus; probably Ben-Hadad II was the Aramaean king in
question. Highly regarded by his king, Naaman was also useful
to God because he was Yahweh's agent to secure Syrian success
against Israel and thus to bring judgment on the Northern
Kingdom for her idolatry. In spite of all he had going for him,
Naaman was afflicted with "leprosy." This was evidently not
Hansen's Disease, which is clinically known as leprosy today
(and that came to the Near East from India as a result of the
conquests of Alexander the Great), but some form of psoriasis. A

disfiguring skin disease, leprosy led to social ostracism in Israel but evidently, at least in its early stages, did not in Syria.

In those days of uneasy relations between Israel and Syria, there were plundering expeditions across the border, even when there was not open warfare. On one of those raids, the Syrians had taken a young female slave who had found her way into the service of Naaman's wife. She told her mistress about the prophet in Samaria who "would heal him." Apparently her belief in Elisha's supernatural power led to the conclusion that he could heal leprosy. Though Elisha moved about a good bit, evidently he did have a house in Samaria and was there at this time (v. 3; cf. 6:24, 32).

Naaman seized the suggestion and went to the king of Syria with the information. The king eagerly embraced the idea and sent him off with a letter to the king of Israel (probably still Joram). For his part Naaman took a gift that fit his stature in the kingdom: computed at seven hundred fifty pounds of silver, twenty-four thousand ounces of gold, and ten changes of clothing. The letter the king of Syria sent embodied the expectation "that you may cure him." The idea was that the king of Israel would have him cured, because all subjects, of course, were supposed to be obedient to the king—and that included the religious figures of the land.

The letter precipitated a crisis at court, for the Israelite king interpreted this as a means of picking a quarrel with him; if he refused to heal Naaman or could not make good on the Syrian king's wishes, the failure could be used as a pretext for invasion. He tore his robes in great distress and cried, "Am I God," i.e., am I omnipotent like God? He need not have been so upset. It was fairly common for ancient Near Eastern kings to seek medical help from one another; several copies of such requests still exist. Moreover, he did have a great prophet to whom he could turn.

b. Naaman's healing (5:8–19). As noted above, Elisha was probably in Samaria at the time, had promptly heard about the king's consternation, and responded equally promptly. He urged the king to send Naaman to him and he would heal him; then "he [Naaman] would know there is a prophet in Israel." If the king was Joram, he might have wished to snub Elisha as the prophet had done at the beginning of his reign (2 Kings 3:14). Perhaps Elisha was saying that Naaman would recognize there was a true prophet of Yahweh in Israel, even if the king did not.

Evidently the king was glad to be rid of a problem and Naaman went charging up to Elisha's house with his retinue, expecting to be received in a way befitting his rank and perhaps to be asked to do something dramatic to obtain healing. Elisha tested him by simply sending a messenger with the prescription to dip seven times in the Jordan River. It was an act that required simple faith and was susceptible to no magical interpretation. Naaman was furious and stalked off, in effect muttering: "No reception befitting my status, no religious ritual, and a national insult to boot by expecting me to bathe in the Jordan instead of one of the superior rivers of Syria!" The Abana is the Barada that flows through downtown Damascus today, and the Pharpar is the Awaj that flows from Mount Hermon to the marshland southeast of Damascus.

Naaman's staff was much more pragmatic; they were used to doing as they were ordered and were also accustomed to official highhandedness. They did not think it would hurt to follow the prophet's instructions and they prevailed upon their master to do so. "His flesh was restored and became sound like that of a young boy." Naaman was ecstatic and returned to Elisha in a humble spirit of thankfulness "with his entire retinue." This time the prophet was happy to receive him and to acknowledge his praise to Yahweh. But Elisha adamantly refused to accept a gift to avoid any appearance of the chicanery that the false prophets engaged in. Moreover, he wanted to make sure that Naaman knew this was the work of Yahweh alone.

Then Naaman made two requests. First, he wanted to take some Palestinian soil home with him to build an altar to Yahweh, evidently still a slave to the polytheistic notion that a god could be worshiped acceptably only on his own land. Second, he asked for understanding if his official duties required him to be involved in the worship of idols, specifically the worship of Rimmon, the Aramaean manifestation of the storm-god. Elisha's answer was noncommittal: "Go in peace," wishing the peace of God on Naaman's trip and perhaps the further guidance and grace of God as he struggled through the problem of serving Yahweh in a polytheistic world.

c. Gehazi's punishment (5:20–27). It was a glorious story of divine cleansing and the conversion of a non-Israelite. But what a sad ending! Cupidity reared its ugly head. The great wealth of Naaman riding off eastward with the general was more than Gehazi could resist. The battle with materialism is not one that has to be fought by modern believers alone. Gehazi's sin is doubly heinous. He had seen the mighty power of God demonstrated in raising from the dead at Shunem, the healing of Naaman, and presumably in many other ways as he had served Elisha. Moreover, he had heard the prophet refuse Naaman's gifts to avoid a charge of trying to profit personally from the power of God that he wielded. Now the servant descended from the high road into the valley as he ran after filthy lucre. Mere avarice was not sin enough; he lied to Naaman and to Elisha, and he misrepresented the prophet and abused the prophet's name.

In paraphrase, Elisha asked in verse 26, "Is this the time to take money and goods for that which God has done in order to acquire property for one's self?" And perhaps he was saying in the first part of the verse, "My heart was with you in absolute agony when the man got down from his chariot and you destroyed all I had tried to accomplish with him by refusing the gift." It was appropriate that all the debilitating effects of Naaman's leprosy should now plague Gehazi the rest of his days.

6. Elisha and the Floating Axhead (6:1–7)

The communal living quarters of the prophetic guild had become too small and they sought a larger facility. The NIV is incorrect in referring to a structure where they met with Elisha (6:1); the true intent of the Hebrew is, "The place where we dwell under your charge" (RSV). Probably the "place" where they were then was Jericho. They proposed to go to the Jordan to cut wood for a new communal structure. Along its banks is the Zor (a thicket still a mile wide), where they could fell willow, acacia, tamarisk, and other trees that would provide wood for the light sort of building adequate for living in the Jordan Valley.

Probably they intended to carry the wood a little father south
into the Jericho oasis and build new quarters there. The Zor
itself was a thick jungle infested with wild animals and malarial
mosquitoes. Elisha approved their plan and agreed to go with
them to launch the project.

While they were cutting down trees, the iron axhead of one
of them flew off its handle and fell into the water. The workman
was dismayed because it was "begged," not "borrowed," as in
some versions. In other words, this poor son of the prophets had
asked or begged this fairly hard-to-get or expensive item from
someone; now he had lost it and had no money to get another.
Evidently the prophetic guild was extremely poor and constantly lived marginally. Elisha worked a miracle and retrieved
the axhead. The lesson of the miracle seems to be that God cares
for His own and that He may even supernaturally meet their
needs in the little and big challenges of daily living.

K. Wars with Syria and Deliverance of Samaria (6:8–8:15)

1. Guerrilla Warfare (6:8–23)

To be sure, Elisha is as active in this section of 2 Kings as
he was in the last one, but the previously noted miracles were of
a more private sort, and those described here involved national
affairs.

Evidently, marauding bands of Syrians engaged in guerrilla
warfare entered Israelite territory periodically after Ahab's
attack on Ramoth Gilead (1 Kings 22), taking whatever plunder
they could carry away. One such band had taken captive the girl
who had become a slave in Naaman's household (2 Kings 5:2).
This section alludes to a whole series of these attacks during the
reign of Joram (v. 23); the reference is not to large military
forces invading the land.

As the Syrians planned one after another of these attacks,
Elisha provided valuable intelligence and frustrated their
efforts. The reason for Yahweh's assistance to Joram is not
exactly clear; possibly it was to demonstrate His great power to
the king and his court. The Hebrew of verse 9 is open to two
interpretations. The NIV properly translates, "Beware of passing
that place," but the question is whether one is to "avoid this

place" (NEB) because of an ambush or a trap set there by a band of men, or whether one is not to pass up the place in the sense of ignoring it or leaving it unfortified in the face of imminent attack. Following the latter interpretation, the JB translates, "Be on your guard at this place." In any case, "not once or twice" Elisha warned the Israelite king of Syrian moves, and the king of Aram was "greatly frustrated" or "disturbed" and sought to ferret out the traitor in the camp. His officers had excellent intelligence-gathering facilities and learned, after the fact, the part Elisha had had in his failures. The Syrian king, probably Ben-Hadad II, then ordered that his men discover where Elisha was so he could capture him and stop the interference with his military moves. When the report came in that Elisha was at Dothan, about ten miles north of Samaria, the king sent a small expeditionary force against it during the night.

In the morning Elisha's servant was frightened by the threatening force; but Elisha prayed that the servant would see the superior divine force protecting them, that he would be translated into an ecstatic state in which he might see the fiery horses and chariots that symbolized the protecting power of heaven. Then he prayed that the Syrians would be struck with blindness, the kind of blindness in which they could see but not recognize correctly the objects in their sight. In this state they could be deceptively led the ten miles to Samaria where Elisha took them to the king of Israel. The prophet then persuaded the king to feed the men well and send them back home. The object of this episode apparently was to show the Syrians that they were powerless when they tangled with a prophet of the true God and, of course, with God Himself. "So the Aramaean raiding parties stopped invading the territory of Israel" (v. 23).

2. Siege of Samaria (6:24–7:2)

That did not mean the Syrian forces would not again try to subdue Israel. Several months later they came in force and besieged Samaria. As the siege dragged on, food supplies gave out and conditions became desperate. The head of a donkey (an unclean animal that was not supposed to be eaten in Israel) was selling for eighty shekels of silver (two pounds, NIV margin) and a fourth of a cab (about one-half pint) of "dove's dung" for five shekels (about two ounces). "Dove's dung" is the literal translation of the Hebrew and that may be intended; Josephus notes that cow's dung was eaten during Titus's siege of Jerusalem in A.D. 70.[14] But it is also taken as a popular term for carob pods, and the JB renders it "wild onions." Worse yet, a woman reported a case of cannibalism to the king. (Josephus recorded an instance of this during the Roman siege of Jerusalem.)[15] When Joram heard about that, he completely fell apart and determined to cut off Elisha's head that very day.

The king may have decided to take out his spite on Elisha because (1) he held him responsible for the people's distress by predicting a seven-year famine (8:1ff.) that put them in a weakened position at the beginning of the siege; or (2) because he concluded that Elisha's urging him to withstand the Syrians, promising deliverance, had prolonged the suffering and made it more severe. The promises of relief had been made often enough; "Why should I wait for Yahweh any longer?" (v. 33), he asked. When the king was determining to execute Elisha, the prophet was sitting with "the elders," the leading citizens of the capital, no doubt discussing what could be done to deal with the emergency. Elisha had God's warning that the king was sending an executioner, and he knew the king would follow close behind. So he ordered the elders to bar the door until the king arrived, and then he could deal with the situation, i.e., promise imminent relief.

Joram said, "Why should I wait . . . longer?" Elisha said, in effect, "Wait one more day," for the next day the famine would be over. A seah (5–7 quarts) of fine meal or two seahs of barley could again be bought at the gate of Samaria (the open market inside the city gate) for a shekel (probably double the usual price, but at least it would be available). The king's "adjutant" or "aide-de-camp" wondered how this could happen, even if "Yahweh should open the sluice gates of heaven." Even if God should cause a downpour of rain and end the famine, they would have to wait for the harvest. Elisha's response was that though the aide would see fulfillment of the prediction, because of his disbelief he would not enjoy the benefits of it.

---

[14] Josephus, *Wars* V.13.7.
[15] Ibid., VI.3.4.

3. The Siege Lifted (7:3–20)

Late that afternoon four lepers who camped outside the gates of Samaria evaluated their situation. They concluded that if they stayed where they were they would starve because lack of movement of people around them eliminated the opportunity to beg. It was senseless to go into the city because food supplies there were virtually non-existent. They finally decided that their best option was to surrender to the Syrians, from whom they might get some food. If the Syrians killed them, they had lost nothing because they would die anyway.

So at "dusk" (v. 5) the four approached the Syrian camp, only to find it abandoned. Evidently the Syrians had fled only minutes before ("in the dusk," v. 7), at the "sound" of horses and chariots. Some commentators interpret the sound to be a rumor that an enemy force was upon them. Others accept it as a literal sound of an enemy host; so JPS translates, "the din of a huge army" (v. 6). Of course, it is possible that both are true; the rumor could simply be the explanation of the sound that was heard. Again, there is some debate over who the Aramaeans thought were coming to help Israel. The Hittites were powerful Hittite city-states located in Syria. After the Hittite Empire broke up about 1200 B.C., Hittite remnants formed into city-states in Syria and maintained themselves there with varying fortunes until the last of them fell to the Assyrians in 709 B.C. But whether we should read *Miṣrayim* (Egypt) or *Muṣri* (Cappadocians, adjacent to the Hittites in Asia Minor) as allied with the Hittites in this passage is not clear. Of course, the end result is the same; the Syrians had fled in panic, leaving even the "horses" (evidently chariot horses that they did not have time to hitch up) and "donkeys" (pack animals they did not have time to load).

The lepers walked into the abandoned camp, ate their fill, rifled a couple of tents, and hid their plunder. But finally they concluded that if they waited until morning to report their discovery they would be "punished." (Parenthetically, verse 9 contains a message applicable to the contemporary church: "This is a day of good news, and we are keeping silent!" Like the lepers of old, therefore, we may incur punishment.) So they told the good news to the city gatekeepers, who in turn reported to the king. Joram interpreted the Syrian action as a ruse and believed they had set up an ambush for the Israelites.

One of the king's officers suggested that they should check out the report, however. The Hebrew of verses 13 and 14 is difficult but the general intent is clear. The officer was saying that the fate of the scouts might be like that of the rest of them in Samaria: they would die, but they should discover the truth. He proposed that five horses be sent; verse 14 may be interpreted to mean that two chariot teams or two horsemen actually went out. The latter would have been more efficient in the hilly terrain. When the scouts went out to reconnoiter, probably along the road to Beth Shan and the Jordan, they discovered the way littered with "clothing and gear" that the army had jettisoned in their headlong flight. Probably what they left behind was largely plunder that they now found expendable; presumably the "gear" did not include weapons or shields.

When the scouts did not encounter any enemy soldiers all the way to the Jordan, they rushed back to Samaria with the good news. As the frenzied mob stampeded out the gate of Samaria to plunder the enemy camp for food and valuables, they trampled to death the official who had belittled the promise that the siege would be lifted. There was indeed food for sale in the market the next day, but the aide was not alive to eat it, as Elisha had predicted.

4. Restoration of the Shunammite's Land (8:1–6)

This account continues the story of the Shunammite woman, broken off in 2 Kings 4:37. Commonly, this event is thought to have taken place before the healing of Naaman because Gehazi contracted leprosy at that point and presumably would no longer be active socially. But it is entirely possible that the narrative is generally in chronological order. Gehazi was not at this time in Elisha's service and apparently had found refuge or even a position at the palace. Some believe that his leprosy had been healed by this time or at the least was not socially restrictive. The seven-year famine would then have taken place during the latter part of Joram's reign, and this appeal probably occurred at the very end of his reign.

On Elisha's instruction the Shunammite had fled her home because of a famine; the self-sufficiency expressed in 4:13 was gone. The "somewhere else" of verse 1 turned out to be the Philistine plain, where rainfall generally is adequate for agricultural pursuits. While the woman was gone, the unoccupied property had reverted to the crown and perhaps had been taken over by another private party. When the famine was over, the Shunammite sought to regain her property; she "went to lodge a claim" or "complaint," a legal term (v. 3). Very likely by this time her aged husband had died, for there is no reference to his being involved in the proceedings. Her son would still have been a minor and therefore not a party to the appeal.

While the Shunammite was on the way to see the king, the king had engaged Gehazi in a rehearsal of Elisha's marvelous works. "While" or "just as" Gehazi was telling about Elisha's restoration of the Shunammite's son, in she came to make her plea. The king was so overwhelmed by the sequence of events that he appointed an official to deal with the case, with the result that she got more than she had requested: the land *and* the revenues from it since she had fled. Parenthetically, it may not be too farfetched to suggest that Gehazi was one of the four lepers at the gate of Samaria and that he had some access to Joram after the siege of the city was lifted. And since Elisha had figured prominently during the siege, it was only logical that his name would have come up in the conversation.

5. Hazael's Accession to the Throne (8:7–15)

Why Elisha went to Damascus the text does not state; perhaps it was to fulfill the commission given to Elijah at Horeb to anoint Hazael king of Syria (1 Kings 19:15). If this visit was subsequent to Naaman's healing, it helps to explain the prophet's acceptance at the Syrian court.

A particularly puzzling detail of this account is the fact that Assyrian records make Hazael the successor to and usurper against Hadadeser; and this passage names Hazael as the usurper against Ben-Hadad. Various suggestions have been offered to solve the problem; of the more acceptable are these: (1) Ben-Hadad was the throne name and Hadadeser was a personal name; they were one and the same. (2) Hadadeser was

followed by a Ben-Hadad (who ruled briefly) and he in turn by
Hazael (the Assyrians telescoped the history and ignored the
insignificant Ben-Hadad).

A second major problem in this passage concerns Elisha's
supposed lie to Ben-Hadad (v. 10). The best explanation seems
to be that the first half of the reply indicates that the disease was
not life threatening and it would not kill him, but that Elisha
knew he would die from an unrelated cause. Hazael reported
only the first half of Elisha's reply.

The third problem involves the understanding of the very
concise or cryptic Hebrew of verse 11. The preferable interpretation is that Elisha apparently went into a prophetic trance and
stared at Hazael for a long time ("his face went rigid and his look
grew fixed," (JB), looking past his face and seeing the terrible
atrocities that his armies would perpetrate against Israel. Hazael
was "embarrassed" to be looked at in this way; finally Elisha
burst into tears and subsequently explained the reason for his
sorrow; that Hazael was to become king and that he would bring
great suffering on Israel.

The very next day Hazael assassinated the king by suffocat-
ing him with a "twisted thick cloth," in such a way as to make it
appear he had died of natural causes, and usurped the throne in
Damascus. Whether Elisha was still in town, Scripture does not
say. Hazael then ruled from 841 to 801 B.C. during the reigns of
Joram, Jehu, and Jehoahaz in Israel and Ahaziah, Athaliah, and
Joash in Judah.

L. Jehoram of Judah (8:16–24)

Though Jehoshaphat was a good king as far as his religious
and internal political policies were concerned, he left a bad
example for his son Jehoram in his cooperation with the dynasty
of Ahab in three major projects, as noted earlier, and the
marriage of his son to Athaliah, daughter of Ahab and Jezebel.
Eventually the influence from the north impacted on Judah, and
Jehoram "followed the [religious] example of the kings of
Israel" (v. 18). The depth of his religious and moral degradation
is seen in the construction of a temple to Baal in Jerusalem
(2 Kings 11:18) and his murder of his six brothers, possible
rivals to the throne (2 Chron. 21:12ff.), who were considered to

be better men than he. But because of the Davidic covenant, Yahweh did not blot out his line or his kingdom (v. 19).

Jehoram suffered important territorial losses; "at the same time" (v. 22) both Edom and Libnah revolted. Edom may have entertained ideas of rebellion ever since Jehoram's father Jehoshaphat had suffered defeat at the hands of the Moabites (2 Kings 3). Now they were successful in breaking away. Jehoram mustered his forces at Zair, evidently northeast of Hebron near the Edomite frontier, and the Edomites surrounded them there. The Hebrew of verse 21 is difficult, but apparently his chariot corps broke out of the encirclement at night and got away; the army was left to escape as best it could. The NIV follows this interpretation. Thereafter Edom was never fully subject to Judah again. Libnah, in the western foothills of the Shephelah, was a frontier town at the edge of the Philistine plain. The loss of these two dependencies weakened Judah's control of important commercial routes.

Jehoram had been coregent with his father since 853, but he became sole ruler in 848, in the fifth year of Joram, the king of Israel. Thirty-two when he became king, he reigned for eight years, until 841. He died of a terrible intestinal disease, "with no one to regret him" (2 Chron. 21:20).

M. Ahaziah of Judah (8:25–29)

When Jehoram died, his twenty-two year old son Ahaziah took the throne. Unfortunately Ahaziah was too closely tied to the house of Ahab. His domineering mother, Athaliah, daughter of Ahab and Jezebel, saw to it that the Baal temple was maintained in Jerusalem; and Ahaziah found himself caught up in the idolatry of the house of Ahab (v. 27). Moreover, Athaliah ensured that the foreign policy of Judah supported that of Israel. The statement that Ahaziah "went with" his uncle Joram of Israel against Syria (v. 28) evidently does not mean that he personally joined him in battle but that he gave general support to the military policies of Israel. When Joram came back wounded from another battle at Ramoth Gilead, he stopped at his secondary palace at Jezreel to recuperate instead of going all the way back to Samaria. Then Ahaziah went to see his uncle and arrived just in time to get caught up in Jehu's revolt and his

campaign to exterminate the house of Ahab. Ahaziah fled to
Megiddo, mortally wounded, and died there, having ruled less
than a year (841, cf. 2 Kings 9:27–29).

N. Jehu's Revolution (9:1–37)

1. The Anointing of Jehu (9:1–10)

The time had arrived for judgment on the house of Ahab. It
was an appropriate time, for the king lay wounded and in a
weakened condition. Thus, he was removed from the army
circle so that they were more free to plot a revolt. The army was
mustered for war and stood ready to support their commander
against the civilian establishment. And to broaden the impact of
judgment on the dynasty, the king's nephew was visiting from
Jerusalem and could be trapped in the assassination web.

Elisha took the initiative, evidently under God's command,
and sent one of the young members of the prophetic guild to
anoint Jehu king. Coming on orders of Elisha and the authority
of Yahweh, this act had full validity, in spite of the youth and
anonymity of the prophet. Elisha told the young man to "tuck up
your cloak," to tie up his long flowing robe around his waist so
he could move more swiftly, and to take a flask of anointing oil
to Ramoth-Gilead on the eastern frontier where Israelite forces
were still conducting warfare against the Syrians. There he was
to search out Jehu, commander of the army, take him to an inner
room and privately anoint him king, and then to leave quickly,
not out of fear but to avoid becoming embroiled in the
insurrectionary activities. What he was to say to Jehu is
elaborated in verses 6–10. This private anointing parallels
Samuel's anointing of Saul (1 Sam. 9:16; 10:1; 15:1) and David
(1 Sam. 16:12, 13ff.) and was intended to give this new dynasty
religious approval and legitimacy.

When the young prophet arrived at Ramoth-Gilead, he
found the army officers "sitting together," many believe in the
process of hatching a plot against the monarchy. It is instructive
to note that when the officers found out about the anointing they
seemed instantly ready to elevate Jehu to the kingship. Evidently it was not a new thought to them. Verses 6–10 list an
accumulation of curses against the evil kings of Israel that are

now coming to a head with the destruction of the house of Ahab. "Slave [in bondage] or free" (v. 8) indicates the widespread nature of the purge; it was to include those locked up and forsaken (cf. 2 Kings 14:26).

2. Jehu Proclaimed King (9:11–13)

"Is all well? Why did this madman come to you?" the junior officers demanded. Their derogatory characterization of the prophet arose from their view of the ecstatic behavior of some members of the prophetic community when in a state of holy inspiration. Jehu tried to be evasive and said, in effect, "You know he is mad and says nothing rational." But they were not content because they surmised that the message must have been important. The NEB "Nonsense" (v. 12) gives a more contemporary ring than the literal translation of the Hebrew, "It's a lie."

Seemingly, Jehu did not need much coaxing to tell them that the prophet had anointed him king over Israel. Nor did the men need any prodding to support their commander enthusiastically for the kingship. Lacking a throne, they took their large cloaks, in which they wrapped themselves to keep warm, and spread them on bare stone steps leading to the second floor of the house where they were meeting and seated Jehu there. Then they blew the shophar or ram's horn, used to announce danger, important public events, or festivity (cf. 2 Sam. 15:10; 1 Kings 1:34, 39) and shouted, "Jehu is king."

3. Jehu's Journey to Jezreel (9:14–20)

Evidently by this time, the Israelites had taken control of Ramoth-Gilead (vv. 14, 15), and Jehu gave a command that no one be permitted to leave the city and warn Joram in Jezreel of what was transpiring. Then he hitched up his chariot and raced with a cavalry platoon to Jezreel. When the lookout on the defense tower of Jezreel saw the troops coming, he immediately informed the king, who ordered a messenger to discover whether they came peacefully and if all was well. When the horseman came with his inquiry, Jehu responded, "What do you have to do with peace?" Interpreted in the light of verse 22, this means there could be no peace as long as the practices of Jezebel were tolerated. Jehu refused to let the horseman return.

Joram ordered a second scout to inquire of the advancing men. The result was the same. But now the platoon was close enough so it could be seen that Jehu, the furious chariot driver (or hot rodder) of ancient Israel, a man who drove with a distinctive reckless abandon, was approaching.

4. The Beginnings of Jehu's Judicial Purges (9:21–37)

At this point Joram concluded that he had better go out in person to deal with the situation. Not suspecting any foul play, he gave orders to "harness" his chariot. It was foolhardy for him to go without a bodyguard to face an armed cavalry unit. Worse, Ahaziah, also unprotected, decided to join him. The two kings met the advancing troop at the site of Naboth's former property, which was appropriate in view of the ensuing conversation and the purpose and nature of the revolt.

When accosted, Jehu indicated that the main reason for his revolt was religious (cf. 2 Kings 10:17–27). The "harlotries" of Jezebel (v. 22) probably indicates that she had not only caused Israel to be unfaithful to her God, but also that her allegiance to Baal had involved the practice of prostitution in fertility rites; and "sorceries" applies to evil arts connected with foreign cults (divining, dreams, amulets, etc.) that had such popular appeal in Israel. After his first brief contact with Jehu, Joram realized that revolution was in the air. He "wheeled about" and fled, yelling warnings to Ahaziah. "Then Jehu drew his bow with all his might" and shot Joram in the back so that the arrow pierced his heart and "issued from his chest" (JPS, v. 24) and he died. Then, to fulfill the judgment on the house of Ahab for the murder of Naboth and his sons and confiscation of his property, Jehu ordered his aide to throw Joram's body on Naboth's land and leave it there. It is clear from this passage that Naboth's vineyard was not located contiguous to the royal palace but was a very desirable piece of property outside of town but not far from the palace.

When Ahaziah saw what was going on, he fled up the road past Beth Haggan, probably modern Jenin (7 miles south of Jezreel). Jehu's men wounded him in his chariot, but he managed to drive on to Megiddo where he died. His body was then taken to Jerusalem. From a divine standpoint, Ahaziah's death may be seen as part of the judgment on the house of Ahab. From a human perspective, he may have been removed to avoid blood revenge on Jehu. The death of Ahaziah sufficiently weakened the Judean monarchy for several years to the extent that it was in no position to seek revenge against the house of Jehu.

Having dealt with Joram and Ahaziah, Jehu now went to town to dispatch the queen mother, Jezebel. After the death of Joram, stories flew through Jezreel about the revolution. While Jehu's cavalry unit was off chasing Ahaziah, Jezebel had time to size up the situation and to recognize that shortly she, too, would be killed. She decided to depart this life in style, painting her eyes with antimony trisulphide to highlight them, as Egyptian royalty was accustomed to do (see, e.g., the well-known Queen Nefertiti or King Tutankhamon), and carefully arranging her hair. Then she looked out an "open window," clearly to be seen—not protected from public stares by lattice-work.

As Jehu came through the city gate, Jezebel was ready with her most sarcastic taunt, "Is all well, Zimri, murderer of your master?" In other words, she was comparing him as killer of his king, Joram, to Zimri, who had killed Elah and the remaining members of the house of Baasha and then lasted as king for only seven days. Her voice must have dripped with acid as she implied that his fate would be like that of Zimri. Undaunted, Jehu simply called up and asked who was on his side. When two or three harem attendants (perhaps eunuchs) indicated they were, Jehu ordered them to throw her out the window. The fall and the trampling by horses of Jehu's cavalry unit killed the nefarious queen.

Jehu then went into Jezreel to "eat and drink," acting as if nothing had happened and showing his utter disdain for Jezebel. During the meal he gave orders for her honorable burial, and the historian records the grisly details of her ignominious end. Jehu himself recognized what had taken place as the fulfillment of Elijah's judgment against Jezebel. What happened to the house of Ahab was a dramatic demonstration of the fact that there is proximate justice (often terrible in its manifestation) for sin, in addition to eternal punishment.

For Further Study

1. Draw up a list of the advantages and disadvantages to Israel and Judah of the alliance between them.

2. With the help of a concordance, locate references to Elijah in the New Testament and try to discover the significance or teaching of each.

3. Discuss Elijah as a man of faith.

4. Compare the personalities and ministries of Elijah and Elisha.

5. Detail specific ways in which Yahweh was proved to be the true God on Mount Carmel.

6. Try to tabulate evidence that Elijah was not the only one left in the Northern Kingdom to serve God.

7. Tabulate reasons why Ahab came under the judgment of God.

8. List the miracles of Elisha and try to discover the special purpose of each (e.g., to accredit the message of the prophet).

9. With the help of a Bible dictionary, try to compile a brief history of relations between Israel and Moab.

Chapter 6

Renewed Hostilities Between the Kingdoms and the Fall of Samaria

(2 Kings 10:1–17:41)

With the demise of the house of Ahab, the alliance between Israel and Judah broke down. Of course, there was no love lost between the two royal houses while Athaliah dominated in Judah and Jehu ruled in Israel after obliterating all her relatives there. Subsequently, reform-minded kings in Judah did not want to cooperate with apostate kings of Israel. There were even times when open warfare broke out between the two kingdoms.

A. Jehu's Extermination of Princes and Priests (10:1–36)

1. The Massacre of Ahab's Family (10:1–11)

But internal affairs dominate first. Jehu must establish himself on the throne and fulfill the charge of Yahweh through Elisha the prophet. Jehu leaps off the page as almost larger than life, as utterly ruthless and a quite brilliant politician. First he throws down the gauntlet at the feet of the bureaucracy in Samaria, the crown possession of the Omride dynasty and the base of its power. It turns out that there were about seventy "sons" or male "descendants" of the house of Ahab (v. 1); Jehu was concerned with this larger progeny and not Joram's ("your master's," v. 2) sons alone. All of these were potential rivals for the throne and presumed worshipers of Baal.

He wrote to the "officers of Jezreel" (military commanders of the city who had apparently fled to Samaria after the death of the king), the local elders, and the guardians responsible for the younger members of the family, to choose one of the princes and make him king and fight for him. He implies that they have considerable military strength: chariots, weapons, and a fortified city. Clearly this group had no stomach for such a confrontation. "They were utterly terrified" (v. 4) either because they were cowards, felt outwitted by Jehu, or recognized that the rebellion was widespread and that it would succeed. So they fell into Jehu's trap and promised him unconditional support. The group that responded was essentially the same as that addressed, except that it now included the "chief steward of the palace" and "the city commandant."

Once he had their promise of unconditional loyalty, Jehu demanded proof of that loyalty by ordering them to send the heads of all seventy princes by the next day. They obeyed the command and Jehu demonstrated his callousness by heaping the baskets containing the heads in piles on either side of the gate of Jezreel. That act symbolized his complete control and was designed, like Assyrian treatment of dead enemies, to intimidate viewers into complete subjection.

The next morning Jehu stood before the gate and harangued the "people," probably soldiers and general populace in the vicinity. He exonerated them of all guilt in the rebellion against Joram, assuming that responsibility himself. The question of who was responsible for killing the descendants of Ahab remained unanswered. They could know that various officials of Samaria had done it, but he did not divulge the fact that his command had dictated it. The inference in verse 10 is that a higher decree had directed the judgment executed on the house of Ahab and that Jehu was not really guilty. Jehu's liquidation of Ahab's house was so thorough that it included not only relatives but governing officials as well (v. 11). In fact, his political effectiveness seems to have suffered because he killed too many individuals who knew how to make the machinery of government work.

2. Killing of the Judeans (10:12–14)

The next incident requires some digging to discover what may have been going on. On the face of it, Jehu encountered some Judeans at Beit Qad, some four miles northeast of Jenin, quite off the beaten track that led from Samaria through Jenin to

Jezreel. The group identified themselves as "brothers" or "relatives" or "kinsmen" of Ahaziah, who had come north to visit or "pay their respects to the sons of the king and of the queen mother." Jehu ordered that they be taken captive and then had all forty-two of them massacred. The action could merely be interpreted as part of Jehu's effort to exterminate the relatives of Ahab.

But there are suspicious aspects to the account. The Judeans must have known of the death of Joram and probably the rest of Ahab's relatives in Samaria. They were *north* of Samaria when encountered. Moreover, they were well off the main road, perhaps to avoid detection. Further, it should be noted, then, that the Hebrew translated "brother" could also mean "fellow soldier" (cf. 9:2, "brother officers"). So what may have been going on here is that a group of relatives and Judean soldiers had come north at the command of Athaliah to avenge the death of the kings of Judah and Israel and their relatives. Under the circumstances, Jehu would have had no mercy on the commando force. Possibly he was leading a military patrol to capture them when he found them at Beit Qad. As an alternate interpretation, this group may have come north with Ahaziah. When he was killed, they may have started south via this little-traveled route.

3. The Support of Jehonadab (10:15–17)

As Jehu went on his way to Samaria he met Jehonadab, son of Rechab, founder of the Rechabites, an ascetic group that believed that the nomadic and simple life was the true way of Yahweh (Jer. 35). This clan was connected with the Kenites (1 Chron. 2:55), and possibly they were metal workers. Jehonadab's friendship for Jehu is probably to demonstrate support of the more conservative factions in Israel for the new dynasty. Jehu welcomed this support, and he sought to strengthen it by showing how zealous he was to destroy Ahab's relatives and Baal worship in Samaria.

4. Massacre of the Priests of Baal (10:18–28)

Upon arrival in Samaria Jehu "outwitted" (v. 19, NEB) the prophets of Baal or acted "deceptively" (NIV) in trapping them.

He pretended that his zeal for Baal would be much greater than that of Ahab, who had served Baal only "a little" (v. 18) by comparison. He planned a great "sacrifice" (v. 19) for Baal, which may be a play on words because the word is also used for the "slaughter" of apostates (1 Kings 13:2; 2 Kings 23:20). He made sure that all the prophets or priests of Baal came to the sacrifice and then made certain they would be clearly identified, by dressing them in festal robes or vestments. Next he posted eighty "guards and officers" (evidently members of an elite infantry unit that constituted the palace bodyguard) at all the entrances to the temple. Jehu himself officiated at the offering to Baal; and "just as" he finished, he gave the signal to the guards to attack. From the way Jehu planned the grisly event, one gets a chilling view of his character.

Then they brought out the sacred stone of Baal and "burned it" (v. 26) and "demolished" it (v. 27). A stone cannot be burned; evidently what happened is that they heated it red hot and then threw cold water on it and smashed it into fragments. Finally they tore down the temple and used the location for a latrine (literally, "the place of dung"), parallel to the allusion to the remains of Jezebel in 9:37.

5. Concluding Comments of the Reign of Jehu (10:29–36)

Jehu won God's commendation for destroying Baal worship and the house of Ahab, but he, like all the other kings of Israel, followed in the steps of Jeroboam in maintaining calf worship at Dan and Bethel. So for his degree of faithfulness to God's instructions he had a promise of a dynasty lasting four generations: Jehoahaz, Jehoash, Jeroboam II, and Zechariah. For his degree of unfaithfulness, God began to "whittle Israel down" (v. 32).

What happened historically was this. In 841, the year of his accession, Jehu was forced to pay tribute to Shalmaneser III of Assyria when Shalmaneser invaded the Westland. This is recorded on Shalmaneser's Black Obelisk. But Jehu had relative peace during the years 841 to 838 B.C. while Shalmaneser was harassing Damascus. After 838 Assyria quit pressuring Syria, and Hazael was free to move against Israel in order to strengthen his rear. Eventually he took nearly all of Israel's holdings in Transjordan and held them until Jeroboam II managed to conquer them (2 Kings 14:25). Jehu's reign lasted twenty-eight years (841–814) and his son Jehoahaz succeeded him.

B. Athaliah and the Accession of Joash (11:1–20)

When Jehu liquidated Ahab's line in Israel, he could at least claim that they were all potential political rivals, that none of them was related to him, and that he was carrying out God's commission. Athaliah of Judah could not hide behind any of those screens as she massacred the royal family, except that some of them might be political rivals. She was cruel and ambitious, willing to sacrifice the dearest of her relatives in her drive for power. She was not even very intelligent in her determination to dominate. As it was, she lasted only about six years as queen; she could have retained power much longer than that as regent for the infant Joash or another minor.

Instead of being remembered for anything worthwhile, her six-year reign was little more than an unfortunate interlude in the progression of the Davidic dynasty. To underscore the illegitimacy of her reign, there is no formal introduction or conclusion to it. Her effort to destroy "all those of royal stock" (v. 1) was greatly facilitated by Jehu's killing some of the royal relatives in Israel (10:12–14).

But Athaliah did not kill off all the blood line. Jehosheba, daughter of Joram and sister of Ahaziah, rescued her nephew, Ahaziah's infant son Joash, and hid him in the "bedchamber," presumably the priests' dormitory within the temple area. Jehosheba was actually the wife of the high priest Jehoiada (2 Chron. 22:11), which explains why Joash was brought up in the priests' quarters in the temple. There he could pass as one of the priests' children or a young devotee from another family.

When the young Joash was seven and when Athaliah had ruled for six years, Jehoiada took steps to install him in office. He sent for the captain of hundreds (military unit of a hundred; in the New Testament, a centurion) of the "Carites" (identification uncertain, possibly the Cherethites) and of the "palace guard," and made a "pact" with them. When he had a guarantee of their loyalty, he revealed to them the existence of the crown prince and presented a plan for his induction to office.

The details of the plan are spelled out in verses 5 to 7 and probably would have been clear to someone living then, but the modern reader has difficulty visualizing the layout of the structures and gates and understanding the meaning of some of the Hebrew words. The general nature of the plan is clear enough, however, and runs as follows. On a normal weekday two companies of soldiers stood guard duty in the palace and one company in the temple. On the sabbath just the reverse was true. And on the sabbath two platoons went off duty (had a rest, v. 7). So there were five platoons that served on a rotation basis.

Jehoiada planned to strike for Joash at the beginning of the sabbath. All five platoons would normally be coming or going then, and their movement on this occasion would create no suspicion. He would completely secure the palace and adjacent gates and the route from the palace to the temple, with the three companies that were to serve. The two companies that should go on leave would be retained in the temple as a bodyguard for the prince and were to maintain tight security for him (v. 8). Then Jehoiada would distribute "spears and shields" to the commanders, probably gear specially consecrated for use in the temple.

Finally all was in readiness. The guards formed a huge semicircle around the altar and the temple from the south corner to the north corner (v. 11) to guard the area where the coronation was to take place. Jehoiada then brought out Joash and crowned him and presented him with the "testimony," variously interpreted as regulations governing the conduct of kingship in Judah, the covenant between God and the Davidic king, a copy of the law, and the demands made upon him in his new office. It must have included the king's obligations associated with the Davidic covenant. Finally Jehoiada proclaimed Joash king, and he and his sons anointed the youthful monarch.

The "people"—troops, priests, and others who had come to the temple for sabbath observances—clapped their hands and shouted, "Long live the king," and made such a din that Athaliah heard it and came to investigate. She sized up the situation at once. Jehoiada commanded that she be taken "outside the precincts" of the temple and that any of her followers be killed; probably she had not come to the temple alone. So the commanders of the platoons seized her and executed her by the horse gate of the palace.

Then Jehoiada made a public covenant that renewed the alliance between the king and Yahweh and between Judah and Yahweh, and confirmed the acceptance of Joash by the people (v. 17). As Jehu had demolished the temple of Baal in Samaria to obliterate all vestiges of the previous regime, so now six years later a popular revolt in Jerusalem destroyed the temple of Baal and its priest (v. 18). Meanwhile, and to complete the process, Jehoiada formed a grand procession of priests, military guard, and common people to usher the new king from the temple to the palace and properly install him on the throne. The people "rejoiced" and the city was "at peace," not "quiet" (as in some versions); they apparently had quite a celebration.

C. Joash and the Temple Repairs (11:21–12:21)

1. The Character of His Reign (11:21–12:3)

Joash was one of the better kings of Judah. During his minority, he could not get very far out of line because the high priest Jehoiada supervised his conduct. As he grew older, he continued under the influence of the high priest (v. 2; 2 Chron. 24:2). But when Jehoiada died, the idolatrous princes of Judah exerted influence over Joash; and he was even a party to the stoning of Jehoiada's son Zechariah for his reproof of the king and his nobles (2 Chron. 24:17–22). Apparently even during the lifetime of Jehoiada, however, the king and the high priest could not bring the populace to full support of the central sanctuary. The fact that they continued to sacrifice and burn incense in the high places (v. 3) does not necessarily indicate that they fell into idolatry; their offerings could have been made to Yahweh. It only means that they did not fully follow the Mosaic requirements for tabernacle/temple worship. Joash ruled for forty years (835–796), coming to the throne at the age of seven and in the seventh year of Jehu.

2. Repair of the Temple (12:4–16)

With the passage of time, and especially as a result of
Athaliah's depredations (2 Chron. 24:7), the temple had fallen
into a sorry state. Evidently, too, the priests had failed to assume
their responsibility for maintenance. Joash took leadership in
launching a fund drive and a plan for repair (2 Chron. 24:4–5).
Probably in earlier years the royal treasury had shouldered the
responsibility for upkeep, but now Joash called for solicitation
from the general public.

First he sent the priests and Levites out to collect money for
repairs (2 Chron. 24:5). The Hebrew of 2 Kings 12:4, 5 is
difficult, and translators and commentators produce quite different results. Evidently, dues or taxes of various kinds and
freewill offerings are involved. "Money from the holy things"
may be money from sacred dues or money set aside for
manufacture and purchase of sacred utensils. This plan of
collection evidently did not work and probably for two reasons:
the priests were not sufficiently aggressive in collecting the
money, and the revenues were insufficient for both capital
improvements and support of the priests. Therefore they took
care of themselves and left the temple in a dilapidated state.

Finally in the king's twenty-third year, when he was thirty,
he lost his patience totally and took a new approach to the
problem. The word translated "acquaintances" (vv. 5–7) in
many of the versions might better be rendered "treasurers" or
"assessors" or "tellers." The priests lost the responsibility of
collecting for repairs and for making them, and royal authority
supplanted their power.

A collection chest was installed in the temple into which
offerings for repairs could be placed. The "money" (vv. 10, 11)
was not coins (coinage was not invented until over a century
later in Asia Minor) but weighed-out silver. When the chest was
largely full, the king's fiscal officer and priest took charge of
opening it and counting its contents or weighing the silver and
putting it in bags. Then the money was transferred to the
foremen who had charge of the construction and repair, and they
paid the carpenters and masons and the suppliers of materials.
As the chief priest and the royal fiscal officer supervised the

process, they were satisfied that the work was carried out properly and that the foremen or overseers dealt honestly and therefore did not require a detailed accounting.

With all this pressure on raising money for repairs of the temple, the priests were not to be neglected. Their support was to come from guilt offerings and sin offerings. Leviticus 5:15–19 describes the procedure of the guilt offering and the giving of one-fifth of the restitution price as a tax for the priests.

3. Ransom of Jerusalem (12:17–18)

"At that time" (v. 17), probably soon after Joash began to collect money for temple repairs, Hazael of Syria launched an attack westward. Assyria was occupied elsewhere and presented no threat to Hazael, who had been expanding at the expense of Israel (2 Kings 10:32–33). Hazael probably marched through the territory of weakened Israel and conquered Gath in the plain of Philistia. Then he threatened Jerusalem on his eastward march home. Joash saved a sacking of his capital and bought time to prepare for a future attack by collecting the valuable objects of the temple and palace and presenting them to Hazael. It is interesting to note that evil Jehoram and Ahaziah had presented donations to the temple along with pious Jehoshaphat and Joash.

4. Summary of Joash's Reign (12:19–21)

Near the end of his reign, as Joash suffered from battle wounds inflicted at the hands of the Syrians (2 Chron. 24:25), two men (an Ammonite and a Moabite, 2 Chron. 24:26), possibly professional soldiers, assassinated him while he lay incapacitated in Beth Millo, a place near Jerusalem of uncertain location. The 2 Chronicles reference indicates that this assassination was to avenge the death of Jehoiada's son. Joash's son Amaziah ascended the throne without incident.

D. Jehoahaz of Israel and Defeat by Syria (13:1–9)

Jehoahaz enjoyed a peaceful succession from his violent father Jehu in the twenty-third year of Joash of Judah, and reigned for seventeen years (814–798). But that did not mean he was to enjoy peace and prosperity. The sacred historian's theological concerns are always in evidence, and both Israel and Judah are constantly evaluated in terms of faithfulness to Yahweh. Jehu had exterminated Baal worship, but neither he nor Jehoahaz had turned away from the idolatrous worship system of Jeroboam I. Therefore Yahweh's anger "blazed out" (v. 3, JB) against the Israelites, and He "repeatedly delivered them" into the hands of Hazael and his son Ben-Hadad. This oppression continued throughout the reign of Jehoahaz (v. 22).

The biblical philosophy of history commonly envisions Israel's subjection to a foreign power as a result of Yahweh's displeasure. That concept was not unique to Israel in the ancient Near East, however, for those supernaturally oriented peoples who believed they had to court the favor of their gods to enjoy national or international prosperity. For example, the Moabite Stone ascribes Israel's oppression of Moab to the perceived anger of Chemosh against his people, and the Cyrus Cylinder attributes Persian success against the Babylonians to the perceived anger of Marduk against the Babylonian king Nabonidus. The major difference between Yahweh's treatment of his people and the experience of other Near Eastern peoples is that Yahweh not only could really judge but He could also supernaturally rescue His people, and He actually did both on numerous occasions.

The faith of the northern kings was syncretistic; it did not eliminate the worship of Yahweh completely but combined it with facets of pagan devotion. Thus, when kings were pressed to the wall, they might sincerely turn to Yahweh for relief. Jehoahaz did and God sent "a deliverer" (v. 5). Some identify this person with Adad-nirari III of Assyria, who invaded Syria in 806 B.C. and exacted heavy tribute. Thus Israel would have gained relief. Others argue that the inclusion of the Elisha account (vv. 14–19) in this context points to the prophet's activity in gaining relief for Israel. In any case, penitence was not deep-rooted; the people continued in the ways of Jeroboam (v. 6). Either the respite was very brief and came during Jehoahaz's administration, or it was more extensive and followed the victories of Jehoash.

At the depth of Israelite weakness, the military forces were reduced to ten chariots, as compared with the two thousand that

Ahab contributed to the combined force that had met Shalmaneser III at Qarqar a half century earlier. The army, too, was only
a fraction of what it had been. As with the other kings of Israel
and Judah, only the briefest sketch of Jehoahaz appears in
Scripture; the reader is invited to investigate further in the
annals of the kings of Israel.

E. Jehoash of Israel and Partial Recovery (13:10–25)

Jehoash succeeded his father in the thirty-seventh year of
Joash, king of Judah, and reigned sixteen years (798–782). As
was true of all the other kings of the Northern Kingdom, he
followed the religious example of Jeroboam I and maintained
the calf worship at Dan and Bethel (v. 11). "His war against
Amaziah of Judah" anticipates exploits narrated in chapter 14.

After dropping out of sight for some forty to fifty years,
Elisha appears on the stage of history once more, this time as an
old man and at the point of death. Along with Elisha, the "sons
of the prophets" also faded from the narrative. What Elisha had
been doing all this time is not known, but he must have
maintained a witness for Yahweh and must have continued to
enjoy the respect of the court. Whether the prophet sent for
Jehoash or whether the king heard of Elisha's eminent demise
and decided to visit him, is not stated. The fact that the king
"went down" to see Elisha is not much of a clue to his
whereabouts because going down could refer to altitude, or a
southerly direction, or even a lower social position. Some have
thought that he was in his house in a lower part of Samaria and
that he was later buried in his ancestral home at Abel-meholah,
east of the Jordan.

The king's greeting, "My father! My father!" indicates a
close relationship to the prophet. The meaning of "the chariotry
of Israel and its cavalry" (v. 14) is not clear (cf. 2:12 where
Elisha spoke similarly on the departure of Elijah), but the first-
century Jewish historian Josephus thought it signified that
Elisha was departing this life and leaving the king (spiritually)
unarmed before the Syrians.[1] The prophet could help ensure
that Yahweh would fight his battles. If this was the meaning, the

---

[1] Josephus, *Antiquities*, IX.8.6.

prophet sought to comfort the king with two symbolic actions; these need not be interpreted as sympathetic magic, as many commentators do. First, he told Jehoash to take a bow in his hands and shoot an arrow. Elisha put his hands on the king's hands, symbolic of prophetic support and of divine help in pursuing the king's anti-Syrian policy. Jehoash was to shoot an arrow out the east window, in the general direction of Aram or Syria. Elisha declared Jehoash would vanquish Syria at Aphek, evidently the Aphek in the Valley of Jezreel. Then Elisha instructed the king to take arrows and strike the ground with them, presumably an indication of the king's determination in pursuing the war effort. When he struck the ground only three times, Elisha rebuked him, perhaps for a lack of determination in pursuing the enemy. He would defeat Syria three times, but he might have utterly destroyed his old enemy.

Verses 20 and 21 record a curious event following the death of the prophet, who probably had been buried in a cave, the entrance to which was covered by a stone. Some Israelites were burying a man when a band of Moabite marauders came upon them. In their rush to dispose of the body, they pulled away the stone covering the mouth of the cave where Elisha was buried and threw in the corpse they were carrying. When it touched the bones of Elisha, it sprang to life once more. Evidently these men told about this miracle far and wide so that it became general knowledge. This resurrection helped to underscore the power in the word, ministry, and person of Elisha and to the king would have provided an encouragement that Elisha's promise of victory over the Syrians would be fulfilled.

The chapter closes with an account of Israelite recovery. Though Syria had oppressed Israel all the days of Jehoahaz, to the point that his military capability was virtually annihilated, Yahweh did not blot out Israel entirely. The Abrahamic covenant applied to all Israel, not just Judah (v. 23), and God would honor His commitment to His people. After the death of Hazael, probably in 806 B.C., his son Ben-Hadad succeeded him. Hazael suffered attacks from Adad-nirari III of Assyria (810–783 B.C.) in 802 and 796. These so weakened Syria that Israel was able to recapture territory lost to Syria during the reign of Jehoahaz. As promised, Jehoash enjoyed three victories over Ben-Hadad.

Thus began the recovery of Israel that during the rule of the final king of the Jehu dynasty, Jeroboam II, would reach significant proportions.

F. Amaziah of Judah (14:1–22)

1. Introductory Statement (14:1–6)

Customarily in the books of Kings the text is replete with chronological references that are both a help and a source of difficulty. The references aid in construction of an exact chronology, but the extent of them sometimes creates a problem of resolving apparent discrepancies. In the second year of Jehoash of Israel, Amaziah began to reign in Judah (796) at the age of twenty-five. The problem arises with his twenty-nine year reign (v. 2), for there is no room in the chronology for him to have ruled that long. Thiele has resolved the difficulty with a long coregency between Amaziah and Azariah or Uzziah (792–767). The explanation is that when Amaziah was taken prisoner to Israel (v. 13), his son, Azariah, then sixteen, was elevated to the throne (v. 21).[2] Presumably Amaziah was released at an early date (no later than 782, when Jehoash died) and returned to Judah to live. His reign would officially comprise the years from his accession to the throne until his death. Amaziah is classified as a good king but he fell short of David's performance (v. 3), possibly an ominous hint of his later apostasy. As was true of his father Joash (12:3), Amaziah did not remove the high places, either (v. 4). But although worship there is assumed to be wrong (i.e., not in conformity with Mosaic worship patterns), nothing is said about a toleration of idolatry. Apparently there was a brief period of political instability after the death of Joash, but when Amaziah got the kingdom "secure in his hand" (v. 5), he executed the assassins of his father. Probably his motive in so doing was to strengthen his hold on the kingdom and to avenge the death of his father. That there was no general purge seems clear from verse 6, for he did not even put to death the sons of the assassins, and thus he followed the restrictions of Deuteronomy 24:16.

---

[2] Thiele, *Mysterious Numbers*, 109–10.

2. Military Actions (14:7–14)

Edom had been lost to Judah from the days of Joram (2 Kings 8:20–22) and Amaziah now sought to recover it and the route through it to the Gulf of Aqaba and Judah's seaport at Ezion-geber. To ensure success he had hired one hundred thousand mercenaries from Israel (2 Chron. 25:6), but a prophet of God warned against employment of these men and Amaziah sent them home. The Israelites were furious, probably at the loss of a chance to get booty; on the way home they plundered and destroyed some cities of Judah (2 Chron. 25:10–13). Amaziah pursued his Edomite campaign, leaving the squaring of accounts with Israel until later. He had a great victory over Edom in the "Valley of Salt." Though there are differences of opinion on the matter, the valley must be the Arabah south of the Dead Sea and Sela is to be located there. This conclusion seems to fit conditions better than the identification of Sela with Petra in the mountain fastnesses southeast of the Dead Sea. After his signal victory over the Edomites, Amaziah carried Edomite gods back to Jerusalem and worshiped them (2 Chron. 25:14); for his idolatrous breach God determined to destroy Amaziah (2 Chron. 25:15–16). This sets the stage for the war with Israel.

With the Edomite conflict behind him, Amaziah sent a delegation to Jehoash, proposing that they "arrange a meeting" or "meet face to face" (v. 8). This could have been an invitation to a discussion of matters of mutual concern or a polite invitation to battle. However the invitation may have been intended, Jehoash made conflict inevitable by his haughty reply (vv. 9–10). Probably neither king was in a mood to lie down and play dead. Jehoash had been enjoying victories over Syria, and Amaziah had just trounced Edom. The two kings prepared for war. Instead of descending on Jerusalem from the north where defense was easier, Jehoash moved along the valley of Sorek into the central highlands of Judah. The two armies met at Beth Shemesh, about fifteen miles west of Jerusalem. There is no hint as to why the Israelites were so successful, but apparently Judean morale snapped completely and the army fled the field, deserting even the king himself, who was captured by the enemy. As noted above, there was a theological reason for Judean defeat.

Then the Israelites advanced on Jerusalem and broke down a six-hundred-foot segment of the wall, from the Ephraim Gate (thought to be about where the present Damascus Gate is located) westward to the corner gate. Probably they only broke through the wall here but did not demolish it, because Uzziah later had only to repair the wall (2 Chron. 26:9). Then from this high ground to the north of the city he was in a good position to plunder the temple and palace treasuries, taking what he possibly felt was justly his for payment of his one hundred thousand troops hired by Amaziah. He also took "hostages," possibly as a pledge of further payment in the future; the temple treasury must not have offered him all he expected at this time, because Hazael of Syria had so recently plundered it (2 Kings 12:18).

3. *Concluding Summary (14:15–22)*

In these verses the reader meets the usual invitation to consult the annals of the kings of Israel and Judah for further information on Jehoash of Israel and Amaziah of Judah. But additionally they tell of a conspiracy against Amaziah. The reason for this is not stated; though commentators engage in speculation on the subject, they have not produced anything concrete. What is clear is that the opposition was widespread. When confronted with it in Jerusalem, Amaziah fled to the military stronghold at Lachish, thirty miles southwest of Jerusalem. The army units there did not close ranks behind him and the assassins from Jerusalem killed him. His son Azariah (Uzziah) then succeeded him. On the view of the coregency noted above, he would have been sixteen at the time of accession and would now have reigned alone. Though Uzziah did many things, he is especially remembered here for rebuilding Judah's seaport on the Red Sea (Gulf of Aqaba), possibly because his father had taken control of Edom. For detail on the reign of Uzziah, see 2 Kings 15:1–7 and 2 Chronicles 26.

G. Prosperity of the Two Kingdoms (14:23–15:7)

During the days of Uzziah of Judah (792–740) and Jeroboam II of Israel (793–753) the two Hebrew kingdoms were powerful once more. Together they controlled most of the territory David had ruled at the height of the united Hebrew kingdom. This resurgence of power was due in part to the weakness of Assyrian monarchs during the first half of the eighth century B.C.

1. Israel Under Jeroboam II (14:23–29)

Jeroboam's reign is said to have begun in the fifteenth year of Amaziah of Judah or in 782 (v. 23), but he was coregent with his father Jehoash for twelve years before that; so his total reign of forty-one years began in 793 and continued until his death in 753. Like all the other kings of Israel before him, he maintained the official cult established by Jeroboam I, but in spite of that he had several things going for him religiously. First, as previously noted, God had promised that Jehu's dynasty would enjoy a certain amount of divine provision down into the fourth generation. Second, the prophet Jonah had given him a divine commitment concerning the expansion of his borders (v. 25). Third, God was moved with compassion by the sufferings of Israel (2 Kings 13:5–7); and since He had not specifically issued a prophetic utterance for Israel's obliteration in punishment for her sins, He was free to act in grace (vv. 26, 27).

Jeroboam expanded the borders of Israel in the north to the "entrance to Hamath" or "Lebo-Hamath" and in the south to the "sea of the Arabah." The "entrance to Hamath" may refer to a general area south of Hamath that would give access to the Euphrates; it was the northern border of the kingdom of Solomon (1 Kings 8:65). Some identify it as a city, Lebo-Hamath, about fifty miles north of Damascus. The "sea of the Arabah" must be the Dead Sea (cf. Deut. 3:17) and indicates establishment of the border at the north end of the Dead Sea (the old Moabite-Israelite frontier) or farther south toward the Arnon. The prophetic pronouncement of Jonah, of which this is said to be a fulfillment, does not appear elsewhere in the Old Testament. Its inclusion here does much to establish the historicity of that prophet whose book has often been maligned as only legend or parable.

Israel's territorial expansion under Jeroboam II must have taken place during the latter half of his reign; Assyrian weakness of activity elsewhere would have permitted it then. Moreover, it would have taken an extended period of time for Jeroboam to build up his military establishment and infrastructure to permit expansionist moves. Evidently, increased prosperity both facilitated expansion and resulted from it.

Verse 28 is very difficult in the Hebrew; literally it reads, "how he recovered both Damascus and Hamath for Judah in Israel." Commentators and translators have tried various emendations of the text. One proposal is that "Judah" refers to Jaudi, a state in northeastern Spain, so the reading would be "Hamath in Jaudi for Israel." Others believe that the verse indicates some cooperation between Israel and Judah in this expansionist effort. Whatever else one may say about it, at the minimum, it claims Israelite control of both Damascus and Hamath. When Jeroboam died, his son Zechariah succeeded him on the throne.

2. Judah Under Uzziah (15:1–7)

Like his contemporary in the north, Uzziah enjoyed great success during his reign. As noted, his father Amaziah had regained Judean control over Edom; that made possible Uzziah's restoration of Eloth (Elath) on the Gulf of Aqaba and hence the redevelopment of Judean maritime activity there. Uzziah also had great military success against the Philistines in the west and Arabians in the south. The Ammonites in the east acknowledged his suzerainty and became tributary to him. Internally, he repaired the walls of Jerusalem and fortified other centers, enjoyed economic prosperity, and built up the size of the army and outfitted it with conventional and sophisticated weaponry (for elaboration see 2 Chron. 26).

"His fame spread far and wide, for he was greatly helped until he became powerful. But after Uzziah became powerful, his pride led to his downfall" (2 Chron. 26:15–16, NIV). Uzziah, like many of the rest of us, could not be trusted with too much success or too much power. We may not like it when some inadequacies or weaknesses prevent us from flying high, but we may be much better off when God keeps us on a short leash. Then, in dependence on Him, we may do really effective work. The apostle Paul found that to be true. When God refused to remove Paul's "thorn in the flesh," He promised, "my power is made perfect in weakness" (2 Cor. 12:9, NIV).

Uzziah in his pride tried to usurp priestly powers and offer incense in the temple, even though courageous priests tried to stop him. For his sin God smote him with leprosy on the spot (2 Chron. 26:16–20), and he went to live "in the house of quarantine" or "in isolated quarters" (v. 5) for the rest of his life. His son Jotham then governed as coregent and de facto king. Jotham's beginning of the coregency in 750 dates Uzziah's blunder, and his death in 740 dates the call of the prophet Isaiah (Isa. 6:1). His total reign of fifty-two years (792–740) included long coregencies with his father (792–767) and with his son (750–740).

H. The Last Days of Israel (15:8–17:41)

The sacred historian now hurries through brief sketches of the last kings of Israel. The high point of success under Jeroboam II was destined to be short lived. Tiglath-pileser III (744–727) of Assyria restored the power of the monarchy there and launched aggressive expansion that included moves into Syria and Palestine. Israel, ripe for judgment as a result of her long apostasy, finally succumbed to the Assyrian juggernaut and was hauled off into captivity. As is clear from the rest of this chapter, however, Israel's greatest problems were not external. Political instability, complicated by political assassinations, robbed the state of the cohesive force needed to stand up to foreign invasion when it finally occurred.

1. Zechariah of Israel (15:8–12)

Zechariah, son of Jeroboam, came to the throne late in 753, and like all the other Israelite kings before him, subscribed to the state cult instituted by Jeroboam I. After only six months on the throne, he succumbed to an assassination attempt by Shallum. If "Jabesh" (v. 10) is understood as a place instead of a person, then he came from east of Jordan and support is given to the thesis that some of the revolts during Israel's latter days reflected a rivalry between tribes on the east and the west of the Jordan. The assassination "in front of the people" (v. 10, NIV) is the translation of a word that in several manuscripts is replaced by "at Ibleam." The reference in verse 12 is to the promise made to Jehu in 10:30, 31 that his dynasty would last for four generations. His descendants Jehoahaz, Jehoash, Jeroboam II, and Zechariah had ruled Israel for about ninety years.

2. Shallum of Israel (15:13–15)

Shallum ruled for only one month early in 752. Then Manahem, son of Gadi, took the field against him. "Gadi" probably refers to his father rather than to his tribal connection; in coming from Tirzah (capital of Israel from the time of Baasha to Omri), he should have been from the tribe of Manasseh. He could be viewed as the leader of a Manasseh faction, as some commentators believe, or he might simply have been the leader or a member of the Jehu camp that sought to avenge the assassination of Zechariah. According to Josephus, Menahem had been the commander-in-chief of Jeroboam II's army.[3]

3. Menahem of Israel and Tribute to Assyria (15:16–22)

Apparently as Menahem was consolidating his power, he attacked Tiphsah (site uncertain, possibly located about six miles southwest of Shechem), and the inhabitants refused to acknowledge his kingship; perhaps supporters or officials of the administration of Shallum were holed up there. On taking the place, Menahem sacked it and cruelly murdered all the pregnant women, presumably in an effort to intimidate other towns into submission. Such brutality was a common feature of ancient Near Eastern warfare and one should not conclude that the Hebrews were much better than their contemporaries.

After Menahem established himself on the throne, he managed to rule for ten years (752–742) and followed the religious example of Jeroboam I. Since the sacred historian is now focusing on the decline of Israel and its imminent demise at the hands of the Assyrians, the one event signaled out for comment in the reign of Menahem is the invasion of Pul or

[3] Josephus, *Antiquities*, IX.11.1.

Tiglath-pileser III. From Assyrian records it is known that Pul
was campaigning in the Mediterranean area from 743 to 738, and
it appears that the contact with Menahem occurred in 743 or
742. Scholars used to assert that the Bible was in error in using
the name Pul to refer to the Assyrian ruler, but now it is known
that he was so addressed in Babylonian circles.

It is necessary to ask at this point what was really going on
in Israel. There is no mention of Tiglath-pileser's actual
invasion; the Hebrew says merely that he "had come against the
land." There is no reference to destruction or casualties either.
The stated purpose for Menahem's payment was to gain "his
support in strengthening his hold on the kingdom" (v. 19).
Hobbs makes a convincing case that this was not tribute in the
usual sense of the term but payment for help, as Ahaz of Judah
was to make later.[4] At this time Pekah (see below) was actually
ruling the part of Israel east of Jordan and Menahem wanted
Assyrian help in consolidating his hold on the kingdom. To
obtain the desired sum of a thousand talents of silver (three
million shekels), Menahem exacted fifty shekels from each
wealthy man; thus, as LaSor points out, there were sixty
thousand upper class persons in Israel at that time.[5] It does not
seem that Menahem got much for his money. The Assyrians did
withdraw from the area and let him alone, but they did not put
any pressure on Pekah to recognize his sovereignty.

4. Pekahiah of Israel (15:23–26)

When Menahem died, his son Pekahiah took the throne and
ruled for two years (742–740), following the usual pattern of
subscribing to Jeroboam's apostasy. Pekah, still ruling east of
the Jordan, may have accepted a high post in the government of
Pekahiah (v. 25), but continued to rule as a virtual independent.
Finally he made a move to take over the entire kingdom and
used a posse of fifty trusted associates from Gilead to liquidate
Pekahiah (v. 25).

---

[4]Hobbs, 2 Kings, 199.
[5]LaSor, "1 and 2 Kings," 359.

5. *Pekah of Israel (15:27–31)*

Even though Pekah ruled only about eight years over all Israel, his reign is reckoned as lasting twenty years (752–732), counting from the time of his rise to power in the area of Israel east of the Jordan. Religiously, he continued the worship system of his predecessors, now described with monotonous regularity by the sacred historian. But just when the reader is tempted to take this as a matter of course, suddenly the impact of it hits like a bombshell. God's patience with Israel has finally run out! The most important event of Pekah's reign was the loss of the whole northern section of the country to Assyria in 732, evidently as a result of the appeal of Ahaz to Assyria (see chapter 16). As punishment for Israel's idolatry, the captivity has begun. Tiglath-pileser tells about this conquest in his annals and states that he placed Hoshea over them as king.[6] Whether Hoshea came to power as a result of Assyrian intervention or a popular uprising is not clear, but he did become a tributary to the Assyrian king.

6. *Jotham of Judah (15:32–38)*

Jotham began to rule when his father Uzziah became a leper in 750 and ruled until 732, sharing a coregency with his father until 740 and with his son Ahaz from 735 until his death. Though classified as one of Judah's good kings, like several others he did not remove the high places. This passage ignores Jotham's successful Ammonite wars and the tribute received from the Ammonites and his extensive building activity recorded in 2 Chronicles 27:3–5. Most of that construction seems to have been fortification, probably in anticipation of the attacks of Rezin of Syria and Pekah of Israel that began during his reign. Those kings would become a real scourge to Judah during the following reign of Ahaz. In connection with those attacks one should read Isaiah 7:1–8:8.

7. *Ahaz of Judah vs. Israel (16:1–20)*

Ahaz was one of the most repulsive of all the kings of Judah. The comment that, compared to David he did not do what was

---

[6]Thomas, *Documents*, 55.

right in God's eyes, is the height of understatement. "He followed the example of the kings of Israel" (v. 3) might be interpreted as involving a syncretistic approach—combining Yahwism with pagan worship. But 2 Chronicles 28:2 makes it clear that that included making images for Baal. He even "made his son to pass through the fire," as an actual burnt offering "after the sordid fashion of the nations whom Yahweh had dispossessed for the Israelites" (v. 3). Apparently some crisis had instigated such an extreme course of action. Evidently he also de-emphasized the place of the central sanctuary in Jerusalem as he encouraged sacrifices in a multiplicity of high places all over the country (v. 4). This wicked king began his rule as a coregency with his father Jotham in 735, probably because of Jotham's ill health (Jotham died in 732 at the age of 43), and continued for sixteen years (732–715). Isaiah the prophet ministered in Judah during all those dark days of apostasy (Isa. 1:1).

Because of the apostasy of King Ahaz, God brought great suffering upon Judah in the form of invasion and rebellion (2 Chron. 28:5, 19). As Assyria threatened the Westland, Syria and Israel sought to persuade Judah to join them in a coalition against Assyria. Ahaz refused to cooperate and Rezin of Syria and Pekah of Israel attacked in an effort to force Ahaz to do so. The allies decimated Judah's army and even killed the king's son and some of his chief officers. Then they virtually depopulated a whole section of Judah and carried the inhabitants off into slavery. But as a result of the intercession of a prophet named Oded, the Israelites returned all the captives (see 2 Chron. 28:5–15 for an account of the war).

Taking advantage of the weakness of Judah, Edom struck to regain control of Elath, which they had lost to Judah in the days of Azariah (2 Kings 14:22). That the Edomites were successful against Judah at this time is clear from 2 Chronicles 28:17, and an apparent copyist's error was responsible for recording "Aram" (Syria) for "Edom" in 2 Kings 16:6 (NASB retains "Aram" but NIV has "Aram" and substitutes "Edomites"). To make matters worse, the Philistines also encroached on Judean territory (2 Chron. 28:18).

In his desperation Ahaz stripped the treasury of the temple

and palace and sent the silver and gold to Tiglath-pileser as tribute, reducing Judah to vassal status to Assyria. In doing so he pled with the Assyrians to rescue him from Syria and Israel. (He need not have done so, however, because the prophet Isaiah had gone to Ahaz with a message from God that foretold the destruction of Syria and Israel, Isa. 7:1–9, and offered a miraculous "sign" of deliverance, 7:10–11, which Ahaz refused.) Tiglath-pileser was happy to oblige. In 732 he obliterated the kingdom of Syria and reduced it to provincial status within the Assyrian Empire. In the same campaign he also defeated Israel, annexed her northern districts, and carried off numerous captives (2 Kings 15:29). Tiglath-pileser recorded his successes on a tablet, excavated at Nimrud (Calah).[7] The tribute of Ahaz he inscribed on the palace wall at Nimrud.[8] Second Chronicles 28:20 indicates Tiglath-pileser came against Ahaz anyway and afflicted (besieged, distressed) him instead of strengthening him, i.e., pillaged Judah. This one verse describes the fulfillment of Isaiah 7:17–25; 8:4–8.

While Tiglath-pileser was consolidating his control in Damascus, Ahaz went there to make obeisance and probably to pay tribute. In Damascus he saw an altar he liked and sent a pattern of it to Jerusalem with orders that one like it be installed in the temple area (v. 10). Hobbs flatly rejects the common critical idea that this altar was of Assyrian design and that adoption of it was an expression of subservience to Assyria. He observes that this was built in honor of the gods of Syria (2 Chron. 28:23) and that known Assyrian altars were not designed for uses to which this one was put in Jerusalem.[9]

It appears from verse 14 that the new altar was placed directly in front of the sanctuary entrance and that the old bronze altar was moved to the north side of the temple. Verse 15 seems to indicate that the use of the new altar had little if anything to do with apostasy, for the usual offerings prescribed in the Mosaic ritual were offered to Yahweh on it. Perhaps the new altar alleviated some of the inadequacies of the old altar as recognized in 1 Kings 8:64. The acceptability to Uriah, the

[7] Ibid., Thomas, 55.
[8] Ibid., 56.
[9] Hobbs, 215.

priest, of the altar and sacrifices performed on it supports the orthodoxy of the new arrangement; evidently this is the same priest that the prophet Isaiah regarded highly (Isa. 8:2). Verse 16 indicates the division of responsibilities between king and priest. The king was the chief executive officer of the state and the temple, and the priest was his immediate subordinate in charge of the temple.

Changes in the temple furniture (v. 17) have been attributed to the need to find sources for tribute to Assyria, but that is not specifically stated. The removal of the Sabbath canopy (a dais for the throne) and the royal entryway of the temple "in deference to the king of Assyria," indicates some demotion of the Judean king.

8. *Hoshea and the Fall of Samaria (17:1–41)*

a. The fall of the city (17:1–6). When Hoshea assumed the throne of Israel in 732 B.C., he took control of a greatly truncated and greatly weakened state. Only the tiny province of Samaria remained under his control. Though he is described as not quite so bad as his predecessors (v. 2), that slight improvement could do no good. The cumulative effect of the sins of Israel's kings and people made the land ripe for judgment. The days of the kingdom of Israel were numbered.

The son of Tiglath-pileser III, Shalmaneser V, came to the Assyrian throne in 727 B.C., and at first Hoshea apparently paid him tribute. The NIV translation of verse 3 is preferable, with its rendering in the English past perfect: "had been Shalmaneser's vassal" and "had paid him tribute." The verse should be regarded as a kind of topic sentence with development following. There is no evidence for two invasions of Shalmaneser (vv. 3–5). After initial subservience Hoshea developed a false hope that he could rebel successfully against Assyria with Egyptian help, and stopped the annual tribute payments. There has been extensive discussion, with no conclusive identification, of who the Egyptian king, So, was. It is not important to the narrative to know who he was.

It is easy to conclude from reading verse 4 that Shalmaneser caught Hoshea and imprisoned him before the siege of Samaria. But the verse is probably only a summary statement about the king: he had been a vassal, he rebelled, and was finally seized and imprisoned. If he had been taken before the siege, the people probably would have chosen a new ruler. In any case, Shalmaneser invaded Israel, subdued the countryside, and launched a three-year siege of Samaria (2 Kings 17:5; 18:9–10). Apparently the siege took place during 725, 724, and 723, with the fall in 723. Since parts of years counted as years, the siege needed to last only one full year and parts of two others, or less than a total of two years. Increasingly, scholars are attributing the fall to Shalmaneser, who died in 722.[10]

Sargon II (721–705) used to be given credit for the victory because he took the credit, claiming to have taken the city and deporting 27,290 people.[11] At most, he probably engaged in some mopping-up activity later on. And 27,290 is a very large number for him to have deported from the city; more than likely this was a number taken from the region. The Israelites that Shalmaneser or Sargon seem to have deported were settled in northern Mesopotamia in Gozan (probably area of Tell Halah) on the Khabur River, an important tributary of the Euphrates; in Halah, either an alternate spelling of Calah or possibly Chalchitis on the west bank of the Tigris; and in the mountains of Media, east of Mesopotamia.

b. Reason for captivity (17:7–23). The kings and the people of Israel had received abundant warning that their departure from the ways of Yahweh would result in destruction of their kingdom and captivity to a foreign power. The God who had previously rescued them from bondage in Egypt (v. 7) had handed Israel over to the Assyrians (v. 23). Now that judgment had fallen, the sacred historian presents a summary indictment of Israel's conduct. "All this happened because the Israelites had sinned against Yahweh their God" is the generalization. What follows is a bill of particulars. The failure of the Israelites fell basically into three categories. First, they "walked in the manner of the nations Yahweh had driven out before them." This consisted in worshiping other gods that were "worthless idols"; multiplication of pagan high places with their sacred stones and Asherah poles; bowing down to the starry host of

---

[10] Thiele, 163–172.
[11] Thomas, 58–63.

heaven—the deification of God's creation and polytheistic worship of it; child sacrifice—sacrifice of sons and daughters; a practice of divination and sorcery—the effort to manipulate forces beyond the human. Second, they walked in practices that their evil kings had introduced. This included especially worship of the "two idols cast in the shape of calves" and Baal worship. Third, they blatantly rejected God's decrees and His covenant. They did not trust in Yahweh (v. 14); i.e., they did not reckon Him to be reliable or worthy of their trust or confidence.

c. Repeopling of Samaria (17:24–41). Assyrian repeopling of Samaria took place long after the deportation of Israelites from the area and followed a general plan of mixing peoples so that organized nationalistic revolts would not occur in the future. Of the groups coming in, many identify "Cuthah" with Tel Ibrahim, about fifteen miles northeast of Babylon; "Avva" is unknown; "Hamath" is probably Hamath on the Orontes in Syria; and "Sepharvaim" has been variously identified, but not with certainty. When these peoples came into Samaria, they had no knowledge of Yahweh whatsoever. Molestation by lions led the populace to inform the king of Assyria that the misfortunes had befallen them because they did not know what the local god of the land required. The king of Assyria permitted a priest to return to instruct the settlers in the worship of Yahweh, and he took up his residence in Bethel, one of the cult centers of the state of Israel. How orthodox his instruction was, we have no way of knowing.   .

For their part, the people of the land had no intention to convert to Yahweh worship but in a syncretistic fashion mixed elements of Yahweh worship with their own cultic practices. "Nergal" was the Mesopotamian god of the underworld. Anammelech may be a reference to the Mesopotamian sun god Anu. The other pagan gods mentioned in this passage cannot be certainly identified. The religious development portrayed here provides a backdrop for the understanding of conditions at the time of the restoration as recorded in Ezra and Nehemiah and for an appreciation of why orthodox Jews later would shun the Samaritan faith with its various aberrations.

For Further Study

1. Formulate a character analysis of Jehu.

2. How real was Joash's faith in Yahweh?

3. Review the political and military situation that made possible the prosperity and expansion of Israel and Judah during the reigns of Jeroboam II (Israel) and Uzziah (Judah) during the first half of the eighth century B.C. Note the territorial extent of each kingdom at this time.

4. On taking Tiphsah, Menahem of Israel cruelly murdered the pregnant women. Can you find other examples of Israelite cruelty to civilians or dismemberment of dead enemy bodies to support the idea that Israelites sometimes followed the cruel practices of their Near Eastern neighbors?

5. Try to tabulate items that made Ahaz so repulsive in God's eyes.

6. Construct a bill of particulars of God's indictment of Israel and His reasons for sending her into captivity.

Chapter 7

The Surviving Kingdom of Judah
(2 Kings 18:1–25:30)

Apostasy and corruption had eaten away at the vitals of Israel until the state toppled and fell to the Assyrians. Now that colossus stood poised on the border of Judah some ten miles to the north of Jerusalem. Judah was destined to eke out an existence for another century, however, given a reprieve from divine judgment by the reforms of Hezekiah and Josiah. But the evil excesses of Manasseh sent Judah full throttle down the road of moral deterioration, and the last kings of Judah pushed her over the brink into the pit of destruction. The sins that had corrupted the Northern Kingdom and had led to its extinction were at work in Judah, too, and finally resulted in overthrow of the state and the captivity of her people.

A. The Reign of Hezekiah (18:1–20:21)

1. His Reforms (18:1–12)

Hezekiah was the very best king in the history of Judah, from the standpoint of his trust in God and faithfulness to His commandments (v. 5). In fact, unlike some of the other kings of Judah who started well, he did not apostatize later in life (v. 6). He stacked up well in comparison with David, too, doing right as David had done (v. 3). This commendation is bestowed on only three other Judean kings: Asa (1 Kings 15:11); Jehoshaphat (2 Chron. 17:3); and Josiah; (2 Kings 22:2).

His faithfulness to God is revealed in several actions. First, he "abolished the high places," breaking in pieces the pillars and cutting down the Asherah poles. While Yahweh might be worshiped at these places, as previously indicated, they were susceptible to pagan use and apparently were increasingly so employed. Second, he "smashed" or pulverized the bronze serpent that Moses had made in connection with the lifting of God's judgment in the wilderness (see Num. 21:4–9). Called "Nehushtan" (the bronze thing), it had become a stumbling block to the Israelites; they had been offering sacrifices to it. The serpent was a fertility symbol in ancient Canaanite religion, and it is possible that by this time the populace had forgotten about Mosaic connections, and associated Canaanite connotations with it instead. Then, third, as the Chronicler pointed out, he cleansed and reconsecrated the temple (2 Chron. 29:3–36). Fourth, he celebrated the Passover and other feast days (2 Chron. 30). Finally, Hezekiah encouraged a number of other reforms connected with offerings, the priesthood, and the service of the temple (2 Chron. 31:2–21).

God blessed Hezekiah for his faithfulness; among his successes was the reconquest of territory lost to the Philistines during the days of Ahaz (v. 8). Probably this victory came after the death of Sargon II in 705 when there was some uncertainty about Assyrian control in the region. Hezekiah would have attacked to weaken Assyrian domination of territory on his western flank and to open communication links with Egypt. "From watchtower to fortified town" indicates the success of military action wherever he went.

It is not easy to determine when Hezekiah ruled. Verse 13 refers to Sennacherib's attack as occurring during his fourteenth year. That attack (if Sennacherib invaded only once) took place in 701 and puts the beginning of his twenty-nine year reign in 715. But verse 1 says he began to reign in the third year of Hoshea, which would be 729/8 B.C., when Hezekiah was twelve or thirteen. If he started to rule in 729, his administration would have terminated in 701, the year of Sennacherib's attack. But in the midst of the attack, Hezekiah received a promise of fifteen additional years of life (2 Kings 20:6). One may argue that he had a coregency with his father Ahaz, and his independent reign began in 715. But when coregencies occurred, the person who joined the coregency dated his reign from that time and not from the year when he began to reign alone. Most commentators begin Hezekiah's reign in 715. Clearly the fall of the Northern Kingdom had occurred before he began to rule; during his first year he rededicated the temple after Ahaz's excesses (2 Chron. 29:3) and then sent word to all Israel and Judah from Dan to Beersheba to participate in the Passover (2 Chron. 30:1, 5). He could not have done that before 722 B.C. The account of the fall of the Northern Kingdom, reported in verses 9–12, tallies with the report given in chapter 17, and the places where the deportees were settled are the same.

2. Deliverance from Sennacherib's Invasion (18:13–19:37)

a. Sennacherib's attack (18:13–18). King Sennacherib of Assyria in 701 on his third military campaign invaded Phoenicia and Palestine, swooped down on the Philistine territory that Hezekiah had taken and reclaimed it for Assyria, and then methodically reduced Judea. He conquered the "fortified cities of Judah" (v. 13), forty-six in all according to his inscriptions, making Jerusalem completely vulnerable. He took over two hundred thousand captives and untold quantities of booty.[1] Sennacherib's siege of Lachish, a bastion second in importance to Jerusalem, especially consumed his energies; and he covered two whole walls of his palace with reliefs depicting the siege and capture of the city. While Sennacherib was engaged in that operation, Hezekiah felt the squeeze so intensely that he offered the Assyrian "whatever you impose" in terms of tribute (v. 14). In order to meet the demands, Hezekiah could not find enough in palace and temple treasuries; he had to strip the decorative gold from the walls of the temple.

But tribute did not satisfy Sennacherib; he seemed to want nothing less than the total capitulation of Judea. He sent the Tartan, the Rabsaris, and the Rebshakeh with a large military force. These were not proper names but titles of officials. The

---

[1] Thomas, *Documents*, 66–67. Gordon Franz in his M.A. thesis, "The Hezekiah/Sennacherib Chronology Problem Reconsidered," Columbia Biblical Seminary, Columbia, SC, 1987, argues that Sennacherib made two incursions against Judah, the first in Hezekiah's fourteenth year (713/12 B.C.) and the second in 701 B.C. He dates Hezekiah's reign 727 to 698 B.C.

Tartan was the chief commander of the Assyrian army, a "second commander" under the king. The Rabsaris, literally "chief eunuch," was possibly the head of the king's bodyguard and held an important military post. The Rabshakeh was another officer who may have been a kind of secretary of state. They stopped at "the aqueduct of the upper pool," a location that has been endlessly discussed; perhaps it was a slight elevation at the northwest part of the city. Of course, they called for the king, but what they got were top-level royal representatives with undesignated major administrative responsibilities: Eliakim, a kind of minister of state; Shebna, a secretary or scribe; and Joah, the archivist—all members of the king's inner circle.

b. The Rabshakeh's propaganda war (18:19–35). In verses 19–25 the Rabshakeh made a pretty little speech in which he tried to undermine the confidence of Jerusalem's inhabitants by (1) showing the worthlessness of depending on Egypt, (2) questioning their dependence on God, (3) asserting the inadequacy of their military prowess, and (4) claiming that the Assyrians themselves had been sent by Yahweh to destroy Judah. He said in effect, "you can't trust in your own military capability (v. 20), the Egyptians (v. 21), or Yahweh because you have demolished his high places (v. 22)." Then he taunted the Hebrews to make a wager; the Assyrians were willing to bet that if they gave the Hebrews two thousand horses they could not find the trained men to ride them.

Up to this point, the Rabshakeh's speech had been designed for Hezekiah's official delegation and evidently was in Hebrew. Hezekiah's men wanted the further contents of the parley to be restricted to the official bodies also, and sought to prevent morale-destroying aspects from reaching the ears of Jerusalem's defenders. Therefore they requested that the language used thereafter be Aramaic (the diplomatic language of Western Asia and known to the trained leadership of the court) and not Hebrew.

But the Assyrians were engaged in propaganda warfare and appealed over the heads of the king and his advisors directly to the people. The Rabshakeh may have known Hebrew, but more likely spoke through an interpreter. He now presses his appeal for surrender. As a kind of introductory thought, he vividly portrays the dire circumstances to which a populace that endures a long siege may be reduced: "doomed to eat their own dung and drink their own urine" (v. 27). As a corollary to his assertion of Judean military weakness (vv. 23, 24), the Rabshakeh next seeks to undermine Hezekiah's leadership: "Do not let Hezekiah delude you . . . " (v. 29); "Do not let Hezekiah persuade you . . . " (v. 30); "Do not listen to Hezekiah," . . . (v. 31).

Then the Assyrian promises the Judeans security, peace, and prosperity if they will surrender (v. 31). That, of course, is an elusive hope. The statement itself speaks of deportation ("until I come and take you away," v. 31) with all the horrors of long, forced marches; relocation; and slave status. As a kind of parody on "Better red than dead," the Rabshakeh is urging, "Better Assyrian than dead," or "Better slave than dead."

Finally, the Rabshakeh describes the inability of national deities to save their peoples from the Assyrians (vv. 33–35). In lumping Yahweh with all these impotent gods and in denying that He can save Jerusalem from the Assyrians, Rabshakeh was overreaching himself and daring Yahweh to prove Himself.

c. Judean remorse and God's promise (18:36–19:7). At this point there is a major scene change in the drama. Obedient, both the soldiers on the wall and the official delegation refrained from answering the Assyrians. Perhaps they merely said, "We'll take your statement to our king." With clothes torn, a common act of remorse, the trio of the king's advisors reported on all the Rabshakeh's propaganda and braggadocio. The ball was in the king's court, so to speak.

The king also adopted the traditional signs of remorse and distress by tearing his clothes and putting on sackcloth (coarse goats' hair clothing) and then went into the temple to seek God's help in this crisis. Meanwhile, he sent off his trusted trio to the prophet Isaiah begging his intercession. The suddenness with which the historian introduced Isaiah and the way in which he brought him into the narratives implies that the original readers would have known about the prophet. In his message to Isaiah, Hezekiah groaned that it is a day of distress, of divine chastisement, and of God's rejection of the people. The people are so weak that they are like a woman in labor who does not have the strength to bring forth her child. "It may be that Yahweh will hear [take note of, and punish] the words of the Rabshakeh." Those words were, after all, ridicule of "the living God," who is to be contrasted with the lifeless idols whose devotees the Assyrians have overcome elsewhere.

The struggle now shifts to a confrontation between Yahweh and His mockers. The Assyrians have overreached themselves. For His name's sake Yahweh must intervene and prove that He is living and powerful. In his desperate weakness and loneliness Hezekiah begged for an intercessor to pray for the remnant, for Jerusalem—all that was left of the kingdom of Judah. The response of Isaiah is immediate. The king is not to fear the blasphemous words of Sennacherib's subordinates; on hearing a certain report he would return home and there he would meet a violent death. His mission was to be aborted.

d. Assyrian movements and Sennacherib's letter (19:8–13). At this point Lachish apparently fell to Sennacherib. The struggle there had been fierce. Recent excavations at the site show that the Assyrians threw up a siege ramp against the wall at the southeast corner and that the defenders erected a counter ramp against them inside the wall. After the fall of Lachish (30 miles southwest of Jerusalem), Sennacherib moved a few miles northward against Libnah and closer to Jerusalem, tightening the noose on the capital.

About this time, too, word came that Tirhakah (of the Cushite or Sudanese dynasty that had taken over Egypt), an ally of Hezekiah, was marching north against Sennacherib. Mention of this leader used to throw commentators into confusion because older information implied that he would have been too young (only about nine) to lead a campaign in 701, and that a second Sennacherib invasion must have become involved with him in the 680s. Moreover, Tirhakah was not king at the time. Now it is known that Tirhakah was twenty in 701 when his brother Shebitku summoned him to assume leadership of the campaign into Judah. Tirhakah was the crown prince, but by the time the 2 Kings and Isaiah 36 accounts were penned he had become king.[2]

---

[2] Archer, 294.

Possibly Sennacherib got the idea that Hezekiah would conclude he was "home free" while the Assyrian was off fighting the Egyptians. So he sent a letter to Hezekiah to the effect that he need not expect his god to deliver him from the Assyrians: he would not be any more successful in doing so than the gods of other nations had been. Verses 10–13 cover some of the same ground as the Rabshakeh had gone over earlier.

e. Hezekiah's prayer (19:14–19). Faced with this additional challenge, Hezekiah entered the temple himself to pray. He spread out the letter (written on an animal skin or papyrus) before God and then prayed over it. It was a remarkable prayer, especially because the petitioner did not have the benefit of most of the biblical canon we now enjoy, and because he was a busy political leader. He recognized Yahweh as Israel's God, in covenant relation to her, and the real ruler of Judah. His omnipotent power included sovereignty over all the kingdoms of the earth and His creation of heaven and earth. In talking to God about the defiance of the Assyrians, Hezekiah understood why the Assyrians could feel they were superior to the gods of those lands; they were gods of wood and stone, "the product of someone's craftsmanship" (v. 18), and not gods at all.

Hezekiah appealed to the living God to deliver His people from Sennacherib. The objective of the king's petition was defense of Yahweh's reputation so that the whole world would acknowledge Him. Twice before, champions of Yahweh had made such an appeal: David when faced by Goliath (1 Sam. 17:46) and Elijah when confronted by the prophets of Baal (1 Kings 18:37). With prayer like this, the fortunes of Judah could be expected to change.

f. Yahweh's answer (19:20–34). Previously, Hezekiah had appealed to Isaiah and the prophet responded. This time Hezekiah had gone directly to God and the answer came by way of His prophet. God almost had to answer the king's prayer, for His name's sake; the Assyrians had said, in effect, that He was impotent and no more able to help His people than the gods of other peoples of Western Asia had been. To "toss" or "shake the head" (v. 21) is a typical gesture of derision (cf. Ps. 22:7). God would intervene because they had really "insulted" and "blasphemed" Him (v. 22); this time they had done so directly, but they had also done so indirectly when abusing His people. "The Holy One of Israel" (v. 22) is a particularly Isaianic descriptive of God. Verse 23 refers to Sennacherib's conquest of Lebanon. Digging wells in foreign lands (v. 24) does not appear in Sennacherib's records, but Assyrian accounts do tell of soldiers' digging wells in dry lands. His trampling on the streams of Egypt, perhaps breaking down the banks of irrigation canals, is something that Sennacherib did not do, because he did not reach Egypt; but he defeated Tirhakah and the statement in verse 24 may be accepted as typical Assyrian braggadocio.

In verse 25 Yahweh really takes the wind out of Sennacherib's sails. If he thinks he can trample Yahweh or Yahweh's people underfoot, he should know that Yahweh in His sovereignty has ordained Sennacherib's military successes. Though the subject does not appear in this verse, Isaiah 10:5 even indicates that God used Assyria as a "rod of mine anger" against wayward Israel. Moreover, God raises up and deposes the rulers of the earth at His good pleasure (Dan. 2:21). Verse 26 paints a picture of people under siege, as vulnerable as grass on the rooftops of mud houses or on the thatched roof of stone houses when the hot rays of a summer sun dries it up.

Yahweh in His omniscience knew all about the Assyrian, especially about how he had "raged" against" Him (v. 27). "Because," in direct response to Sennacherib's arrogance and raging, Yahweh would "put my hook in your nose" (as Assyrian monuments portrayed captives being led by cords passed through rings in their noses), in like fashion God would make Sennacherib return home by the way he had come (v. 28).

To Hezekiah God promised a sign, not that He would send Sennacherib away, but that He would restore Judah. Though in the midst of the ravages of war the Hebrews had been unable to plant crops, they would be able to harvest some food that year and the next from seed that had been sown naturally. In the third year there would be a full recovery with a return to the normal cycle of sowing and reaping. If the Assyrians remained in the land from spring to fall of 701, they prevented the harvest of that year and the fall plowing and sowing that would be necessary for the harvest of 700. Therefore, an ordinary agricultural cycle would not return until 699. God's care for the populace during the transitional period would be a sign of His preservation and multiplication of the remnant; they would "take root" and "bear fruit," i.e., achieve a degree of prosperity once more.

Now, finally, in verses 32–34 God gives the specific response to Hezekiah's prayer. Sennacherib would "not enter this city," but that did not mean merely that his attack on it would not be successful. "He will not shoot an arrow at it"; he would not even mount an attack on Jerusalem. In fact, he would not even prepare to attack: "He will not pile up a siege ramp against it." God Himself would save the city "for my sake," i.e., His own reputation (cf. v. 19), and "for the sake of my servant David" (the promise of the Davidic covenant in such passages as 2 Sam. 7 and 1 Kings 11:13).

g. Fulfillment of God's promise (19:35–37). The fulfillment was prompt. "That very night the angel of death struck down 185,000 men in the Assyrian camp." The number seems excessive, and one of the greatest problems in the Old Testament is the transcription of numbers. The Assyrians could and did amass large armies. For example, Shalmaneser III moved across the Euphrates westward with an army of one hundred twenty thousand men in 845.[3] But after the one hundred eighty-five thousand died on this occasion, there was apparently a substantial army left to return to Assyria. If one assumes that the figure is accurate, it might be arrived at by including Assyrian fighting men, camp servants, Judean defectors or impressments into the Assyrian force, and even some captives (many of whom may have become collaborators). The parallel passage in 2 Chronicles 32:21 leaves unspecified the number of men killed. Another explanation is that the Hebrew of 2 Kings 19:35 could be translated "one hundred and eighty and five thousand," i.e., $100 + 80 + 5,000 = 5,180$.

Scripture never discusses such details as how these masses of men were buried or whether further plague was incurred from handling the dead bodies. Sennacherib probably recognized this as a supernatural event, at least as some displeasure of the local gods, and withdrew in disgrace. Naturally, he would

---

[3] Saggs, *The Might That Was Assyria*, 253.

not mention a catastrophe of this magnitude in his records. He merely said of Hezekiah: "He himself I shut up like a caged bird within Jerusalem, his royal city," and then went on to list the booty and tribute collected on the campaign.[4] Sennacherib returned to Nineveh, to be assassinated there almost twenty years later, in 682, by his sons Adrammelech and Sharezer, who escaped to the land of Ararat or Urartu (v. 37). The Assyrian records do not give the names of the assassins but state that one of his sons killed him. They also allude to a civil war after Sennacherib's son Esarhaddon came to power; during the struggle he defeated his enemies and pursued them in the direction of Urartu.

3. Hezekiah's Illness and Recovery (20:1–11)

"In those days" is not one of the indefinite references of time that appears in the Old Testament. Evidently here it connects with the defeat of Sennacherib, for the additional fifteen years of life would have brought his reign to 686, the commonly accepted year of his death. Isaiah the prophet went to Hezekiah with the instruction to "put your house in order," for he was about to die. The "order" might involve making a testament or will, giving one's last instructions, and perhaps also naming a successor. Naming a successor would avoid the kind of strife that occurred during David's last days.

Hezekiah turned "to the wall," evidently for private communion with God and "wept bitterly," protesting his "wholehearted devotion" to Yahweh. Some commentators see this as a rather self-serving prayer and find it to be in contrast to the kind of life Hezekiah had apparently lived before God. They score him for a lack of penitence in his final hours. But one needs to look at the circumstances. In the first place, in Hezekiah's society, such an announcement would likely be taken as a pronouncement of judgment for some failure or heinous sin; he had tried to be faithful. Second, evidently the Assyrian issue had not yet been resolved, because verse 6 puts deliverance from Sennacherib in the future. Hezekiah did not want to give the Assyrians the advantage and to leave his people leaderless at

---

[4]Thomas, 67.

such a crucial time. Third, if putting his house in order involved naming a successor, he was in trouble because his son Manasseh was still too young to be king. Fourth, it was only natural that as a hardworking, dedicated sovereign he wanted to continue living and reigning.

The details of his prayer are not recorded, but the answer is. It was swift in coming: "before Isaiah had left the middle court" or "the middle city," the area between the palace and the temple, God spoke to him. The message to Hezekiah was that he would live for fifteen more years and that he would see the deliverance of Jerusalem from the hand of the Assyrians. This additional period of time would permit the maturation of the crown prince and would give Hezekiah time to pull the kingdom back together after the terrible depredations of the Assyrians.

The instruction to prepare a poultice of figs to be applied to the boil or sore or infection that was life threatening does not imply that the sore was a minor illness that could be cured by a simple folk remedy. This act of healing might be put in the same category as Naaman's dipping in the Jordan for healing from his leprosy. The application of the poultice was in obedience to the instruction of the man of God who had brought two specific commands from God in the last couple of hours or so. In accepting the poultice, the king accepted God's promise of healing, and the poultice as a symbol of God's remediation. In "three days" he was to be well enough to get out of bed and go to worship God in the temple.

But for all his faithfulness to God and strength of personal faith, Hezekiah needed some additional evidence that God really would heal him and that the Assyrian problem would be solved. He asked for a sign, and God through Isaiah granted him one. The sign agreed on concerned the shortening of the shadow on the steps. Evidently Hezekiah lay in a room on an upper story or in an elevated area approached by steps that King Ahaz had built during his reign. As the day would wear on, the shadows cast by the sun would lengthen on the steps. As a sign of God's working, the shadow went back ten steps instead of forward. What happened with the refraction of light, one can only speculate; it is not necessary to conclude that God had to interfere with the movement of the sun in the heavens. The Hebrew seems clearly to refer to "steps" here. There is no support for the idea sometimes broached that the discussion concerned a sundial and that the request was for the sun to go backward ten degrees on the sundial.

4. Embassy from Babylon (20:12–19)

"At this time," in the midst of Sennacherib's attack and Hezekiah's illness, a delegation came from Merodach-baladan of Babylon. The historical situation was this. Merodach-baladan was a Chaldean prince who had been trying to establish his power in Babylon during the days of Tiglath-pileser III, Sargon II, and Sennacherib and had had running battles with all three of them. In 703 Merodach-baladan had organized a Chaldean insurrection in Babylonia, but Sennacherib forced him out of Babylon and set up a puppet king in the city. While Sennacherib was busy with Hezekiah, Merodach-baladan planned another rebellion in Babylon. In 700 Sennacherib was forced to launch another campaign against Merodach-baladan, and the Babylonian fled to Elam and finally passed off the stage of history.

In the wake of Sennacherib's fiasco at Jerusalem, Merodach-baladan sent a delegation to wish him well and presumably to establish some sort of alliance with him. If Hezekiah could be successful on one end of the Assyrian Empire and Merodach-baladan on the other, perhaps there was some hope for both of them. As a long shot, possibly the Assyrian Empire could be broken up. Hezekiah rashly showed the Babylonians all his palace and treasury and armory, perhaps in the spirit that, "This is what was used to stop Sennacherib and this is what would be available in an alliance against him in the future." If that was the case, Hezekiah failed to give God the credit for the victory just achieved, which certainly was not on the basis of Judean resources.

Isaiah reacted with suspicion against foreign alliances and sought to encourage dependence on Yahweh alone. Then he uttered a prophecy of Babylonian victory over Judah and deportation of the Judeans to that land. The prophecy need not be viewed as a judgment on Hezekiah but as a statement of fact. If Hezekiah was proud of what he had in Jerusalem, it would all be carried off to Babylon some day. The kingdom of Judah had previously been warned of judgment for her faithlessness.

Hezekiah's days of reform were only an island in a sea of apostasy. With his son Manasseh the tide of wickedness would rise once more and ultimately would engulf the state. The ministry of good kings served to revitalize the state periodically and to postpone the evil day. As a matter of fact, Judah was destined to limp along for another century until judgment fell. Hezekiah's response to Isaiah's prediction of calamity is unexpected. The pious king did, after all, have feet of clay. He seemed almost to shrug it off with the thought: "Will there not be peace and security in my lifetime?" (v. 19, NIV).

5. Summary of Hezekiah's Reign and Death (20:20–21)

After Sennacherib returned to Assyria, Hezekiah was evidently very prosperous and very successful in his administration (2 Chron. 32:27–29), no doubt doing much to rehabilitate the state. One achievement for which he was especially known was his water system, by which he brought water into the city (v. 20). This was a tunnel about 1780 feet long connecting the Gihon Spring on the east side of the city to the pool of Siloam within the walls at the south end of the city. Then he covered the spring so that invaders would not discover it and cut off the city's water supply. This tunnel, still to be seen in Jerusalem, was dug from both ends and is a remarkable feat of engineering. The inscription describing construction has been removed from the tunnel and is now in the Archaeological Museum in Istanbul. When Hezekiah died, his son Manasseh succeeded him as king.

B. The Apostasy of Manasseh and Amon (21:1–26)

1. Manasseh (21:1–18)

After the elevated spiritual tone of Hezekiah's reign, it seems almost inconceivable that Manasseh could turn his back on all that his father had stood for. Then after Amon's continued apostasy there was major reform again under Josiah. Some scholars believe that the religious direction of the state was not so much the result of royal persuasion as the victory of factions in Judea—the one wishing to purify the cult and supported by the prophets, and the other syncretistic in approach and seeking reconciliation with the Assyrians and the priests of foreign gods. Moreover, apostasy seemed to come when the Assyrians were strong, and reform occurred when the Assyrians were in no position to dominate Judean internal affairs.

It is interesting to observe that as a result of divine intervention and then Assyrian preoccupation elsewhere, Hezekiah was able to reform the state. During Hezekiah's latter days Sennacherib was involved with Babylonian revolt and finally destroyed Babylon to cow her citizens into submission. Then Esarhaddon (680–669) and Ashurbanipal (668–627) sought to dominate the Palestinian corridor while they engaged in the conquest of Egypt. That activity coincided with the reign of Manasseh and its pagan orientation. When Assyria lost control in the West after 625, Josiah was free to launch his major reforms without Assyrian interference. These correlations between Hebrew apostasy and Assyrian control in Palestine and Syria point up the importance of looking at the international scene when evaluating Judean internal affairs.

Throughout Manasseh's long and apparently rather prosperous reign, he seems to have been under the domination of Assyria and to have paid regular tribute to her. Assyrian records attest to that fact, but they do not mention Manasseh's enforced visit to the Assyrian king at Babylon as noted in 2 Chronicles 33:10–13.

The sacred historian chose to record in 2 Kings only an indictment of the apostasy of Manasseh, a religious policy that appears to reflect his submission to Assyria. Manasseh began to reign at twelve years of age, probably being made coregent with Hezekiah for about ten years. His total reign of fifty-five years would have then extended from 696 to 642, with a coregency with his father from 696 to 686. Presumably his apostasy did not begin as long as his father lived. Then perhaps the pro-Assyrian party got control of him, and he became the culmination of all rebellion against Yahweh.

Manasseh followed the "disgusting actions of the nations" whom God had driven out of Canaan (v. 2) as follows: (1) rebuilt the high places; (2) erected altars to Baal, as Ahab had done in Israel; (3) instituted worship of the astral deities and built altars for them in the temple; (4) sacrificed his son to the Ammonite god Molech in the Valley of the Hinnom (2 Chron. 33:6); (5) practiced soothsaying and divination, dealt with spiritistic mediums, and engaged in wizardry.

Not only did Manasseh involve himself in all these evil practices, but he also "beguiled" or "seduced" his people so they did greater evil than did the former inhabitants of Canaan before Israel entered (vv. 9, 11). Though none of the writing prophets ministered during Manasseh's reign (with the possible exception of Nahum), his sins were so grievous that later prophets remembered them and pronounced judgment because of them (vv. 10, 12). The news of Judah's disaster would shock all who heard it (v. 12).

Stretching the measuring line and plumb line over Jerusalem refers to the standards by which Judah would be judged, and scouring Jerusalem as one scours a dish (v. 13) applies not only to the totality of judgment but also to the cleansing of corruption by means of this violent act of judgment. The writer wants to leave no doubt of the completeness of judgment, so he piles one figure on top of another: stretching of the measuring line and plumb line, scouring of a dish, forsaking the remnant, and giving Judah over to looting and plundering. And to all the idolatrous sins of Manasseh is added widespread murder that the king himself either initiated or sanctioned (v. 16). "Innocent blood" would include his son and, according to tradition, the prophet Isaiah. This passage leaves nothing unsaid in the description of Manasseh's public sins and the condemnation of the king and his people for their gross iniquity.

Verse 18 states that Manasseh was buried "in the garden of his palace, in the garden of Uzza." This change of burial place is now thought to have resulted from lack of further room in the royal necropolis. In support of that conclusion is the note in 2 Chronicles 32:33 that Hezekiah was buried "in the ascent [or the upper part] of the sepulchers of the sons of David." Recent discoveries of magnificent tombs on the grounds of the École Biblique et Archéologique Francaise, a few hundred yards north of Jerusalem's Old City, have been identified by some as the burial place of Judah's last kings, beginning with Manasseh.[5] Discussion with one of the excavators leads to the conclusion that while these were indeed royal tombs, they were burial places of minor members of the royal family. The kings themselves probably were interred on the southwestern hill, to which the city had now expanded.

2. Amon (21:19–26)

Judging from the sacred historian's comments, Amon was a carbon copy of his father, continuing in all his evil ways. Coming to the throne at twenty-two years of age, he lasted only two years as king of Judah (642–640) until a palace coup was successful in unseating and assassinating him. Why they did so we are left to guess. Perhaps an anti-Assyrian/pro-Egyptian faction sought to realign the policies of state. Egypt was reviving and Ashurbanipal was busy with an Elamite revolt in 642 to 639 B.C.; perhaps some thought Assyria would be too busy to interfere in Judean affairs. If an anti-Assyrian element was responsible for Amon's death, Assyria had nothing to fear, because the conspirators were promptly executed.

Amon's eight-year-old son Josiah was then elevated to the throne. An anti-Assyrian or at least priestly element seems to have dominated the regency during the minority of Josiah, and public policy was destined to take a very different turn under the new king. Though it is tempting to look for political reasons for the assassination of Amon, those responsible for his death may simply have grown sick of his conduct, assuming that he shed innocent blood as his father had.

Two minor notes about Amon hold some interest. First, his mother was from Jotbah, located about twenty miles north of Eilat on the Gulf of Aqaba, and from her family connections she is thought to have been Arabian. Second, Amon was buried in the same place as his father. Perhaps a new burial ground for the kings was being established, assuming that the old one was full (see comment on burial of Manasseh).

---

[5] Hershel Shanks, "Have the Tombs of the Kings of Judah Been Found?," *Biblical Archaeology Review*, July/August 1987, 54–56.

C. Reform Under Josiah (22:1–23:30)

Of all the Judean kings, only Josiah and his great-grand-father Hezekiah received unqualified divine approval. Coming to the throne at age eight (640 B.C.), Josiah began his own spiritual odyssey at the age of sixteen (2 Chron. 34:3); and on reaching his majority in his twelfth year, he launched his reform of the land (2 Chron. 34:3). This would have been about the time of Ashurbanipal's death (627). The Assyrian Empire was now evidently cracking up. Egypt had become independent in 655 B.C. and was making some inroads into Palestine. Nabopolassar won independence for Babylon in 626 B.C. and allied himself with the Medes. Cimmerians and Scythians encroached on Assyria's northern borders.

Under the circumstances, Josiah was free to take an independent political and religious role, and an anti-Assyrian faction (if such were alive) was free to strike for Hebrew monotheism. This is not to imply, however, that the gods Josiah revolted against were Assyrian deities, because clearly what Manasseh and Amon had introduced were Canaanite religious practices and conditions that had existed in the land when the Hebrews invaded. Lifting of Assyrian control in Samaria permitted Josiah to extend his reform not only to Judah and Jerusalem but also throughout the territory of the former Northern Kingdom (2 Chron. 34:6–7).

1. Repair of the Temple (22:1–7)

In his eighteenth year (622–21) Josiah began to repair the temple (cf. 2 Chron. 34:8), but that probably did not mean he began to attend to the needs of the temple at that time. When he began his other reforms, the temple evidently needed a lot of work. It had fallen into disrepair and had suffered the desecration of Manasseh, who had erected pagan altars there. Presumably about his twelfth year or shortly thereafter the king issued orders for collection of funds for major renovation purposes (2 Kings 22:4). Now enough was in hand to start the work.

Josiah sent Shaphan the "scribe" or "secretary," a kind of secretary of state, and other officials (2 Chron. 34:8) to begin the work. Shaphan was a man of some distinction. One son, Ahikam, helped Jeremiah the prophet; another son, Gemariah, was a noble in Jerusalem in the days of King Jehoiakim (Jer. 36:12, 25). A grandson, Gedaliah, served as governor of Judah under the Babylonians after the fall of Jerusalem (Jer. 40:5–41:10). The procedure for repair was about the same as that followed by Joash (2 Kings 12); in fact the king may have simply copied the arrangements from court annals that the sacred historian also used in the composition of 1 Kings. As before, the supervisors proved trustworthy and no accounting of funds was required once they were distributed to the workmen (v. 7; cf. 2 Kings 12:15).

2. Recovery of the Law (22:8–20)

As the temple repairs began, Hilkiah the high priest reported finding there "the Book of the Law." What he found would, of course, have been a scroll with text written in columns, not a book in the modern sense. The nature of the contents has been endlessly debated. The old higher critical view held that the scroll contained part of the book of Deuteronomy, that it had been recently written, and that it was reported "found" to give it prestige. Of course, that view did not accept Mosaic authorship of the Pentateuch. Scholars have modified this position in many ways.

The traditional conservative view on the composition of Deuteronomy argues that God judged Israel and Judah up to that time on the basis of a standard set forth in Mosaic/ Deuteronomic terms. The conduct expected of a king and people was not something new concocted in 621 B.C. Moreover, it is not fair, either, to argue that the book was used to institute and legitimize the reforms of Josiah. Those reforms and the preparation for repair of the temple had begun years earlier; additional sanitizing of the court and society would result from a reading of the law, however.

What the Book of the Law contained, even from a conservative standpoint, is not clear. The whole Pentateuch would have been tremendously bulky in a single roll, but it is possible that it was all there. More likely, only a portion of the first five books of the Old Testament was hidden in this way. Judging from the reforms that followed, at least most of Deuteronomy must have been written on the roll. Deuteronomy 31:9, 24–26 required "this book of the law" to be kept next to the ark of the covenant.

After Shaphan received the book, he read it himself (or part of it, v. 8) and then read it aloud to the king (v. 10), who tore his clothes as a gesture of repentance and distress. Then he decided he should get an evaluation from God about how Judah stood before Him at the moment in the light of the disobedience of "our fathers." "Inquire of Yahweh for me" is a technical expression for seeking a divine oracle. Josiah's concern for "the people" and "the whole of Judah" (v. 13) compares favorably with Hezekiah's apparent self-centeredness near the end of his reign. Josiah sent his whole inner circle of advisors on this important errand: Ahikam (father of Gedaliah, later the Babylonian governor of Judah, 25:22; also aide to Jeremiah who saved him from death, Jer. 26:24), Achbor (whose son Elnathan figured in Jeremiah's arrest, trial, and release, Jer. 26:22), Shaphan, Asaiah (an important senior civil servant), and Hilkiah the priest.

The delegation went to the prophetess Huldah, who was at the center of things in Jerusalem. The contemporary prophets Jeremiah and Zephaniah are not mentioned nor even involved in the reform; apparently they were not in Jerusalem at the time. Critics who doubt other aspects of the Kings narrative tend to accept this as an accurate account because it is so unusual to have a woman speak for Yahweh; this is not the kind of narrative that is likely to have been made up. Her husband was "keeper of the wardrobe," whether at the palace or temple is not stated. Perhaps the latter is to be preferred because Hilkiah the priest seems to have headed this delegation, and the only other time in the book when such an official is mentioned occurs in connection with the temple of Baal (2 Kings 10:22). Huldah lived in the "second quarter" of Jerusalem, generally accepted as the northern extension of the city, which probably developed as a residential area for palace and temple personnel. At the time of Josiah it would have sprawled out westward over the upper Tyropoeon Valley.

Huldah spoke in the style of the classic prophetic tradition and sent a double message: judgment of Jerusalem and a personal promise addressed to Josiah. Judgment is inevitable, she said, and is fast approaching. The catalog of apostasy (v. 17) is like many other summaries, but because of the quality of Josiah's public policies, and especially because of his penitence in the light of God's judgment, "I have listened" (v. 19), said Yahweh. The promise that Josiah would be buried "in peace" (v. 20) usually means that one would die a natural death, but Josiah died fighting the Egyptians. The promise must be understood in a relative sense; when qualified by the last sentence, it means to say that he will be spared the agony of the nation's destruction.

3. Renewal of the Covenant (23:1–3)

Next the king took center stage in the narrative. He called together "the elders," the old family heads (v. 1), the "priests and prophets," and "all the people" (v. 2). "All the people" should not be taken too literally, for they were present in their representatives. Certainly the masses of the population of Jerusalem and Judah did not assemble, nor were they invited. There was not room for more than a few hundred in the area where the gathering occurred. Josiah "read" personally or had a scribe read in his name, with the king standing next to him. The king assumed the role filled earlier by Moses (Exod. 24:3–8) and Joshua (Josh. 8:34–35). He read all the words of the "book of the covenant," not the whole Pentateuch or the whole book of Deuteronomy, but probably the sections promising blessing for obedience and threatening punishment for disobedience (Deut. 27:15–28:68).

The king stood "by the column" in the temple, signifying his authority (cf. 11:14), and made a pact that involved a renewal of the Sinai covenant. The emphasis of the covenant centered on accepting the standards ("confirming the words," v. 3) given in the Law. First Josiah pledged himself to carry out the words of the covenant (not just mechanically but "with all his heart"), then all the people "gave their allegiance" to it. It was eminently fitting to renew this relationship to Yahweh in a time of religious revival.

4. Reform of the Nation (23:4–28)

Then Josiah launched a thoroughgoing cleanup campaign; the mere listing of his activities gives some inkling of how depraved the religious practices of the nation had become, and therefore, the justification of Yahweh in exercising judgment.

Purification started in the temple. The king ordered that articles and vessels used for the worship of Baal and Astarte and the sun, moon, and stars be carted out to the "field of the Kidron," probably to the broader part of the valley just northeast of Jerusalem, and burned there. The spectacle was as much symbolic as physical because stone and metal will not burn. They had to be pulverized after passing through the fire. Verse 4 indicates that cultic vessels dedicated to pagan deities stood in the temple itself. Josiah commanded that the ash and debris of this great bonfire be hauled off to Bethel, an appropriate dumping ground because of its apostate religious connections. Purification of the temple also involved removal of the Asherah pole, destruction of quarters for cult prostitutes (probably both male and female), and places where women wove ritual vestments for Asherah worship (v. 7).

Next Josiah deposed the heathen priests of the high places of Judah who had been appointed by Manasseh and Amon ("kings of Judah"). The high places themselves were not necessarily pagan; sacrifices to Yahweh had been offered in many of them. But at these worship centers priests offered sacrifices to Baal, the sun, moon, and constellations. Possibly in an effort to prevent any future irregularities at the high places, he even destroyed those where pagan worship was not taking place and brought the priests from them into Jerusalem, where they did not minister at the temple but enjoyed public support (vv. 8–9).

Continuing his cleanup in the environs of Jerusalem, Josiah desecrated or destroyed Topheth, probably a fireplace in the valley of the Hinnon to the south of Jerusalem, where children were burned as sacrifices to Molech (v. 10). From the entrance to the temple he took statues or figurines of horses dedicated to the worship of the sun and the chariots of the sun and destroyed them all (v. 11). Ahaz apparently had built an upper room on

one of the buildings at the entrance to the temple and on its roof
had erected altars for worship of the sun or moon or stars. These
Josiah pulled down, along with altars Manasseh had constructed
in the temple courts, and smashed them all and dumped the
rubble in the Kidron Valley. Next, Josiah went after high places
to Ashtoreth, Chemosh, and Molech that had been operating on
the southern end of the Mount of Olives (above the modern
village of Silwan) since the days of Solomon. He smashed any
cultic paraphernalia there, and then desecrated the sites thoroughly by scattering human bones over them.

Having launched a radical reform in Judah, Josiah now
turned his attention to territory of the former kingdom of Israel.
It was possible for him to do that because Assyria had lost all
ability to control the area. Evidently he confined his activities to
the province of Samaria; Galilee does not figure in the narrative
at all. First he went to Bethel, a center of apostasy from
Jeroboam I on, about ten miles north of Jerusalem. There he did
all he could to wreak divine vengeance on the site. He opened
the tombs of priests buried near the high place and burned their
bones on the altar (cf. 1 Kings 13:2–3). But he spared the tomb
of the man of God from Judah who was buried there (vv. 17, 18;
1 Kings 13:30–32). Then he demolished the altar, burned what
was combustible, and pulverized anything that did not burn.
After destroying the high place at Bethel, Josiah moved against
the other high places of Samaria, slaughtering the priests on
their altars and burning human bones on them to desecrate
them. Those killed would not have been Levites, or probably
not even Hebrews, but pagan individuals who had come into
office during the period of Assyrian occupation and the influx of
non-Hebrew peoples.

As a climax of Josiah's reformation, he gave orders for
celebration of the Passover. It took place during the same
eighteenth year of the king's reign (621) when the book of the
Law was found (v. 23). Not since the days of the Judges (since
the days of Samuel, 2 Chron. 35:18) had any Passover been kept
so strictly by everyone, according to all the Mosaic laws; this is
the real meaning of verse 22. Other Passovers had been held,
but had not been so properly observed. For example, the great
Passover of Hezekiah had been moved from the legal time of the

first month to the second month, and many participated without proper purification required by law (2 Chron. 30:2–3, 17–20). What especially distinguished this Passover was that "all Judah and Israel" took part in it (2 Chron. 35:18), and that it was kept in strict accordance with the Mosaic law. An elaborate description of Josiah's keeping of the Passover appears in 2 Chronicles 35:1–19.

Not only did Josiah go after formal and official practices repugnant to Yahweh, but he also moved against informal religious practitioners ("mediums and wizards") and against "teraphim" (household gods used in divination and in imitative magic to promote fertility) and "fetishes."

For all his efforts, Josiah won the height of praise. He tallied well with the Deuteronomistic expectation (Deut. 6:5), loving Yahweh with all his heart, soul, and strength. And he won the assessment that there was no king like him before or after his days (v. 25). He was truly the ideal king. Since the same praise was heaped on Hezekiah (2 Kings 18:5), some evaluation must be made of the statement that before him there was no king like him. In his public policy he forcefully observed Mosaic regulations. He did not seem to be self-centered about the future tragedy of Judah as Hezekiah had been. Nor did he commit a major indiscretion as Hezekiah did in the reception of Merodach-baladan's delegation. There is not even a record of great personal sin as occurred in David's life. His record is quite clean.

But in spite of all the good that can be said about Josiah, God would not reverse the former pronouncements about the fate of Jerusalem and Judah (vv. 26–27). Josiah might postpone the exile but not avoid it. As is clear from contemporary preaching of Jeremiah and the persecution he suffered and from subsequent conduct of the kings and their subjects, Josiah had not been able to effect a thorough conversion of the people. The first ten chapters of Jeremiah especially contain a summary of the prophet's labors in the reign of Josiah, and demonstrate a deep inward apostasy of the people during and after Josiah's reform. The contemporary reproaches of Zephaniah provide further evidence of the basic sinfulness of Judah. The corrupting influences of Manasseh's half century of rule had so thoroughly

fixed the general tendency to apostasy that in spite of all that
Josiah did, there was no real hope of reversal.

5. Death of the Reformer (23:29–30)

Palestine as a land bridge between Europe, Asia, and Africa
periodically suffered as armies of neighboring states charged
across her landscape. The small state of Judah now found herself
in the path of one of those interminable struggles. Nineveh had
fallen in 612 and Assyrian forces held out precariously in the
western part of the country. Pharaoh Necho, son of Psammeti-
chus I (Psamtik), founder of the Twenty-sixth Dynasty, moved
north along the coastal plane to link up with the remnants of the
Assyrian army in 609 B.C. Evidently Josiah wanted to stop any
aid from reaching Judah's old enemy Assyria, and hoped that if
Assyria were left without support she would collapse. Necho
tried to assure Josiah that he had no quarrel with him and that
he merely wanted to move northward (see 2 Chron. 35:20–21);
presumably he did not even intend to march through territory
under Judean control. But Josiah would not listen, and met
Necho in battle at Megiddo, where he sustained a mortal wound
in the conflict and died in Jerusalem shortly thereafter.

After the death of his father, Josiah, Jehoahaz ascended the
throne of Judah. Three months later Necho came back south,
dethroned Jehoahaz, made Josiah's son, Eliakim, king and
changed his name to Jehoiakim. If Necho had no previous plan
to control all of Syria, he certainly did after Josiah's death and
after the demise of Assyrian power. He enjoyed some domination of the area until his forces met Nebuchadnezzar at
Carchemish in May or June of 605. Then Necho's Syrian empire
crumpled like a house of cards, and Babylon established
suzerainty over the region. Jehoiakim, a vassal of Necho,
submitted voluntarily to Nebuchadnezzar, and some Jews
(including Daniel the prophet) were taken as captives or
hostages to Babylon.

D. The Last Days of Judah (23:31–25:30)

1. Jehoahaz and Egyptian Interference (23:31–35)

Jehoahaz, king at twenty-three, was the second son of
Josiah; his brother who succeeded him was two years older

(v. 36). Probably the law of primogeniture was bypassed because of Jehoahaz's known anti-Egyptian views. That "he did
evil" (v. 32) is striking, in view of the exemplary conduct of his
father. Even worse, his brother fell under the same condemnation (v. 37). Unfortunately, the good king Hezekiah also had an
evil son, Manasseh. The sad truth is that there is no guarantee
that the children of great stalwarts of the faith will follow in their
paths. Perhaps Satan works harder on the families of those with
a strong spiritual commitment. And maybe sometimes we, with
Josiah, so rigorously enforce an external conformity to right
conduct that it turns off the younger generation. In any case, it is
clear that Josiah's God-honoring reign was only an interlude in
the downward slide of Judah.

After Necho's abortive attempt to aid Assyria, he concentrated on greater control of Syria and Palestine for Egypt.
Evidently he believed Jehoahaz to be too unsupportive of
Egyptian policies in Judah and summoned him to his headquarters at Riblah, about twenty miles south of Hama in the Beqa',
and made him captive there. Subsequently he sent him to
Egypt, where he eventually died, presumably from natural
causes. Then Necho elevated Josiah's elder son to the throne,
possibly believing he would be a more pliant puppet of Egypt.
The reason for the minor change of his name of Eliakim
(meaning "God establishes") to Jehoiakim ("Yahweh establishes") is not clear; perhaps it placated some elements in
Judah. Necho had demanded tribute from Jehoahaz, which
Jehoiakim now raised by a general assessment on the people of
Judah. The verb "levied" or "exacted" (v. 35) implies the use of
excessive force.

2. Jehoiakim and Nebuchadnezzar's Invasion
(23:36–24:7)

As noted, Jehoiakim was the eldest son of Josiah and his
policies, like those of his brother Jehoahaz, deviated markedly
from his father's. As noted, too, Necho lost his Syrian empire to
the Babylonians after Nebuchadnezzar defeated him at Carchemish in 605. Evidently Nebuchadnezzar did not have to fight
much to extend his control over Syria and Palestine all the way
to the border of Egypt. Though Nebuchadnezzar did not enter

the highlands of Judah, Jehoiakim submitted to him voluntarily and some Jews, including the prophet Daniel, were taken to Babylon at this time.[6] In the midst of this campaign, on August 15/16, 605 B.C., Nabopolassar died in Babylon. Following a speedy notification sent to his son Nebuchadnezzar and an equally speedy return of Nebuchadnezzar to Babylon, the new king arrived in the city September 6/7 and immediately took the throne. After some successful campaigns in Syria and Palestine in subsequent years, in 601 he attacked Egypt and sustained such heavy losses that his imperialistic designs received a severe setback. Jehoiakim seems to have interpreted the situation as an opportunity to strike for independence, for he "rebelled" against Nebuchadnezzar (2 Kings 24:1). Again Judah entertained the elusive hope that it could count on Egyptian help against a powerful force from the north.

Unable to come in person with a Babylonian army, Nebuchadnezzar evidently sent "raiding bands," lightly armed mercenaries, from east of the Jordan (Syrians, Moabites, and Ammonites) to engage in guerrilla activities and weaken the state (v. 2). The historian viewed Yahweh as being behind this effort that was an initial stage of fulfillment of the prophecy of judgment against Judah. Conditions in the kingdom had now reached the point of no return. Jehoiakim ruled for eleven years (609–598) and apparently died in December, 598, about the time Nebuchadnezzar finally sent an army to deal with rebellious Judah. One manuscript of verse 5 states that he was buried in the garden of Uzza, where Manasseh and Amon had also been buried. Second Chronicles 36:6 states that Nebuchadnezzar bound him in shackles to take him to Babylon, but it does not say he actually took him there. To complicate matters, Jeremiah said Jehoiakim did not receive a royal burial (Jer. 22:19). It is impossible at the moment to reconcile these three divergent statements. One possibility is that some partisans of Nebuchadnezzar had captured the king and planned to send him to Babylon but that he was wounded in the attack, which succeeded in putting him in fetters, and that he died in Jerusalem. The brevity of both the Babylonian and Hebrew records of the

---

[6]Wiseman, 26.

period precludes an exact reconciliation. Verse 7 makes it clear that although both Babylon and Egypt had suffered heavy losses in the battle of 601, Egypt had not been able to recoup its losses as Babylon had, and therefore was forced to concede control of Syria and Palestine to Nebuchadnezzar as the Babylonians advanced in 598.

3. Jehoiachin's Reign and Captivity (24:8–16)

When Jehoiakim died, his eighteen-year-old son Jehoiachin came to the throne and continued the evil policies of his father. After Josiah, nothing good could be said for the kings of Judah. While Jehoiachin was trying to consolidate his power in Jerusalem, Babylonian forces were on the way. They must have begun the siege of the city in January of 597, and apparently it did not last much over two months. Jerusalem fell to the Babylonians on the second of Adar, March 15/16, 597 B.C.[7] Evidently the siege began at the hands of the advance guard and concluded after Nebuchadnezzar himself arrived (v. 11). Assyrian and Babylonian sieges were slow torture for an invested city. Since this was the winter season there would have been enough water, but food would have grown increasingly scarce— especially for a population greatly swollen by refugees from the surrounding countryside. Some have attributed the remarkably lenient treatment of the king and his officials to the quick surrender.

Then the Babylonians helped themselves to the spoils of war, thoroughly looting the treasuries of temple and palace, in fulfillment of the prophecy of 2 Kings 20:16. Probably not everything was taken, because Nebuchadnezzar provided for continuation of the religious, economic, and political life of Judah after the first deportation. Therefore Jeremiah 27:19–22 need not be thought of as contradictory when it speaks of furnishings still remaining in the temple during the reign of Zedekiah. Of course, what Jeremiah referred to was largely made of bronze rather than of gold or silver.

The captives deported included the king, his mother, wives, officials, the notables of the land, craftsmen and metal workers,

---

[7]Wiseman, 33.

the 7,000 in the standing army left within the city, and Ezekiel (Ezek. 1:1–3). Some have found a disagreement between the 10,000 of verse 14 and the 7,000 fighting men plus 1,000 craftsmen in verse 16, but it is not necessary to reach such a conclusion. Probably the total was 10,000 and that included 7,000 in the army, 1,000 craftsmen, and 2,000 others (officials, notables, etc.). The total of 3,023 taken in the first captivity as listed in Jeremiah 52:28 might refer to the civilian population of Jerusalem; the army of 7,000 would have come from all Judah and would have been only temporarily in the city. In any case, only the poorest of the land were left (v. 14); all those capable of mounting an effective rebellion and running a viable war effort were carried off.

4. Zedekiah and the Destruction of Jerusalem (24:17–25:21)

Nebuchadnezzar made Mattaniah (subsequently known as Zedekiah), the full brother of Jehoahaz and uncle of Jehoiachin, king on the condition that he would keep the kingdom for him and make no alliance with the Egyptians.[8] Zedekiah, the last king of Judah, reigned for eleven years (597–586) and was classified as an evil king, like Jehoiakim, probably denoting that he also refused to heed the prophetic word. The reason for Judah's troubles in the days of Zedekiah was "Yahweh's anger" with the nation for her apostasy. Therefore he "cast them out of his presence," i.e., out of the land and from the vicinity of the temple, where He especially chose to dwell. From what little there is about Zedekiah in Scripture, he appears to have been a weak and vacillating figure, easily swayed by circumstances (see, e.g., Jer. 27–30).

The sacred historian skipped over the events of Zedekiah's reign down to his ninth year and the rebellion against Nebuchadnezzar. Actually, he had entertained such thoughts before. In his fourth year (595/4) he took part in a conspiratorial movement, and a number of envoys from other countries came to Jerusalem to confer with him (Jer. 27:3). At that time Zedekiah made a visit to Babylon to allay Babylonian suspicions

---

[8]Josephus, *Antiquities*, X.7.1.

(Jer. 51:59). All during his reign the pro-Egyptian faction pressured him to rebel against Babylon, and Jeremiah repeatedly urged him to knuckle under to Babylon (Jer. 21:1–10; 34:1–3; 37:6–10; 38:17–23).

Finally, in his ninth year, Zedekiah decided to rebel, and the inevitable happened: Nebuchadnezzar prepared to attack. The assertion that "Nebuchadnezzar . . . advanced against Jerusalem" (25:1) when he remained at his headquarters at Riblah (v. 6), and his officers conducted the siege (Jer. 38:17), is not a mistake. He masterminded the campaign and his army represented his power and will, and he was therefore present in a very real sense in the persons of his deputies. The beginning of the siege in the ninth year and tenth day of the tenth month of Zedekiah's reign is to be equated with January 15, 588 B.C., according to Thiele.[9] And it continued until the eleventh year, the fourth month, and the ninth day, or July 18, 586.[10] The destruction of the city began a month later, on August 14 (the seventh day of the fifth month, v. 8). There was a temporary lifting of the siege, probably at about the halfway point, when Pharaoh Hophra of Egypt (588–570) invaded Palestine with his army and sent his fleet against Phoenicia (cf. Jer. 37:5–11; Ezek. 17:15–17).

Assyrian and Babylonian sieges of ancient cities were terrifying experiences. They did not merely surround a city and cut off its supplies, but they built siege ramps around it (v. 1). On these they deployed battering rams for breaching the walls, and constructed platforms higher than the city walls in order to rain down arrows and other missiles on the defenders. In the case of Judah they were also busy reducing all the fortified towns (e.g., Lachish and Azekah), as archaeological discoveries indicate, and engaging in psychological warfare to encourage defections. That the latter effort was successful is clear from Jeremiah 38:19, where Zedekiah expressed a fear to surrender because he thought the Babylonians might turn him over to these defectors to make sport of him as they wished. Of course, the real horror of the siege was the "famine" (v. 3) and the

[9] Thiele, *Mysterious Numbers*, 190.
[10] Ibid.

lengths to which people went to get food. As a result of Hezekiah's efforts, the city had an adequate supply of water.

Finally on July 18, 586 the food supplies gave out completely and about the same time the Babylonians breached the wall (vv. 3–4). Probably they broke through the wall on the north of the city where access was easiest. The king and a body of troops fled at night through a narrow passage at the southeast end of the city into the Hinnom Valley and out to Jericho. Presumably this was possible because the Babylonians were concentrated at the north and west of the city; the precipitous slopes on the east and south would have been hard to attack and scaling the walls there would have resulted in unnecessary loss of life. Perhaps the Judeans hoped to get across the Jordan to Moab and Ammon, who had also been involved in the revolt against Babylon (Jer. 27:4). The Babylonians caught up with the refugees on the "plains of Jericho," probably the next day. This area, east of Jericho, offered little or no cover to troops trying to cross it. The Judeans deserted their king in panic and scattered to the winds.

Nothing is said about whether the Babylonians tried to round them up. The Babylonians were after Zedekiah, and they hauled him off to Riblah in northern Syria to face Nebuchadnezzar. The Babylonian king "passed sentence on him" (v. 6), presumably for breaking his covenant of vassalage or treaty obligations and meted out harsh punishment. Nebuchadnezzar's men "butchered" Zedekiah's sons before his eyes and then blinded him to render him powerless and sent him off to Babylon in chains. At thirty-two he had nothing to look forward to but a dark and lonely life in exile.

About a month after the fall of Jerusalem, on August 14, "Nebuzaradan, commander of the guard," came to take charge of liquidating the Judean state and reorganizing government there. "Commander of the guard" is only one possible translation of the Hebrew, but seems to be the best one in this context. What appears in verses 9–12 must be considered a general summary, with verses 13–16 as elaboration. The intent of verse 9 is clear: destruction of every important structure in the city: the temple, palace, and houses of the well-to-do. But the Hebrew is unclear in the latter part of the verse and may mean either important or

"notable buildings" or "houses of the notables." Verse 10
concerns the destruction of protective walls so the inhabitants
could not again stage an effective rebellion against Babylon.
Apparently the destruction was most complete on the east
where stones could be thrown down the slope toward the
Kidron Valley. When Nehemiah rebuilt the walls in 444 B.C., he
constructed a whole new section on the east but had only to
repair the walls elsewhere. Verse 11 alludes to the depopulation
of the city and deportation of its inhabitants, of the defectors to
the enemy, and the upper classes (craftsmen and managerial
types) from the countryside. Some of the lower classes, including farmers and vinedressers, were to remain behind to continue
some form of agricultural life in the land.

Verses 13–17 make clear what the reader of verse 9 must
already imagine. Conquerors do not destroy buildings before
thoroughly looting them. Further comment on items removed
from the palace of the king or houses of the wealthy is
unnecessary, but there had been so much prophecy about
destruction of the temple, and there was so much there, that it
comes in for further treatment. Most of the really valuable things
probably had been carted off to Babylon when Nebuchadnezzar
took the city in 597. No doubt a few gold and silver objects had
been replaced since then (v. 15), but the focus of attention now
is on the bronze—tons of it—that was broken up into manage-
able pieces and taken to Babylon.

Finally Nebuzaradan dealt with a group of people who did
not fit into any of his other categories of deportees or people to
be left behind: leaders of state and ringleaders of the rebellion
against Babylon (vv. 18–21). These included Seraiah, the head
priest; Zephaniah, the deputy priest and the one who was
Zedekiah's agent against Jeremiah (Jer. 21:1; 29:25, etc.); and
three members of the priestly hierarchy. After taking these
religious leaders, he turned his attention to those who held civil
and military posts. First, there was a man who might be
classified as minister of the army; then five members of the
king's privy council; next, the one in charge of the militia (with
special duties in connection with the siege); and finally, sixty of
his petty officers—a total of seventy-two. These were all
believed to be expendable; and after they were paraded before

Nebuchadnezzar at Riblah, they were executed. "Judah went into captivity" (v. 21); the temple had been destroyed and the ruling elite removed by execution or deportation.

5. Gedaliah, the Puppet Governor (25:22–26)

It is clear, though, that some form of life and administration continued after the fall of Jerusalem. The new masters attempted to set up a new government of sorts and appointed Gedaliah governor over the remaining populace, but the physical boundaries of his province are not clear. Gedaliah came from a noble family, and his father Ahikam (2 Kings 22:12) had supported Jeremiah's policy (Jer. 26:24). He was associated with the Jerusalem establishment and the pro-Babylonian group in Jerusalem.

Gedaliah set up his administration at Mizpah, about nine miles north of Jerusalem and not far from Bethel. There some army officers and their men "in the open country" (Jer. 40:7) came to him. Clearly there were bands of troops wandering around the countryside after the collapse of the Judean state. Gedaliah apparently sought to demobilize these troops and return them to a productive way of life once more. He reassured them that they need not fear the Babylonians, who would not oppress them if they settled down and concentrated on their farming. The Babylonians were not interested in complete devastation of the land.

But Ishmael, son of Nethaniah and of royal blood, was perhaps personally ambitious and also anti-Babylonian. Sometime in October, hardly two months after Gedaliah's appointment, Ishmael and his band killed Gedaliah, his Judean administrative assistants, and Babylonian attachés. Johanan, son of Kareah, defeated Ishmael soon thereafter and rescued the large number of captives or hostages he had taken. Subsequently, a band of Judeans, fearful of Babylonian reprisal against them because of Gedaliah's murder, determined to flee to Egypt, in spite of Jeremiah's assurances that they would come to no harm if they remained in the land. These emigrants took Jeremiah with them. A fuller account of all these proceedings appears in Jeremiah 40:7–43:7.

6. Epilogue: Release of Jehoiachin (25:27–30)

After all the terrible tragedy of previous paragraphs, the last paragraph of the book ends on a note of hope. Yahweh had established the Davidic dynasty and protected it even in Babylon. As is now known from tablets found near the Ishtar Gate in Babylon and dating 595–770 (during the reign of Nebuchadnezzar), the crown provided regular rations for Jehoiachin and his five sons.[11] Nebuchadnezzar's son Evil-Merodach (Amel-Marduk) liberalized the policy of his father. Apparently, in one of those acts of generosity ancient Near Eastern monarchs engaged in on their accession to the throne, Amel-Marduk released Jehoiachin from prison. Presumably Jehoiachin had been living in a kind of house-arrest arrangement for deported kings. The accession year of Amel-Marduk would have been 561, the thirty-seventh year of Jehoiachin's exile and the year of his release. The Jews in Babylonia reckoned years by those of Jehoiachin's captivity (e.g., Ezek. 1:2).

To "lift up the head" (v. 27, Hebrew) was a gesture of rehabilitation and here refers to release from prison. To "treat" or "speak kindly" (v. 28) sometimes refers to good relations established through treaty or compact. Allotting him "a seat above those of the other kings," implies a hierarchy of royal prisoners, and putting off prison clothes suggests that he could again wear royal robes. To dine at the king's table was to receive food allowances from the royal treasury. Thus the Davidic king, even in exile, lived in dignity and honor. Yahweh in His sovereign power could and would care for His people while in exile and ultimately would restore them to their land once more. Punishment for sin is not without grace.

* * *

The books of 1 and 2 Kings offer numerous lessons to the people of God in both ancient times and the contemporary world. But above all else, they show how utterly repulsive idolatry is to God and how severely He will punish for it. Clearly, idolatry involves having greater affection for someone

---

[11] Thomas, 84–86.

or something other than God. If God would uproot the kingdoms of Israel and Judah and send them into captivity for their idolatry, what kind of punishment might He reserve for modern members of the Christian church who often have greater love for such Baals as wealth, power, entertainment, sports, hobbies, and prestige than for Yahweh?

For Further Study

1. Evaluate the character of Hezekiah. Illustrate your conclusions with specific reference to his conduct.

2. Study the first ten chapters of Jeremiah to discover the extent or depth of apostasy in Judah during the reign of the good king Josiah.

3. List the aspects of Josiah's reform.

4. Write a fictionalized account of the horrors of the Babylonian siege of Jerusalem beginning in January, 588 B.C. Include reference to the excitement and hope brought on by the Egyptian invasion of Palestine in 587, and an account of the dashed hopes when the Egyptians were routed. Josephus's *Antiquities*, Book X, will help.

5. Write a separate account of the march of the Jewish prisoners to Babylonia after the fall of Jerusalem in 586.

6. Describe forms of idolatry practiced in contemporary society and even in the contemporary church.

Bibliography

Allen, Ronald B. "Elijah the Broken Prophet," *Journal of the Evangelical Theological Society*. Jackson: JETS, 1979.

Archer, Gleason L. *A Survey of Old Testament Introduction*. rev. ed. Chicago: Moody, 1974.

Auld, A. Graeme. *I & II Kings*. Philadelphia: Westminster, 1986.

Bright, John. *A History of Israel*. 3rd ed. Philadelphia: Westminster, 1981.

Brueggemann, Walter. *1 Kings*. Atlanta: John Knox, 1982.

————. *2 Kings*. Atlanta: John Knox, 1982.

Comay, Joan. *The Hebrew Kings*. New York: Morrow, 1977.

Constable, Thomas L. "1 and 2 Kings," *The Bible Knowledge Commentary: Old Testament*. Edited by John F. Walvoord and Roy B. Zuck. Wheaton: Ill.: Victor Books, 1985.

Davis, John J., and John C. Whitcomb. *A History of Israel*. Grand Rapids, Baker: 1980.

Davis, John J. *Moses and the Gods of Egypt*. Grand Rapids: Baker, 1971, 16–37.

DeVries, Simon J. *1 Kings, Word Biblical Commentary*. Vol. 12. Waco, Tex.: Word Books, 1985.

Finegan, Jack. *Light from the Ancient Past*. 2nd ed. Princeton: Princeton U. Press, 1959.

Gates, John T. "I Kings." *The Wycliffe Bible Commentary*. Edited by Charles Pfeiffer and Everett F. Harrison. Chicago: Moody, 1962.

Gray, John. *I & II Kings*. 2nd ed. Philadelphia: Westminster, 1970.

Heaton, E. W. *The Hebrew Kingdoms*. Oxford: Oxford U. Press, 1968.

Hobbs, T. R. 2 *Kings, Word Biblical Commentary.* Vol. 13. Waco, Tex.: Word Books, 1985.

Jamieson, Robert; Andrew R. Fausset; and David Brown. *A Commentary, Critical, Experimental, and Practical on the Old and New Testaments.* Grand Rapids: Eerdmans. 1945 reprint.

Jensen, Irving L. *Jensen's Survey of the Old Testament.* Chicago: Moody, 1978.

Jones, Gwilym H. "1 and 2 Kings," *New Century Bible Commentary.* Grand Rapids: Eerdmans. 2 vols. 1984, 1:133.

Jones, Tom B. *Ancient Civilization.* rev. ed. Chicago: Rand McNally, 1964, 135.

Keil, C. F. and F. Delitezch. "The Books of the Kings," *Biblical Commentary on the Old Testament.* 2nd ed. Edinburgh: T. & T. Clark, n.d.

LaSor, William S. "1 and 2 Kings," *The New Bible Commentary,* rev. ed. Edited by D. Guthrie and J. A. Motyer. Grand Rapids: Eerdmans, 1970.

Long, Burke O. *1 Kings with an Introduction to Historical Literature.* Grand Rapids: Eerdmans, 1984.

Luckenbill, D. D. *Ancient Records of Babylonia and Assyria.* 2 vols. Chicago: U. of Chicago, 1927.

McNeely, Richard I. *First and Second Kings.* Chicago: Moody, 1978.

Meyer, F. B. *Elijah and the Secret of His Power.* London: Morgan and Scott, 1917.

Miller, J. Maxwell, and John H. Hayes. *A History of Ancient Israel and Judah.* Philadelphia: Westminster, 1986.

Montgomery, James A., and Henry S. Gehman. *A Critical and Exegetical Commentary on the Book of Kings.* Edinburgh: T. & T. Clark, 1941.

Nelson, Glueck, *The Other Side of Jordan.* New Haven, Conn.: American Schools of Oriental Research, 1940.

Newsome, James D., Jr. *A Synoptic Harmony of Samuel, Kings and Chronicles.* Grand Rapids: Baker, 1986.

Olmstead, A. T. *History of Assyria.* Chicago: U. of Chicago, 1951.

Parker, Richard A., and Waldo H. Dubberstein. *Babylonian Chronology 626 B.C.–A.D. 45.* Chicago: U. of Chicago, 1942.

Payne, David F. *Kingdoms of the Lord.* Grand Rapids: Eerdmans, 1981.

Pritchard, James B. *Recovering Sarepta, A Phoenician City.* Princeton: Princeton U. Press, 1978.

————. ed. *Ancient Near Eastern Texts Relating to the Old Testament.* 2nd ed. Princeton: Princeton U. Press, 1955.

Saggs, H. W. F. *The Greatness That Was Babylon*. New York: New American Library, 1962.

―――. *The Might That Was Assyria*. London: Sidgwick & Jackson, 1984.

Sivan, Gabriel. *The Bible and Civilization*. New York: *New York Times*, 1973.

Stigers, Harold. "II Kings," *The Wycliffe Bible Commentary*. Edited by Charles Pfeiffer and Everett F. Harrison. Chicago: Moody, 1962.

Thiele, Edwin R. *The Mysterious Numbers of the Hebrew Kings*. rev. ed. Grand Rapids: Zondervan, 1983.

Thomas, D. Winton, ed. *Documents from Old Testament Times*. New York: Harper & Row, 1958.

Vos, Howard F. *An Introduction to Bible Archaeology*. rev. ed. Chicago: Moody, 1983.

Wiseman, D. J. *Chronicles of the Chaldaean Kings*. London: British Museum, 1961.

Wood, Leon J. *A Survey of Israel's History*, rev. by David O'Brien. Grand Rapids: Zondervan, 1986.

Listed below are Bible translations specifically referred to in this study.

The Jerusalem Bible. Garden City, N. Y.: Doubleday, 1966. Referred to in this study as JB.

New American Standard Bible. La Habra, Calif.: Lockman Foundation, 1971. Referred to in this study as NASB.

The New English Bible. Oxford: University Press, 1970. Referred to in this study as NEB.

New International Version. New York: New York Bible Society, 1978. Referred to in this study as NIV.

The New Translation of the Holy Scripture According to the Masoretic Text. Philadelphia: Jewish Publication Society of America, 1982. Referred to in this study as JPS.

The Holy Bible. The Authorized or King James Version. Referred to in this study as KJV.

The Holy Bible. The Revised Standard Version. New York: Thomas Nelson & Sons, 1952. Referred to in this study as RSV.